OTHER KAPLAN BOOKS FOR COLLEGE-BOUND STUDENTS

College Admissions and Financial Aid

Conquer the Cost of College

Parent's Guide to College Admissions

Scholarships

The Unofficial, Unbiased, Insider's Guide to the 320 Most Interesting Colleges

The *Yale Daily News* Guide to Succeeding in College

Test Preparation

SAT & PSAT

SAT Verbal Workbook

SAT Verbal Velocity

SAT Math Workbook

SAT Math Mania

SAT II: Biology

SAT II: Chemistry

SAT II: Mathematics

SAT II: Physics

SAT II: Spanish

SAT II: U.S. History

SAT II: Writing

ACT

SAT*
for Super Busy Students

By Chris Kensler

Simon & Schuster

NEW YORK · LONDON · SINGAPORE · SYDNEY · TORONTO

Kaplan Publishing
Published by Simon & Schuster
1230 Avenue of the Americas
New York, NY 10020

Contributing Editors: Trent Anderson and Seppy Basili
Project Editor: Megan Duffy
Cover Design: Cheung Tai
Production Manager: Michael Shevlin
Executive Editor: Del Franz
Managing Editor: Déa Alessandro

Manufactured in the United States of America
Published simultaneously in Canada

August 2003

10 9 8 7 6 5 4 3 2

ISBN: 0-7432-4766-3

TABLE OF CONTENTS

Chris Kensler majored in English at Indiana University. He has written over a dozen books, covered a presidential campaign for a national news organization, and edited an arts and culture magazine. He is co-founder of the book packager Paper Airplane Projects with his wife and partner, Heather Kern.

This is the perfect SAT prep book for the overextended high schooler with a hyperactive lifestyle. *SAT for Super Busy Students* crunches Kaplan's years of test-prep know-how into a book that's fast, easy to read, and effective.

Here's how. Studying for the SAT is pretty straightforward:

- You learn overall test-taking skills and strategies
- You learn Verbal section skills and strategies
- You learn Math section skills and strategies
- You practice on a simulated SAT

SAT for Super Busy Students teaches the MOST IMPORTANT skills and strategies in 10 super-organized steps. Each *Super Busy* step can be completed in one or two evenings or a few study halls. Each step helps you:

- Know the details of an SAT section (Critical Reading, for example)
- Learn the specific skills that help you with that section or subject
- Master Kaplan's proven strategies for answering SAT questions on that section
- Practice what you've learned before you forget it

SAT for Super Busy Students covers general SAT information and strategies (Step 1), the Verbal section (Steps 2–5), the Math section (Steps 6–9), and stress-relieving and test-day strategies (Step 10). Each step covers its subject in detail. As you progress through the step you are asked multiple-choice questions about what you just read. Each step ends with sample questions that reinforce what you just learned, quickly and effectively. At the end of the book is a timed, full-length practice SAT. Take it, score it, and you're ready for the real deal.

We recommend giving yourself 2–4 weeks to finish the 10 *Super Busy* steps and take the practice SAT. If the SAT is next week, go through steps 1 and 10 and take the practice exam. If you have any time after that, learn the strategies for the subjects you had the most trouble with.

OK, you're busy, so let's start.

Section One

UNDERSTANDING THE *SAT*

Get to Know the SAT

The SAT is a three-hour test that measures reading and math skills. That's the bad part. The good part is that you can improve your score on the SAT without necessarily memorizing a dictionary or becoming a walking calculator. Of course, in this book we'll help you improve your math and verbal skills, but you can also improve your score just by knowing how the SAT is set up and learning how to deal with it. You can improve your score just by knowing what to expect on the SAT. That's what we cover in Step 1:

STEP 1 PREVIEW

Format
Know the different parts of the SAT:
- SAT overview
- Verbal section
- Math section

Strategies
Learn strategies that help you score higher on the SAT:
- Know the physical format
- Know the directions
- Have a plan and stick with it

FORMAT

The SAT is a three-hour, mostly multiple-choice exam. It's divided into seven Math and Verbal sections, which can appear in any order. The sections are broken down like so:

- Two 30-minute Verbal sections containing Analogies, Sentence Completions, and Critical Reading questions

- One 15-minute Verbal section made up solely of Critical Reading questions
- One 30-minute Math section with Quantitative Comparisons and Grid-ins
- One 30-minute Math section testing regular math
- One 15-minute Math section testing regular math
- One 30-minute experimental section (Math or Verbal)

Experimental Section

The experimental section is used by the test makers to try out new questions and does not affect your score. It can show up anywhere on the exam and will look like any Verbal or Math section. DO NOT try to figure out which SAT section is experimental. Treat all the sections as if they count.

Scoring

You gain one point for each correct answer on the SAT and lose a FRACTION of a point for each wrong answer (except with Grid-ins, where you lose nothing for a wrong answer). You do not gain or lose any points for questions you leave blank.

The totals for the 78 Verbal and 60 Math questions are added up to produce two raw scores. These raw scores are then converted into scaled scores, with 200 as the lowest score and 800 the highest. ETS converts your raw score to a scaled score. Each raw point is worth approximately 10 scaled points.

Registering Online

- Check www.collegeboard.com for complete information about registering for the SAT.

- Register online at www.collegeboard.com/sat/html/satform.html. Not all students are eligible to register online; read the instructions and requirements carefully.

- Register early to secure the time you want at the test center you want.

- The basic fee at press time is $26 in the United States. This price includes reports for you, your high school, and up to four colleges and scholarship programs.

Verbal Section

There are three kinds of questions on the Verbal section, broken down like so:

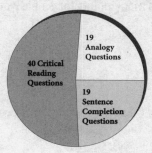

Analogy questions test your ability to understand relationships between words.

Sentence Completions test your ability to see how the parts of a sentence relate. About half will have one word missing from a sentence; the rest will have two words missing. Both types test vocabulary and reasoning skills.

Critical Reading questions test your ability to understand a piece of writing. The passages are long (400–850 words), and at least one passage contains two related readings. Most Critical Reading questions test how well you understand the passage, some make you draw conclusions, and some test your vocabulary.

The three scored Verbal sections on the SAT break down the questions like this:
- One 30-minute section with 9 Sentence Completions, 13 Analogies, and 13 Critical Reading questions
- One 30-minute section with 10 Sentence Completions, 6 Analogies, and 14 Critical Reading questions
- One 15-minute section with 13 Critical Reading questions

The Sentence Completions and Analogies are arranged in order of difficulty. The first few questions in a set are meant to be fairly easy. The middle few questions will be a little harder, and the last few are the most difficult. Keep this in mind as you work.

Critical Reading is NOT arranged by difficulty. Whenever you find yourself spending too much time on a Critical Reading question, you should skip it and return to it later.

How to Approach the SAT Verbal Section

To do well on SAT Verbal, you need to be systematic in your approach to each section and to each question type. Sentence Completions and Analogies are designed to be done relatively quickly. That means you can earn points fast, so you should do these first. Critical Reading takes a lot longer, so don't leave yourself just five minutes to do a passage. We will cover each question type and how to approach it in detail in upcoming steps.

Math Section

There are three kinds of questions on the Math section, broken down like so:

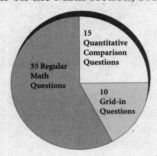

Regular Math questions are straightforward multiple-choice math questions, with five answer choices.

Quantitative Comparisons ask you to compare two quantities. You have to determine if one quantity is larger, if they are both equal, or if you don't have enough information to be able to decide. Quantitative Comparisons test your knowledge of math, your ability to apply that knowledge, and your reasoning ability.

Grid-ins are not multiple-choice questions, either. Instead of picking an answer choice, you write your response in a little grid like this:

These questions test the same math concepts as Regular Math and Quantitative Comparison questions.

Test Tools

Besides the basics—No. 2 pencils, erasers, a photo ID, and your admission ticket—you should bring the following items to the test center:

- Watch or stopwatch that you know how to use
- Calculator that you know how to use
- Snacks for the breaks

How to Approach the SAT Math Section

All sets of SAT Math questions start off with the easiest questions and gradually increase in difficulty. Always be aware of the difficulty level as you go through a Math question set. The later it is in a set, the more traps the question will have. (We go into math traps in detail in Step 8.)

To maximize your Math score, you need to:

1. Work systematically, and
2. Use your time efficiently.

The key to working systematically is to THINK ABOUT THE QUESTION before you look for the answer. A few seconds spent up front looking for traps, thinking about your approach, and deciding whether to tackle the problem now or come back to it later will pay off in points. On basic problems, you may know what to do right away. But on hard problems, the few extra seconds are time well spent.

Q. The only section in the SAT that does NOT have its questions ordered in increasing difficulty is

(A) Verbal Section: Analogies
(B) Math Section: Grid-Ins
(C) Verbal Section: Critical Reading
(D) Math Section: Quantitative Comparisons
(E) Verbal Section: Sentence Completions

Ⓐ Ⓑ Ⓒ Ⓓ Ⓔ   (C)

GENERAL SAT STRATEGIES

We will go into more section-specific strategies in later steps, but for now, let's go over some basic test tips.

Know the SAT's Format

The first time you see an SAT should NOT be on test day. On the day of the test, you should recognize Analogy questions, Quantitative Comparisons, Grid-ins, and the setup of any other question type or section on the test. If you are reading this book in the recommended amount of time (two to four weeks), we will introduce you to the format of each section and question type as you go along. If you are cramming, take 10 minutes now to familiarize yourself with the practice SAT at the back of the book.

Know the Directions

One of the easiest things you can do to help your performance on the SAT is to understand the directions before taking the test. Knowing the instructions beforehand will save you precious time reading them on test day. The directions NEVER change, so learn them now.

If you are completing this book in the recommended amount of time, you will learn each set of directions as you read each chapter. If you are cramming, go to the first page of each chapter and read the directions for each question type.

Have a Plan and Stick with It

Now that you know some basics about how the test is set up, you can approach each section with a plan. Kaplan has come up with a seven-step plan that organizes the way you approach the SAT:

1. Think About the Question Before You Look at the Answers
2. Pace Yourself
3. Know When a Question Is Supposed to Be Easy or Hard
4. Move Around Within a Section
5. Be a Good Guesser
6. Be a Good Gridder
7. Two-Minute Warning: Locate Quick Points

1. Think About the Question Before You Look at the Answers

The people who write the SAT put distractors among the answer choices. Distractors are answer choices that look right, but aren't. If you jump into the answer choices without thinking about what you're looking for, you're much more likely to fall in a test writer's trap. So always think for a second or two about the question before you look at the answers.

2. Pace Yourself

The SAT gives you a lot of questions to answer in a short period of time. To get through a whole section, you can't spend too much time on any one question. Keep moving through the test at a good speed; if you run into a hard question, circle it in your test booklet, skip it, and come back to it later if you have time.

Recommended Time Per Question

Question Type	On Average
Analogies	30 Seconds
Sentence Completions	30 Seconds
Critical Reading*	75 Seconds
Regular Math	70 Seconds
QCs	40 Seconds
Grid-ins	120 Seconds

*Average time for Critical Reading includes time to read the passage. Spend about 40 seconds per question.

This chart doesn't mean that you should spend exactly 30 seconds on every Analogy. The chart is just a guide. Remember, the questions get harder as you move through a problem set. Ideally, you can work through the easy problems at a faster pace and use a little more of your time for the harder ones that come at the end of the set.

3. Know When a Question Is Supposed to Be Easy or Hard

Some SAT questions are more difficult than others. Except for the Critical Reading section, the questions are generally designed to get tougher as you work through a set. Look at the following graphs following the difficulty levels of SAT questions:

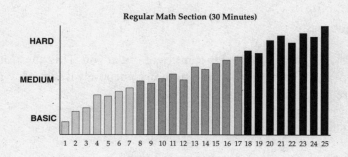

Regular Math Section (30 Minutes)

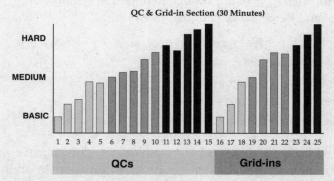

QC & Grid-in Section (30 Minutes)

The difficulty level builds to a peak, falls back to the "basic" level, then starts building again. This is because the difficulty pattern starts over again each time a new question type begins (except for Critical Reading). So if a section begins with a set of Analogy questions, those questions will begin with an easy one and then gradually become more difficult. If the section proceeds to a set of Sentence Completion questions, this set will also progress from easy to difficult.

As you work, always be aware of where you are in a set. When working on the easy problems, you can generally trust your first impulse—the obvious answer is likely to be right. As you get to the end of the problem set, you need to be more suspicious of "obvious answers" because the answer should not come easily. If it does, look at the problem again because the obvious answer is likely to be wrong. It may be a distractor—a wrong answer choice meant to trick you.

Hard SAT questions are usually tough for two reasons:

1. Their answers are not immediately obvious, and
2. The questions do not ask for information in a straightforward way.

Here's an easy question.

> Known for their devotion, dogs were often used as symbols of _____ in Medieval and Renaissance painting.
>
> (A) breakfast
> (B) tidal waves
> (C) fidelity
> (D) campfires
> (E) toothpaste

The correct answer, *fidelity* (C), probably leapt right out at you. This question would likely be at the beginning of a problem set. Easy questions are purposely designed to be easy and their answer choices are purposely obvious.

Now here is virtually the same question, made hard.

> Known for their _____, dogs were often used as symbols of _____ in Medieval and Renaissance painting.
>
> (A) dispassion . . bawdiness
> (B) fidelity . . aloofness
> (C) monogamy . . parsimony
> (D) parity . . diplomacy
> (E) loyalty . . faithfulness

This question would likely be at the end of a problem set. This time the answer is harder to find. For one thing, the answer choices are far more difficult. In addition, the sentence contains two blanks.

The correct answer is (E). Did you fall for (B) because the first word is *fidelity*? (B) is a good example of a distractor. By the time you're done with this book, distractors will be as easy to see as black undies under white linen H&M pants.

4. Move Around Within a Section

On a test at school, you probably spend more time on the hard questions than you do on the easy ones, since hard questions are usually worth more points.

DO NOT DO THIS ON THE SAT.

Easy problems are worth as many points as tough problems, so do the easy problems first. Don't rush through the easy problems just to get to the hard ones. When you run into questions that look tough, circle them in your test booklet and skip them for the time being. (Make sure you skip them on your answer grid too.) Then, if you have time, go back to it AFTER you have answered the easier ones. Sometimes, after you have answered some easier questions, troublesome questions can get easier, too.

Important

You CANNOT skip from section to section. You can only skip around within a section.

If you've started working on a question and get confused, stop and go to the next question. Persistence may pay off in school, but it usually hurts your SAT score because it wastes time. Don't spend so much time answering one tough question that you use up three or four questions' worth of time. That costs you points, especially if you don't get the hard question right.

Remember, the name of the game is to get as many points as possible, so you need to score points as quickly as possible.

Q. What is the best advice for answering questions on the SAT?

(A) Pick the first answer that looks right to you because first impressions are important.

(B) Do not dwell on any one question, even a hard one, until you have tried every question at least once.

(C) Answer every question in order, then go back and check your answers.

(D) Do not read the questions and do not answer the questions, because the test writers are just trying to trick you.

(E) Do the hard questions first because they are worth more points than easy questions.

Ⓐ Ⓑ Ⓒ Ⓓ Ⓔ   (B)

5. Be a Good Guesser

The SAT says there is a penalty for guessing on the SAT. This is not true. There is a "wrong-answer penalty"—if you guess WRONG, you get penalized. Here's how the wrong-answer penalty works:

- If you get an answer wrong on a Quantitative Comparison, which has four answer choices, you lose one third point.
- If you get an answer wrong on other multiple-choice questions, which have five answer choices, you lose one quarter point.
- If you get an answer wrong on a Grid-in Math question, for which you write in your own answers, you lose NOTHING.

These fractions of points are meant to offset the points you might get "accidentally" by guessing the correct answer. If you can eliminate one or more wrong answers, you turn the odds in your favor, and you will actually come out ahead by guessing.

Take a look at this question:

> Known for their devotion, dogs were often used as symbols of _____ in Medieval and Renaissance painting.
>
> (A) breakfast
> (B) tidal waves
> (C) fidelity
> (D) campfires
> (E) toothpaste

Chances are, you recognized that choice (A), *breakfast*, was wrong. You then looked at the next answer choice, and then the next one, and so on, eliminating wrong answers to find the correct answer. This process is usually the best way to work through multiple-choice SAT questions. If still don't know the right answer, but can eliminate one or more wrong answers, YOU SHOULD GUESS.

6. Be a Good Gridder

Don't make mistakes filling out your answer grid. When time is short it's easy to get confused skipping around a section and going back and forth between your test book and your grid. If you misgrid A SINGLE QUESTION, you can misgrid several others before realizing your error—if you realize it at all. You can lose a TON of points this way.

To avoid mistakes on the answer grid:

- **Always circle the answers you choose.** Circling your answers in the test book makes it easier to check your grid against your book.

- **Grid five or more answers at once.** Don't transfer your answers to the grid after every question. Transfer your answers after every five questions, or, in the Critical Reading section, at the end of each reading passage. That way, you won't keep breaking your concentration to mark the grid. You'll save time and improve accuracy.

Important Exception

When time is running out at the end of a section, start gridding one by one so you don't get caught at the end with ungridded answers.

- **Circle the questions you skip.** Put a big circle in your test book around the number of any questions you skip, so they'll be easy to locate when you return to them. Also, if you realize later that you accidentally skipped a box on the grid, you can more easily check your grid against your book to see where you went wrong.

- **Write in your booklet.** Take notes, circle hard questions, underline things, etc. Proctors collect booklets at the end of each testing session, but the booklets are not examined or reused.

7. Two-Minute Warning: Locate Quick Points

When you start to run out of time, locate and answer any of the quick points that remain. For example, some Critical Reading questions will ask you to identify the meaning of a particular word in the passage. These can be done at the last minute, even if you haven't read the passage. And on most Quantitative Comparisons, even the hardest ones, you can quickly eliminate at least one answer, improving your chances of guessing correctly.

CONCLUSION

These SAT facts and strategies underpin the upcoming Verbal and Math steps. Use what you've learned here on the practice questions. By the time you finish this book and are ready to take the practice test, these strategies will come as naturally to you as saying "I can tell from the six minutes we spent in the hot tub that I could build a life with him" comes to a contestant on *The Bachelor*.

Section Two

UNDERSTANDING THE VERBAL SECTION

STEP TWO

Analogy Questions

Short-term prepping for Analogies can gain you more points than any other Verbal question type. Analogies can be frightening at first because they don't look like anything you've ever seen before, but once you get used to them, you'll be able to get an Analogy question right even when you don't know what most of the words mean. Here's your outline for Step 2:

STEP 2 PREVIEW

Format

Know what an Analogy question is:
- Overview
- The strong, definite connection

Bridge-Building Strategies

Learn how to tackle Analogy questions:
- Three simple steps
- Identify the parts of speech
- Nine common bridges

Practice

Use it before you lose it (13 questions / 8 minutes)

FORMAT

Each of the SAT's two 30-minute Verbal sections contains a set of Analogies. You'll probably see one set of 13 and one set of six (that's 19 total). The 19 Analogies count for about 1/4 of your Verbal score.

An analogy question looks like this:

FLAKE : SNOW ::

(A) storm : hail
(B) drop : rain
(C) field : wheat
(D) stack : hay
(E) cloud : fog

The instructions for SAT Analogies read as follows: "Choose the lettered pair of words that is related in the same way as the pair in capital letters."

The two words in capital letters are called *stem words*. In our example, the answer is (B). A FLAKE is a small unit of SNOW like a *drop* is a small unit of *rain*.

The Strong, Definite Connection

There is a strong, definite connection between the two stem words in every Analogy question. For example, the words "pick" and "guitar" have a strong, definite connection. A *pick* can be used to play a *guitar*. PICK : GUITAR could be an SAT question stem. On the other hand, the words "pick" and "shoe" do NOT have a strong, definite connection. A *pick* and a *shoe* have nothing to do with each other. PICK : SHOE would never be a question stem.

You need to identify this relationship, and then to look for a similar relationship among the answer pairs. The best way to pinpoint the relationship between the stem words is to build a bridge. A bridge is a short sentence that relates the two words. Often, a bridge reads like a definition of one of the two words. For instance: "A pick can be used to play a guitar."

The ability to build these bridges is your key to Analogy success. Your bridge needs to capture the strong, definite connection between the words.

Q. Which of the following stem word pairs would NOT be on the SAT?

(A) RUN : FAST ::
(B) HOUSE : ROOF ::
(C) GREEN : GRASS ::
(D) GUITAR : TREE ::
(E) MEAN : NICE ::

Ⓐ Ⓑ Ⓒ Ⓓ Ⓔ   (D)

BRIDGE-BUILDING STRATEGIES

The strategies that follow work hand in hand in hand with one another. Think of them as the Charlie's Angels of SAT strategies. Each has strengths, each has weaknesses, but together, they kick Analogy section booty.

The Three Steps

Kaplan has come up with three simple steps to building an Analogy bridge:

1. Build a bridge between the stem words.
2. Plug in the answer choices.
3. Adjust your bridge, if you need to.

Look at the following stem words. We've left out the answer choices because you need to focus first on the stem.

> LILY : FLOWER ::

Now (1) build your bridge.

The best bridge here is, "A LILY is, by definition, a type of FLOWER."

Now (2) take the bridge you have built and plug in the answer choices. Be sure to try all five choices. If only one pair fits, that's the correct answer.

> LILY : FLOWER ::
>
> (A) rose : thorn
> (B) cocoon : butterfly
> (C) brick : building
> (D) maple : tree
> (E) sky : airplane

Here's how plugging in the answer choices should have worked:

> (A) A *rose* is a type of *thorn*? No.
> (B) A *cocoon* is a type of *butterfly*? No.
> (C) A *brick* is a type of *building*? No.
> (D) A *maple* is a type of *tree*? Yes.
> (E) A *sky* is a type of *airplane*? No.

We've got four no's and only one yes, so the answer is (D).

If no answer choice seems to fit, your bridge is too specific and you should go back and (3) adjust it. If more than one answer choice fits, your bridge is too general. Look at this example:

SNAKE : SLITHER ::

(A) egg : hatch
(B) wolf : howl
(C) rabbit : hop
(D) turtle : snap
(E) tarantula : bite

With a simple bridge, such as "a SNAKE SLITHERS," all of the answer choices make sense: an *egg hatches*, a *wolf howls*, a *rabbit hops*, a *turtle snaps*, and a *tarantula bites*. If this happens to you, go back build another bridge, this time making it more specific. Think carefully about what *slither* means.

New bridge: "SLITHERING is how a SNAKE gets around."

(A) *Hatching* is how an *egg* gets around? No.
(B) *Howling* is how a *wolf* gets around? No.
(C) *Hopping* is how a *rabbit* gets around? Yes.
(D) *Snapping* is how a *turtle* gets around? No.
(E) *Biting* is how a *tarantula* gets around? No.

Four no's and one yes; the answer is (C).

If you still can't narrow it down, build a new bridge and plug in again.

Q. What are the three steps to building a bridge?

(A) Build your bridge, plug in the answers choices, adjust bridge if necessary.
(B) Build your bridge, adjust your bridge, pick your answer choice.
(C) Pick your answer choice, put it on the bridge, blow up the bridge if necessary.
(D) Bridge your choice, choose an adjustment, and rebuild the steps.
(E) Pick your answer choice, adjust bridge if necessary, choose another answer choice.

Ⓐ Ⓑ Ⓒ Ⓓ Ⓔ   (A)

KAPLAN

Identify the Part of Speech

Sometimes a stem word has more than one part of speech. For example, the word "light" can be a noun, verb, or adjective. When you're not sure what part of speech a stem word is, look at the answer choices directly beneath that word.

The words in a vertical row are ALWAYS all the same part of speech. So you might see this:

VERB : NOUN ::

(A) verb : noun
(B) verb : noun
(C) verb : noun
(D) verb : noun
(E) verb : noun

Or this:

ADJECTIVE : NOUN ::

(A) adjective : noun
(B) adjective : noun
(C) adjective : noun
(D) .adjective : noun
(E) adjective : noun

But you'll NEVER see this on an SAT Analogy:

NOUN : NOUN ::

(A) verb : noun
(B) noun : noun
(C) verb : verb
(D) verb : noun
(E) verb : noun

To establish the part of speech of a stem word, you usually don't have to look further than choice (A). So how would you think through the following example?

PINE : DESIRE ::

(A) laugh : sorrow
(B) drink : thirst
(C) watch : interest
(D) listen : awe
(E) starve : hunger

The word "pine" can be a noun, but not here. You can't build a bridge between a tree with needlelike leaves and "desire." At least we hope you can't. Try another part of speech. A glance at the answer choices below pine (*laugh, drink, watch, listen,* and *starve*) tells you *pine* is being used as a verb.

What about "desire"? It could be a noun or a verb, too, but the answer choices beneath it (*sorrow, thirst, interest, awe,* and *hunger*) tell you it's used as a noun.

You've probably heard of someone pining away from unrequited love. As a verb, *pine* means "to yearn or suffer from longing." A good bridge would be: "By definition, to PINE is to suffer from extreme DESIRE." Plugging in the answer choices, you get:

    (A) To *laugh* is to suffer from extreme *sorrow*? No.
    (B) To *drink* is to suffer from extreme *thirst*? No.
    (C) To *watch* is to suffer from extreme *interest*? No.
    (D) To *listen* is to suffer from extreme *awe*? No.
    (E) To *starve* is to suffer from extreme *hunger*? Yes.

The answer is (E).

Nine Common Bridges

It's easier to build bridges when you know the types of bridges that have appeared before on the SAT. The nine bridges that follow appear over and over again on the SAT. Common bridges may take different forms, depending on what parts of speech are used, but the underlying concepts are what matter. Try to know these, or at least learn to recognize them, by test day.

Bridge 1: Description

In many Analogies, one stem word is a person, place, or thing, and the other word is a characteristic of that person, place, or thing. Look at these examples:

        PAUPER : POOR—A PAUPER is always POOR.

        GENIUS : INTELLIGENT—A GENIUS is always INTELLIGENT.

This bridge can also describe a person, place, or thing by what it is *not.*

        PAUPER : WEALTHY—A PAUPER is never WEALTHY.

        GENIUS : STUPID—A GENIUS is never STUPID.

The common bridges that follow are themes on this. As you read on, fill in each blank with a stem word that YOU think will complete the bridge.

Bridge 2: Characteristic Actions

        An INSOMNIAC can't _____.

        A GLUTTON likes to _____.

Bridge 3: Lack

Something MURKY lacks _____.
A PESSIMIST lacks _____.

Bridge 4: Categories

✗MEASLES is a type of _illnesse_.
A BARRACUDA is a type of _fish_.

Bridge 5: Size/Degree

To SPEAK very quietly is to _whisper_.
To LIKE strongly is to _love_.

Bridge 6: Causing/Stopping

✗ A REMEDY stops or cures a(n) _illness_.
An OBSTACLE prevents _progress_.

Bridge 7: Places

A JUDGE works in a(n) _court_.
✗A PLAY is performed on a(n) _Stage_.

Bridge 8: Function

GILLS are used for _breathing_.
A PAINTBRUSH is used to _paint_.

Bridge 9: Part/Whole

✗An ARMY is made up of _soilders_.
A CROWD is made up of many _people_.

Answers for Nine Common Bridges

Your answers may vary from these. As long as you recognized the relationship, that's OK.

Characteristic Actions

An INSOMNIAC can't SLEEP.
A GLUTTON likes to EAT.

Lack

Something MURKY lacks CLARITY.
A PESSIMIST lacks OPTIMISM.

Categories

MEASLES is a type of ILLNESS.
A BARRACUDA is a type of FISH.

Size/Degree

To SPEAK very quietly is to WHISPER.
To LIKE strongly is to LOVE (or ADORE).

Causing/Stopping

A REMEDY stops or cures an ILLNESS.
An OBSTACLE prevents PROGRESS (or MOVEMENT).

Places

A JUDGE works in a COURTROOM.
A PLAY is performed on a STAGE (or in a THEATER).

Function

GILLS are used for BREATHING.
A PAINTBRUSH is used to PAINT.

Part/Whole

An ARMY is made up of SOLDIERS.
A CROWD is made up of many PEOPLE.

PRACTICE

Analogy Questions

Number of Minutes—8; Number of Questions—13

Choose the lettered pair of words that is related in the same way as the pair in capital letters.

1. NOVEL : CHAPTER ::

    (A) painting : frame
    (B) poem : rhyme
    (C) film : festival
    (D) symphony : movement
    (E) article : summary

2. CHAMPION : SUPPORT ::

    (A) score : defeat
    (B) validate : confirmation
    (C) amend : error
    (D) invoke : penalty
    (E) defile : honor

3. RELATIVES : FAMILY ::

    (A) writers : anthology
    (B) singers : musical
    (C) secretaries : office
    (D) actors : play
    (E) teachers : faculty

4. COUNTERFEIT : FAKE ::

    (A) opinion : justified
    (B) imitation : genuine
    (C) condensation : abbreviated
    (D) installment : lengthy
    (E) delicacy : expensive

5. ARCHITECT : BUILDINGS ::

   (A) doctor : patients
   (B) composer : operas
   (C) designer : models
   (D) judge : lawyers
   (E) chef : ingredients

6. DEFEAT : TROUNCE ::

   (A) dislike : abhor
   (B) expand : abridge
   (C) replace: succeed
   (D) mock : nullify
   (E) suggest : prevaricate

7. TRANSGRESS : LAW ::

   (A) exceed : limit
   (B) engage : taboo
   (C) stalk : prey
   (D) remedy : ill
   (E) vie : competition

8. ABSCOND : LEAVE ::

   (A) concede : defeat
   (B) spurn : decline
   (C) frown : cry
   (D) spy : observe
   (E) stride : move

9. ENERVATE : IMPOTENT ::

   (A) dupe : credulous
   (B) obviate : evident
   (C) vacillate : indecisive
   (D) kindle : flammable
   (E) stratify : layered

10. PEERLESS : EQUAL ::

    (A) pragmatic : sense
    (B) sophomoric : maturity
    (C) glib : remark
    (D) vigilant : observation
    (E) arable : land

11. ONEROUS : BURDEN ::

    (A) generous : contribution
    (B) bothersome : irritant
    (C) scripted : dialogue
    (D) nuptial : ceremony
    (E) antique : valuable:

12. LACONIC : BREVITY ::

    (A) desultory : inhibition
    (B) meticulous : veracity
    (C) heretical : evil
    (D) capacious : restriction
    (E) surreptitious : secrecy

13. FRANGIBLE : BREAK ::

    (A) foreseeable : divine
    (B) invariable : change
    (C) reprehensible : emulate
    (D) ostensible : result
    (E) impalpable : touch

Answers and Explanations

1. (D)

The stem bridge is: a CHAPTER is part of a NOVEL. A *frame* isn't part of a *painting* (A); a *festival* isn't part of a *film* (C); a *summary* isn't part of an *article* (E). Be careful with (B). While a *rhyme* is often part of a *poem*, it does not have to be. There are plenty of poems without rhymes. Therefore, (D) "a *movement* is part of a *symphony*" is the correct answer.

2. (B)

Before jumping into this analogy, you need to discern if CHAMPION is a noun or a verb. Remember, the best way to figure this out is to scan all of the first words in the answer choices. Since *validate*, *amend*, *invoke*, and *defile* are clearly verbs, you know that

CHAMPION is a verb as well. A good bridge, then, would be: to CHAMPION means to give SUPPORT. Similarly, "to *validate* means to give *confirmation*." None of the other choices express this relationship: to *score* does not mean to *defeat* (A); to *amend* does not mean to *error* (C); to *invoke* does not mean to *penalty* (D); and to *defile* does not mean to *honor* (E).

3. (E)

This bridge is pretty straightforward: RELATIVES make up a FAMILY. Look for the choice with the same relationship. Don't pick an answer just because the two words are closely related, as in choices (C) and (D). *Secretaries* don't make up an *office*; they work there. Similarly, *actors* don't make up a *play* by themselves. But (E) *teachers* do make up a *faculty*.

4. (C)

A stem bridge could be: a COUNTERFEIT is, by definition, FAKE. The only answer choice that fits the bridge is (C), a "*condensation* is, by definition, *abbreviated*." A *delicacy* is usually an expensive gourmet food, but is not by definition *expensive* (E).

5. (B)

This is an example of an Analogy in which you must make your bridge specific. If your bridge was: an ARCHITECT makes BUILDINGS, there would be two possible answer choices; (B) and (C) would both work. You need to tweak your bridge. Try this: BUILDINGS are *created* by ARCHITECTS. *Models* are not necessarily created by *designers* (C), but *operas* are created by *composers* (B).

6. (A)

Note that both words in this stem are verbs—and you know that the SAT often tests relationships of degree. Here's your bridge: to TROUNCE means to DEFEAT thoroughly. Answer choices (B), (C), and (D) are relatively easy to eliminate. To *abridge* is to shorten, and to *nullify* is to negate. (E) has a word that you might not know: *prevaricate*. Plug it into the bridge and see how it sounds: "To *prevaricate* means to *suggest* thoroughly." This sentence does not sound nearly as strong as (A): "To *abhor* is to *dislike* thoroughly." Yes.

7. (A)

Even if you don't know what TRANSGRESS means, you still have an excellent chance of getting this question right. LAW is a noun. TRANSGRESS is a verb. What are the verbs that come to mind when dealing with the law? We obey laws. We disobey laws. TRANSGRESS has a negative charge (or connotation). Therefore, pick a negative-sounding bridge: to TRANSGRESS a LAW is to disobey it. Plug in (A)—"To *exceed* a *limit* is to disobey it." It sounds correct. No other choice has the same relationship. To *vie* means to engage in *competition*, not to disobey it (E). None of the other possibilities come close.

8. (D)

This is a tough one. Your bridge has to be very specific: To ABSCOND is to LEAVE in a secretive manner. *Concede* (A) doesn't mean *defeat*, nor does *frown* (C) mean *cry*. Both can be eliminated right off the bat. To *spurn* is to *decline* in a rude manner, but not an unlawful one (B). (E) does not fit your bridge at all—to *stride* is to *move* smoothly and quickly. The best choice is (D), "to *spy* is to *observe* in a secretive manner."

9. (E)

Even if you don't know what ENERVATE means, you can figure out this question. You know that ENERVATE must have a strong relationship to IMPOTENT, and that ENERVATE is a negative-sounding word. To ENERVATE, then, means "to make IMPOTENT." The bridges for (A) and (D) aren't even close to ours, so both can be tossed out: Someone who is *credulous* can be easily *duped*; to *kindle* is to start a fire. To *obviate* is to make not *evident* (B), and to *vacillate* is to **be** *indecisive*, not to make indecisive (C). The answer, then, is (E), "to *stratify* is to make *layered*."

10. (B)

To be PEERLESS is to have no EQUAL. Even if you don't know the exact definition of *sophomoric*, you've probably heard at least one teacher use the word to describe the cut-up who sits in the back row and makes noises with his armpit during class. To be *sophomoric*, then, is to have no *maturity* (B). While the word pairs in (A), (C), and (E) all have something to do with each other, none of them are related closely enough: To be *pragmatic* is to use good *sense*; a *glib remark* is casual; *arable land* is fertile. To be *vigilant* is to have *observation*, not the opposite, so (D) is also wrong.

11. (B)

A word as ugly as ONEROUS must be negative; to be ONEROUS, then, is to be a BURDEN. (A) and (D) make don't even come close to this bridge, so both are wrong (*nuptial* has to do with weddings). To be *scripted* is not to be a *dialogue* (C), necessarily; silent movies were scripted, and they had no dialogue at all. Similarly, my rusty 1968 Buick Skylark is *antique*, but it's unfortunately not *valuable* (E). The best choice here is (B), "to be *bothersome* is to be an *irritant*."

12. (E)

This question features numerous big words and a difficult bridge: to be LACONIC is to be marked by BREVITY. Don't let big words scare you; skip the ones you don't know. *Surreptitious* means "secret," so this choice fits our bridge perfectly: "to be *surreptitious* is to be marked by *secrecy*" (E). You could get this answer without knowing what most of the big words in this question mean. *Desultory* means "random" and has nothing to do with *inhibition* (A). *Veracity* means "truthfulness," and has no relation to *meticulous* (B). *Capacious* means "big," and something big is not marked by *restriction* (D). Finally, while zealots might claim that to be *heretical* is to be *evil*, there is nothing in the definition of *heretical* (going against an established system of beliefs) that equates it with *evil* (C).

13. (A)

If you remove the N and the B from the word FRANGIBLE, you're left with "fragile." Both words mean the same thing. The word FRANGIBLE only exists for poets to rhyme with "tangible" and for ETS test makers to confuse you. The bridge is: you can BREAK something that is FRANGIBLE (remember—you can reverse the order of the words in the stem as long as you reverse the words in the answer choices as well). The answer, then, is (A): you can *divine*—or predict—something that is *foreseeable*. You can't *change* something that is *invariable* (B), nor can you *touch* something that is *impalpable* (E). The other two options make no sense. Something *reprehensible* is worthy of punishment, and to *emulate* is to copy (C). *Ostensible* (D) means "apparent."

STEP THREE

Sentence Completion Questions

Sentence Completions are probably the most student-friendly question type on the Verbal section. Unlike Analogies, they give you some context in which to think about vocabulary words, and unlike Critical Reading, they require you to pay attention to just one sentence at a time. Here's the outline for how to approach Sentence Completions:

STEP 3 PREVIEW

Format

Know what a Sentence Completion question is:

- Overview

Strategies

Learn how to tackle Sentence Completion questions:

- Kaplan's Four-Step Method for Sentence Completions

- Picking up on clues and predicting answers

- Handling hard or tricky questions

- When else fails—guess!

Practice

Use it before you lose it (9 questions / 7 minutes)

FORMAT

There are 19 Sentence Completion questions on the SAT. The 19 Sentence Completions count for about one quarter of your Verbal score. You'll probably see one set of nine and one set of 10 in each of the 30-minute Verbal sections.

The instructions for Sentence Completions look something like this: "Select the lettered word or set of words that best completes the sentence."

The questions look like this:

> Today's small, portable computers contrast markedly with the earliest electronic computers, which were - - - - - .
>
> (A) effective
> (B) invented
> (C) useful
> (D) destructive
> (E) enormous

In this example, the new, small, portable computers are contrasted with old computers. You can infer that old computers must be the opposite of small and portable, so (E), *enormous*, is right.

STRATEGIES

Master these strategies, and you're on your way to acing the Sentence Completions.

Four-Step Method for Sentence Completions

This is Kaplan's most powerful method for tackling Sentence Completions. It also works wonders on stubborn grass stains.

1. Read the sentence for clue words.

Think about the sentence for a second or two. Figure out what the sentence means, taking special note of the "clue words." A word like *but* tells you to expect a CONTRAST coming up; a word like *moreover* tells you that what follows is a CONTINUATION of the same idea. Clue words such as *and, but, such as*, and *although* tell you how the parts of the sentence will relate to each other.

2. Predict the answer.

Decide what sort of word should fill the blank or blanks. Do this BEFORE looking at the answer choices. You don't have to make an exact prediction; a rough idea of the kind of word you'll need will do. It's often enough simply to predict whether the missing word is positive or negative.

3. Select the best match.

Compare your prediction to each answer choice. Read EVERY answer choice before deciding.

4. Plug your answer choice into the sentence.

Put your answer choice in the blank or blanks. You should be able to come up with your final answer. Only one choice should really make sense. If you've gone through the four steps and more than one choice seems possible, eliminate the choices you can, guess, and move on. If all of the choices look great or all of the choices look terrible, circle the question and come back when you're done with the section.

Let's unleash the powers of the Four-Step Method on a sample question.

> The king's - - - - decisions as a diplomat and administrator led to his legendary reputation as a just and - - - - ruler.
>
> (A) quick . . capricious
> (B) equitable . . wise
> (C) immoral . . perceptive
> (D) generous . . witty
> (E) clever . . uneducated

1. Read the sentence for clue words.

The clue here is the phrase *led to*. You know that the kind of decisions the king made gave him a reputation as a just and - - - - ruler. So whatever goes in both blanks must be consistent with *just*.

2. Predict the answer.

Both blanks must contain words that are similar in meaning. Because of his - - - - decisions, the king is viewed as a just and - - - - ruler. So if the king's decisions were good, he'd be remembered as a good ruler, and if his decisions were bad, he'd be remembered as a bad ruler. *Just*, which means "fair," is a positive-sounding word; you can predict that both blanks will be similar in meaning, and that both will be positive words. You can write a "+" in the blanks or over the columns of answer choices to remind you.

3. Select the best match.

One way to do this is to determine which answers are both positive and similar. In (A), *quick* and *capricious* aren't both positive and similar. (*Capricious* means "erratic or fickle.") In (B), *equitable* means "fair." *Equitable* and *wise* are similar, and they're both positive. When you plug them in, they make sense, so (B) looks right. But check out the others to be sure. In (C), *immoral* and *perceptive* aren't similar at all. *Perceptive* is positive but *immoral* is not. In (D), *generous* and *witty* are both positive adjectives, but they aren't really similar and they don't make sense in the sentence. *Generous* decisions would not give one a reputation as a *witty* ruler. In (E), *clever* and *uneducated* aren't similar. *Clever* is positive, but *uneducated* isn't.

4. Plug your answer choice into the sentence.

"The king's equitable decisions as a diplomat and administrator led to his legendary reputation as a just and wise ruler." (B) makes sense in the sentence. So (B)'s your answer.

Q. A clue word in a Sentence Completion question

(A) tells you whether a Sentence Completion question is hard or easy
(B) tells you how the parts of the sentence will relate to each other
(C) tells you whether to spend time on the question or skip to the next one
(D) tells you whether you need to improve your vocabulary or not
(E) tells you how a sentence is constructed

Ⓐ Ⓑ Ⓒ Ⓓ Ⓔ   (B)

Picking Up on Clues

To do well on Sentence Completions, you need to understand how a sentence fits together. Clue words help you do this. The more clues you get, the clearer the sentence becomes, and the better you can predict what goes in the blanks. So let's delve further into the fascinating subject of clue words. Take a look at this example.

> Though some have derided it as - - - - , the search for extraterrestrial intelligence has actually become a respectable scientific endeavor.

Here, the word *though* is an important clue. *Though* contrasts the way some have derided, belittled, or ridiculed the search for extraterrestrial intelligence, with the fact that that search has become respectable. Another clue is *actually*. *Actually* completes the contrast: <u>Though</u> some see the search one way, it has <u>actually</u> become respectable.

You know that whatever goes in the blank must complete the contrast implied by the word *though*. So, to fill in the blank, you need a word that would be used to describe the opposite of a respectable scientific endeavor. *Useless* or *trivial* would be good predictions for the blank.

Let's put your deeper understanding of clue words to the test. Use clue words to predict the answers to the two questions below. First, look at the sentences without the answer choices and:

- Circle clue words.
- Think of a word or phrase that might go in each blank.
- Write your prediction below each sentence.

1. One striking aspect of Caribbean music is its - - - - of many African musical - - - - , such as call-and-response singing and polyrhythms.

Predictions: _____   _____

2. Although Cézanne was inspired by the Impressionists, he - - - - their emphasis on the effects of light and - - - - an independent approach to painting that emphasized form.

Predictions: _____   _____

Here are the questions with their answer choices (and with their clue words italicized). Find the right answer to each question, referring to the predictions you just made.

1. One striking aspect of Caribbean music is its - - - - of many African musical - - - - , *such as* call-and-response singing and polyrhythms.

    (A) recruitment . . groups
    (B) proficiency . . events
    (C) expectation . . ideas
    (D) absorption . . forms
    (E) condescension . . priorities

2. *Although* Cézanne was inspired by the Impressionists, he - - - - their emphasis on the effects of light and - - - - an independent approach to painting that emphasized form.

    (A) accepted . . developed
    (B) rejected . . evolved
    (C) encouraged . . submerged
    (D   dismissed . . aborted
    (E) nurtured . . founded

The answers to the questions are (D) and (B), respectively. In question 1, *such as* tells you that the second blank must be something (genres, practices, forms) of which call-and-response singing and polyrhythms are examples. *Although* in question 2 tells you that the first blank must contrast with Cézanne's being "inspired" by the Impressionists.

Hard or Tricky Questions

Sentence Completions go from easiest to hardest—the higher the question number, the harder the question, so the last few Sentence Completions in a set are usually pretty difficult. If you're getting stuck, we have a few special techniques to pull you through:

1. Avoid tricky wrong answers.
2. Take apart tough sentences.
3. Work around tough vocabulary.

1. Avoid tricky wrong answers.

Towards the end of a set, watch out for tricky answer choices. Avoid:

- Opposites of the correct answer
- Words that sound right because they're hard
- Two-blankers in which one word fits but the other doesn't

The following example would be the seventh question out of a 10-problem set.

> Granted that Janyce is extremely - - - - , it is still difficult to imagine her as a professional comedian.
>
> (A) dull
> (B) garrulous
> (C) effusive
> (D) conservative
> (E) witty

Read this sentence carefully or you may get tricked. If you read too quickly, you might think, "If Janyce is hard to imagine as a comedian, she's probably extremely dull or conservative. So I'll pick either (A) or (D)." But the sentence is saying something else.

Remember to pick up the clues. The key here is the clue word *granted*. It's another way of saying *although*. So the sentence means, "Sure Janyce is funny, but she's no professional comedian." Therefore, the word in the blank must resemble "funny." That means (E), *witty*, is correct.

Now don't pick an answer just because it sounds hard. *Garrulous* means "talkative" and *effusive* means "overly expressive." You might be tempted to pick one of these simply because they sound impressive. But they're put there to trick you. Don't choose them without good reason.

Now let's look at a two-blank sentence. The following example is another seventh question out of a 10-problem set.

> When the state government discovered that thermal pollution was killing valuable fish, legislation was passed to - - - - the dumping of hot liquid wastes into rivers and to - - - - the fish population.
>
> (A) discourage . . decimate
> (B) regulate . . quantify
> (C) facilitate . . appease
> (D) discontinue . . devastate
> (E) prohibit . . protect

Look at all the choices. Check out the first blank first. Legislation was not passed to *facilitate* dumping, so that eliminates choice (C). The other four are all possible.

Now check the second blanks. The legislature wouldn't pass a law to *decimate*, or *quantify*, or *devastate* the fish population, so (A), (B), and (D) are wrong. Only choice (E), *prohibit . . protect*, fits for both blanks. The legislature might well pass a law to *prohibit* dumping hot liquids and to *protect* fish.

2. Take apart tough sentences.

Look at the following example, the seventh question of a nine-problem set.

> Although this small and selective publishing house is famous for its - - - - standards, several of its recent novels have a mainly popular appeal.
>
> (A) proletarian
> (B) naturalistic
> (C) discriminating
> (D) imitative
> (E) precarious

What if you were stumped, and had no idea which word to pick? Try this strategy. The process might go like this:

(A) *Proletarian* standards? Hmmm . . . sounds weird.
(B) *Naturalistic* standards? Not great.
(C) *Discriminating* standards? Sounds familiar.
(D) *Imitative* standards? Weird.
(E) *Precarious* standards? Nope.

(C) sounds best and, as it turns out, is correct. Although the small publishing house has *discriminating*, or picky, standards, several of its recent novels appeal to a general audience.

Now try a complex sentence with two blanks. Remember our rules:

- Try the easier blank first.
- Save time by eliminating all choices that won't work for one blank.

The following example is the fifth question out of a nine-problem set.

> These latest employment statistics from the present administration are so loosely documented, carelessly explained, and potentially misleading that even the most loyal senators will - - - - the - - - - of the presidential appointees who produced them.
>
> (A) perceive . . intelligence
> (B) understand . . tenacity
> (C) recognize . . incompetence
> (D) praise . . rigor
> (E) denounce . . loyalty

It's not so easy to see what goes in the first blank, so try the second blank. You need a word to describe presidential appointees who produced the "loosely documented," "carelessly explained," and "misleading" statistics. So it's got to be negative. The only second-word answer choice that's definitely negative is (C), *incompetence*, or inability to perform a task. Now try *recognize* in the first blank. It fits, too. (C) must be correct.

3. Work around tough vocabulary.

The following example is the second question out of a nine-problem set.

> Despite her - - - - of public speaking experience, the student council member was surprisingly cogent, and expressed the concerns of her classmates persuasively.
>
> (A) hope
> (B) depth
> (C) method
> (D) lack
> (E) union

If you don't know what *cogent* means, work around it. From the sentence, especially the clue word *and*, you know that *cogent* goes with "expressed the concerns of her classmates persuasively." So you don't have to worry about what *cogent* means. All you need to know is that the student council member was persuasive despite a - - - - of speaking experience.

Only (D), *lack*, fits. "Despite her lack of public speaking experience, the student council member expressed the concerns of her classmates persuasively." (By the way, *cogent* means "convincing, believable," roughly the same as "expressing concern persuasively.")

Let's look at another Sentence Completion problem. This time the tough vocabulary is in the answer choices. This example is the sixth question out of nine questions.

> Advances in technology occur at such a fast pace that dictionaries have difficulty incorporating the - - - - that emerge as names for new inventions.
>
> (A) colloquialisms
> (B) euphemisms
> (C) compensations
> (D) neologisms
> (E) clichés

Whatever goes in the blank has to describe "names for new inventions." If you don't know what the words *colloquialisms* or *euphemisms* mean, don't give up. Rule out as many choices as you can, and guess among the remaining ones.

You can eliminate (C) and (E) right off the bat. They don't describe names for new inventions. Now you can make an educated guess. Again, educated guessing will help your score more than guessing blindly or skipping the question.

By studying word roots (see Step 5, Building Your Vocabulary), you might know that *neo-* means "new," so the word *neologisms* might be the best choice for names of new inventions. In fact, it's the right answer. *Neologisms* are newly coined words.

If All Else Fails—Guess!

If you're really stumped, don't be afraid to guess. Eliminate all answer choices that seem wrong and guess from the remaining choices.

Now get ready to practice the strategies you've learned on this Sentence Completions problem set.

PRACTICE

Sentence Completion Questions

Number of Minutes—7; Number of Questions—9

Select the lettered word or set of words that best completes the sentence.

1. The stranger was actually smaller than he looked; looming up suddenly in the dark alley, he was - - - - in the eyes of the beholder by the alarm he inspired.

   (A) worsened
   (B) magnified
   (C) disparaged
   (D) disfigured
   (E) admonished

2. Although the risk of a nuclear accident remained - - - - , the public's concern about such an accident gradually - - - - .

   (A) steady . . waned
   (B) acute . . persisted
   (C) unclear . . shifted
   (D) obvious . . endured
   (E) pressing . . remained

3. Prior to the American entrance into World War I, President Woodrow Wilson strove to maintain the - - - - of the United States, warning both sides against encroachments on American interests.

   (A) involvement
   (B) belligerence
   (C) versatility
   (D) magnanimity
   (E) neutrality

4. The graceful curves of the colonial-era buildings that dominated the old part of the city contrasted sharply with the modern, - - - - subway stations and made the latter appear glaringly out of place.

   (A) festive
   (B) grimy
   (C) angular
   (D) gigantic
   (E) efficient

5. The discovery of the Dead Sea Scrolls in the 1940s quickly - - - - the popular imagination, but the precise significance of the scrolls is still - - - - by scholars.

   (A) impressed . . understood
   (B) alarmed . . obscured
   (C) troubled . . perceived
   (D) sparked . . disputed
   (E) eluded . . debated

6. Dietitians warn of the dangers of anorexia, an illness that can cause people with relatively normal physiques to starve themselves until they are too - - - - to survive.

   (A) glutted
   (B) lachrymose
   (C) emaciated
   (D) superfluous
   (E) satiated

7. Recent editions of the Chinese classic *Tao Te Ching*, based on manuscripts more authoritative than those hitherto available, have rendered previous editions - - - - - .

   (A) incomprehensible
   (B) interminable
   (C) inaccessible
   (D) obsolete
   (E) illegible

8. Despite their outward resemblance, the brothers could not be more - - - - temperamentally; while one is quiet and circumspect, the other is brash and - - - - - .

   (A inimical . . timid
   (B) passionate . . superficial
   (C) dissimilar . . audacious
   (D) different . . forgiving
   (E) alike . . respectful

9. Her scholarly rigor and capacity for - - - - enabled her to undertake research projects that less - - - - people would have found too difficult and tedious.

   (A) fanaticism . . slothful
   (B) comprehension . . indolent
   (C) analysis . . careless
   (D) negligence . . dedicated
   (E) concentration . . disciplined

Answers and Explanations

1. (B)

The clue here is the phrase "was smaller than he looked." The missing word has to mean "made larger" or "made to seem larger." Choice (B), *magnified*, is the answer. *Disparaged* (C) means "belittled." *Admonished* (E) means "scolded."

2. (A)

The word *although* indicates contrast. The contrast is between the risk and the public's concern. Choice (A) is the only one that presents a clear contrast: the risk didn't decrease, but the public's concern did.

3. (E)

The phrase "warning both sides against encroachments on American interests" indicates that Wilson was attempting to prevent each side from taking an action that would force the United States to get involved in the war. Choice (E), *neutrality*, gets this point across. *Involvement* (A) suggests the opposite of the correct answer. *Belligerence* (B) is the quality of being warlike; *versatility* (C) means being able to handle a variety of different situations; *magnanimity* (D) is generosity.

4. (C)

You're specifically told that there's a contrast between the buildings and the subway stations. Checking the answer choices for a word that contrasts in meaning with "graceful curves," you find that the answer is (C), *angular*, which means "jagged" or "angled."

5. (D)

The word *but* indicates contrast. If you plug in the answer choices, (D) makes the most sense: the public became quickly excited about the issue, but agreement among experts as to the significance of the scrolls has been slower in coming. None of the other choices provides a clear contrast of ideas.

6. (C)

The missing word describes people who "starve themselves" and become malnourished. Choice (C), *emaciated*, which means "extremely thin," is the only choice that really fits. (A) and (E) are the exact opposites of what's needed, and *lachrymose* (B) means "tearful."

7. (D)

If new editions of this book are based on "more authoritative," or more accurate, manuscripts, previous editions would be rendered out-of-date, or *obsolete* (D)—scholars wouldn't use the old editions because the new ones are markedly superior. However, the new edition wouldn't render the old edition *incomprehensible* (A), *interminable* (B), *inaccessible* (C), or *illegible* (E).

8. (C)

The clue word *despite* indicates that the brothers must have different temperaments—making *dissimilar* (C) and *different* (D) both possibilities. The second word has to contrast with "quiet and *circumspect*," and be similar in tone to "*brash*"; *audacious,* or bold, is the only choice that makes sense, so (C) is correct.

9. (E)

It's easier to start with the second blank. You need a word that goes with "*rigor*" and contrasts with finding things "difficult and tedious." *Slothful* (A) and *indolent* (B) both mean "lazy," so they're the opposite of what you need. Only *dedicated* (D) and *disciplined* (E) fit. Eliminate the other choices and try (D) and (E) in the first blank. The correct choice will be a quality held by a dedicated, rigorous scholar, so *concentration* (E) is the answer. *Negligence* (D) is the opposite of what you're looking for.

STEP FOUR

Critical Reading Questions

One of the things the SAT tests is your ability to remember what you just read. It does this in its Critical Reading section. This section counts for about one half of your Verbal score, so doing better on Critical Reading is very important. Here's your outline for Step 4:

STEP 4 PREVIEW

Format

Know the Critical Reading section's components:

- Critical Reading format
- Little Picture questions
- Definition-in-Context questions
- Big Picture questions

Critical Reading Skills

Learn the reading skills needed to do well in the Critical Reading section:

- Skimming
- Paraphrasing
- Making inferences

Critical Reading Strategies

Master the strategies that help you score higher on Critical Reading questions:

- Read, Locate, Think, Scan, Select
- Paired Passages: First things first, second things second
- Running out of time: Two-Minute Warning

Practice

Use it before you lose it (13 questions / 15 minutes)

FORMAT

The Critical Reading section has four passages, each about 400–850 words long (the length of an average newspaper article), that deal with the arts, humanities, social science, and science. One of the four Critical Reading passages is a "paired passage" consisting of two related excerpts.

The instructions for the Critical Reading section are simple: "Answer the questions based on the information in the accompanying passage or passages."

Read them five times, count backwards from 14 in your head, think back to the last time you were happy with your hairstyle, then summarize the instructions below:

_____

_____

You DO NOT want to waste time reading these directions on test day, so make sure you understand them now.

Each reading passage has a short introduction that will say something like this:

> *The following excerpt is from a freestyle rap delivered in 1993 by Snoop D.*
> *Dogg, a leader of the West Coast hip-hop scene.*

DO NOT skip this short introduction. It will help you focus your reading.

The Critical Reading passage follows the short introduction. Most passages read like a story in *Time* or *People* magazine, and typically deal with those magazines' general subject matter, with more emphasis on historical figures and less emphasis on pop singing sensations. The passage is followed by 7–13 multiple-choice questions. The questions follow a logical order: the first few questions ask about the beginning of the passage; the last few questions ask about the end. The questions themselves are also very predictable, since the test makers use a formula to write them.

Paired passage questions also usually follow a specific order. The first few questions relate to the first passage, the next few to the second passage, and the final questions ask about the passages as a pair. This is usually, but not always, the case, like the bounce one's hair often, but not always, gets from one's favorite hair care product.

Critical Reading questions ARE NOT ordered by difficulty. All of the other questions on the SAT are. So don't get bogged down on a hard, early question, because the next one could be easier.

Q. Why should you read a Critical Reading passage's brief introduction?

(A) To focus my reading

(B) To increase the volume of my hair

(C) To focus my eyes

(D) To gauge the passage's difficulty

(E) To focus my camera

Ⓐ Ⓑ Ⓒ Ⓓ Ⓔ   (A)

Three Kinds of Questions

Critical Reading questions ask about three kinds of things:

1. Details from the passage (Little Picture)
2. The definition of a word from the passage (Definition-in-Context)
3. The overall tone and content of the passage (Big Picture)

For the paired passages, you are also asked to compare and contrast the two passages.

Little Picture

About 70 percent are **Little Picture** questions that ask about "snapshots" from the passage: small pieces of information contained in the passage. Little Picture questions usually give you a line reference from the passage to reread or refer you to a particular paragraph in the passage. Little Picture questions can:

- Test whether you understand important information stated in a passage
- Ask you to make inferences or draw conclusions based on a part of a passage
- Ask you to relate parts of a passage to one another

Here's a sample Little Picture question:

22. According to lines 52–56, one difficulty of using a linear representation of time is that

(A) linear representations of time do not meet accepted scientific standards of accuracy

(B) prehistoric eras overlap each other, making linear representation deceptive

(C) the more accurate the scale, the more difficult the map is to copy and study

(D) there are too many events to represent on a single line

(E) our knowledge of pre-Cambrian time is insufficient to construct an accurate linear map

The rest of the questions are divided into "Definition-in-Context" and "Big Picture" questions.

Definition-in-Context

Definition-in-Context questions ask about an even smaller part of the passage than Little Picture questions. They ask about the usage of a single word. These questions DO NOT test your ability to define hard words like "frisson" and "salubrious." They test your ability to infer the meaning of a word from context of the words around it.

In fact, the words tested in these questions will probably be familiar to you—they are usually fairly common words with more than one definition. Many of the answer choices will be correct definitions of the tested word, but only one will work in context. Definition-in-Context questions always have a line reference, and you should always use it. Here's a sample Definition-in-Context question:

29. The word *hardihood* in line 52 could best be replaced by

    (A) endurance
    (B) vitality
    (C) nerve
    (D) opportunity
    (E) stupidity

Context is the most important part of Definition-in-Context questions. Sometimes one of the answer choices will jump out at you. It will be the most common meaning of the word in question, but it is ALMOST NEVER RIGHT.

For example, let's say "curious" is the word being tested. The obvious definition of *curious* is "inquisitive." But, less often, *curious* means "odd," so that's more likely to be the answer. Using context to find the answer will help prevent you from falling for the "obvious choice" trap.

You can use these choices to your advantage, though. If you get stuck on a Definition-in-Context question, eliminate the obvious choice, and guess from the remaining choices.

Big Picture

Big Picture questions test your overall understanding of the passage's main points—the kind of stuff that, if you were driving down the highway, you might see on a billboard advertising the passage. Like this:

THE WRITER THINKS THAT
DOGS ARE BETTER PETS THAN CATS.

Big Picture questions might ask about:
- The main point or purpose of a passage
- The writer's attitude or tone
- The logic behind the writer's argument
- How ideas relate to each other

Here's a sample Big Picture question:

9. The author of Passage 2 cites Shakespeare's status as a landowner in order to

   (A) prove that Shakespeare was a success as a playwright
   (B) refute the claim that Shakespeare had little knowledge of aristocratic life
   (C) prove that Shakespeare didn't depend solely on acting for his living
   (D) dispute the notion that Shakespeare was a commoner
   (E) account for Shakespeare's apparent knowledge of the law

Now that you know what to expect in the Critical Reading section, we'll get to the skills you can develop that will help you score higher on this section.

Q. Critical Reading questions usually ask

   (A) for details from the passage
   (B) about the overall tone and content of the passage
   (C) what the writer is trying to say
   (D) All of the above
   (E) None of the above

   Ⓐ Ⓑ Ⓒ Ⓓ Ⓔ   (D)

CRITICAL READING SKILLS

Mastering these three reading skills will help you score better on the Critical Reading passages:

1. *Skimming*—Reading for a reason, not for pleasure. You are reading Critical Reading passages for one reason: to score points on the SAT. The best way to read for points is to skim (read quickly and lightly). You skim when you look up information in a phone book, or when you read a newspaper article only long enough to get an idea of the story.

2. *Paraphrasing*—Restating something in your own words. You do it all the time in daily life, especially when you are trying to explain questionable behavior, which is probably pretty often.

3. *Making Inferences*—When you deduce information from a statement or situation, you're making inferences. You may infer from the statement "We eat Funyons" that we like Funyons, even though we never actually said we *liked* Funyons. We just said we *eat* Funyons. But it's a good inference.

Skimming for COPPS

Skimming requires that you read (1) quickly and (2) in less detail than usual. These two characteristics make skimming the best way to read Critical Reading passages. You want to read quickly because time is limited, and you want to read in less detail because the Critical Reading questions direct you to the only details you need to know about.

Important

The questions will direct you to the important details in the passage.

Reading the entire passage before you see the questions wastes a lot of time. So skim the passage and look for COPPs. "I should look out for police at the SAT?" you ask. If you're hiding something, yes. But you should look for COPPs, too:

- The **C**ontent of the passage
- The **O**rganization of the passage
- The **P**urpose or **P**oint of view of the writer

Content is what the passage is about: jellybeans, stock car racing, the Middle East.

Organization is how the passage is written. Every passage contains phrases or paragraph breaks that signal that the passage is changing direction.

The writer's **p**urpose is the reason she wrote the passage, and her **p**oint of view is her opinion on the passage's subject matter. Every passage is written for a purpose. The writer wants to make a point, describe a situation, or convince you of something. The SAT is testing your ability to figure out what the writer is trying to get at, so as you're reading, ask yourself these questions:

1. What's the point of this passage?
2. What's this passage all about?
3. Which side is the writer on?

This is THE KEY TO SKIMMING: staying focused on the COPPs, instead of on the uncommonly attractive test proctor. Once you have skimmed a passage, you can go to the questions. The questions will help you to fill in the story's details by directing you back to line references and other important information in the passage. This way, the only details you will know are the ones you need to know to answer the question.

Important

You can tackle whichever Critical Reading passages you like in any order you like within the same section. But once you've read through a passage, answer the questions that go with it.

Q. When I read a Critical Reading passage I should

(A) read every word so I'm prepared to answer any question that may be asked

(B) read every word so I'm better able to avoid the traps set by the test takers

(C) skim the passage to get a general idea of what it's about, then let the questions guide me to its important details

(D) skim the passage and answer only one question so I can get a jump on the Math section

(E) finish quickly then try to make eye contact with the uncommonly attractive test proctor

(C)

Getting hung up on details is the major Critical Reading pitfall. You need to understand the outline of the passage, but you don't need to—and don't want to—remember every single detail. The less time you spend on reading the passages, the more time you'll have to answer the questions, and that's where you score points.

Kaplan's Keys to Skimming

Quick Like a Bunny

The way your eyes move across each line of type and return to the beginning of the next line is your "tracking style." You want your tracking style to be light and quick like a bunny, rather than heavy and deliberate like a . . . that's right, a turtle. Move your eyes lightly over the page, grouping words. Don't read each word separately. You want to increase your reading rate, but don't go too fast, or you won't remember anything.

Don't Talk To Yourself

Subvocalizing means "sounding out" words as you read. Even if you don't move your lips, you're probably subvocalizing if you read one word at a time. Subvocalizing costs you time because you can't read faster than you speak. If you group words, you won't subvocalize.

Keep Asking Yourself Where the Writer Is Going

Each SAT passage takes you on a fascinating journey, and every passage contains phrases or paragraph breaks that signal the next phase of the magical trip. As you skim the passage, notice especially where the writer changes course.

Let's try it out. Read the following paragraphs, letting your eyes "touch" on only two places per line, like a cute little bunny hopping down the page.

The *Catcher in the Rye*, published in <u>1951</u>, is the only novel written by <u>J.D. Salinger</u> in a career that lasted <u>less than twenty years</u>. It is the story of Holden Caulfield, a <u>sensitive, rebellious</u> New York City teen-ager taking his first hesitant <u>steps into adulthood</u>. Holden <u>flees the</u> confines of his <u>snobbish Eastern prep</u> school, searching for <u>innocence and truth,</u> <u>but finds only "phoniness."</u> Filled with <u>humor and pathos</u>, *The Catcher in the Rye* <u>won wide critical</u> acclaim at the <u>time of its publication</u>. In the <u>four decades since</u> then, however, it has become a <u>true phenomenon</u>, selling hundreds of <u>thousands of copies</u> each year, and <u>Holden Caulfield</u> has gained the status of a <u>cultural icon</u>. What accounts for this <u>book's</u> <u>remarkable hold</u> on generation <u>after generation</u> of <u>American youth</u>?

<u>Holden Caulfield is the narrator</u> of *The Catcher in the Rye*, and his narration is a <u>stylistic tour de force</u>, revealing <u>Salinger's masterful ear</u> for the linguistic <u>idioms and rhythms</u> of adolescent speech. <u>Slang evolves</u> <u>continuously</u>, of course, and <u>yesterday's "in" expressions</u> are usually <u>passé by tomorrow</u>. But Holden's <u>characteristic means</u> of expression— <u>the vernacular</u> of a teen-age <u>social misfit, desperately trying</u> to find his niche—<u>transcends the particulars</u> of time and place. Like <u>another 1950s</u> <u>icon</u>, James Dean in *Rebel Without a Cause*, <u>Holden Caulfield has</u> <u>"outlived" his era</u> and become an enduring symbol of <u>sensitive youth</u>, <u>threatened</u> by an indifferent <u>society</u>.

See how your eye takes in whole phrases, though you haven't read every word? That's good skimming.

Paraphrasing

Paraphrasing means condensing a long passage into a few sentences that highlight the most important parts of the long passage. Critical Reading questions often ask you to paraphrase when they ask a Big Picture question: what a passage, or part of it, means. The right answer choice correctly paraphrases the meaning of the passage or excerpt. That means it restates the meaning without losing any important points.

Q. What does paraphrasing do?

(A) It helps you answer questions that involve a pair of phrases

(B) It makes you laugh like you've never laughed before

(C) It helps you answer questions that ask you what a long passage means

(D) It makes you the envy of your peer group

(E) It helps you say in many sentences what a passage says in just a few

Ⓐ Ⓑ Ⓒ Ⓓ Ⓔ   (C)

Kaplan's Keys to Paraphrasing

We have a good way to answer a paraphrasing question:

1. Read the question stem. That's the partial sentence leading to the answer choices.
2. Read the lines the question refers you to, searching for the relevant phrases. (If a question gives you a line reference, be sure to read a line or two before and after it, too.)
3. Think of your own paraphrase for what's being asked.
4. Find a similar answer choice.

Let's try it on this excerpt from a Critical Reading passage:

> No doubt because it painted a less than flattering picture of American life in America for Asian immigrants, *East Goes West* was not well received by contemporary literary critics. According to them, Kang's book displayed a curious lack of insight regarding the American effort to accommodate those who had come over from Korea. The facet of the novel reviewers did find praiseworthy was Han's perseverance and sustained optimism in the face of adversity.

> The passage indicates that the response of critics to *East Goes West* was one of

> (A) irony regarding the difference between Han's expectations and reality
> (B) admiration of the courage and creativity Kang showed in breaking from literary tradition
> (C) confusion about the motivation of the protagonist
> (D) qualified disapproval of Kang's perception of his adopted homeland
> (E) anger that Kang had so viciously attacked American society

Now apply Kaplan's paraphrasing method:

1–2. After reading the stem and relevant lines of the passage, the key phrases should have popped out: "not well received," a "curious lack of insight," and the "facet . . . reviewers did find praiseworthy."
3. Predicted paraphrase: The critics were displeased with Kang's view of the immigrant's experience, but approved of the hero's persistence.
4. Look for the answer choice that means the same as your paraphrase.

Choice (D) comes closest. *Qualified* means "modified" or "limited," so qualified disapproval captures both the negative and the positive reaction the reviewers had. Choice (E) is too negative, and choice (B) is too positive. Choices (A) and (C) don't reflect what the excerpt says. So (D) is the answer.

Now you try. The excerpt below is followed by a space where you should write your own paraphrase. Compare your paraphrase with the answer choices and pick the best approximation.

> Only with effort can the camera be forced to lie: basically it is an honest medium; so the photographer is much more likely to approach nature in a spirit of inquiry, of communion, instead of with the saucy swagger of self-dubbed "artists."
>
> The distinction made in the passage between a photographer and an "artist" can best be summarized as which of the following (summarize the distinction in your own words):

_____

_____

_____

Find the best paraphrase:

    (A) The photographer's job is to record the world, and the artist's is to embellish it.

    (B) The photographer's work is realistic, while the artist's is impressionistic.

    (C) The artist finds his inspiration in the urban environment, the photographer in nature.

    (D) The photographer has a more open and unassuming attitude towards the natural world than the artist does.

    (E) Photographers are more pretentious than artists are.

The answer is (D): A photographer is more open to nature and less pretentious than an "artist" is.

Making Inferences

When you make an inference, you are reaching a conclusion that is only hinted at in the Critical Reading passage. When you infer, you "read between the lines." For example, if you have read the Paraphrasing and Skimming parts of this book, you may infer that, next, we will give you Kaplan's Keys to Making Inferences and some practice making inferences.

Kaplan's Keys to Making Inferences

There are three important parts to good inferring on Critical Reading passages. Remember the skimming COPPs? Now meet the inferring REDs.

- **R**ead a line or two around any line reference you are given in the question.
- Look for **E**vidence in the passage to support an inference.
- **D**on't go too far with inferences. SAT inferences are straightforward and consistent with the overall idea of the passage. They are predictable. They are NOT extreme, complex, or subtle.

Let's practice. Read this passage and answer the question that follows:

> My father was a justice of the peace, and I supposed that he possessed the power of life and death over all men and could hang anybody that offended him. This distinction was enough for me as a general thing; but the desire to become a steamboat man kept intruding, nevertheless. I first wanted to be a cabin boy, so that I could come out with a white apron on and shake a tablecloth over the side, where all my old comrades could see me. Later I thought I would rather be the deck hand who stood on the end of the stage plank with a coil of rope in his hand, because he was particularly conspicuous.

> The author makes the statement that "I supposed he possessed the power of life and death over all men and could hang anybody that offended him" primarily to suggest the

> (A) power held by a justice of the peace in a frontier town
> (B) naive view that he held of his father's importance
> (C) respect that the townspeople had for his father
> (D) possibility of miscarriages of justice on the American frontier
> (E) harsh environment in which he was brought up

The answer is implied here. The author doesn't say "my view of my father's importance at the time was naive." But the idea can be inferred from the excerpt.

As the author explains it, he supposed at the time that his father could kill almost anyone. That probably sounded weird to you, and you also probably wondered why the son was proud of it. But read the rest of the passage and you'll realize the tone is ironic. The author is making fun of his youthful ideas (dad can kill anyone he wants, being a cabin boy is a glamorous job, deck hands get all the attention). So the correct answer has to be (B).

Remember, SAT inferences are straightforward. That's why choices (A) and (E) go too far. Is it realistic that the author's father could hang anyone he wanted? Even if he could, would the author be proud of it? Very unlikely. Do the boy's early assumptions about his father's power indicate anything about the environment he grew up in? No.

Now that you know the Critical Reading skills you need to develop, let's proceed to Kaplan's strategies for getting your best possible score on the Critical Reading portion of the SAT Verbal section.

CRITICAL READING STRATEGIES

Kaplan's strategies for improving your Critical Reading score use the skills we just covered, so if you were pressed for time and skipped right to this page, take five minutes to skim the skills first, then go to the strategies.

Read/Locate/Think/Scan/Select

This is THE MOST IMPORTANT STRATEGY for answering questions in the Critical Reading section. If you only have time to learn one strategy for the section, this is it:

1. *Read* the question stem.
2. *Locate* the material you need.
3. *Think* up YOUR idea of the right answer.
4. *Scan* the answer choices.
5. *Select* your answer.

Let's go through these carefully, in the order you should do them.

1. Read the question stem.

Read the question very carefully. Make sure you understand what the question is asking before you go back to the passage.

2. Locate the material you need.

If the question gives you a line reference, also read the material in the passage that surrounds the line. The surrounding material clarifies what the question is asking. If you're not given a line reference, scan the passage to find the place in the passage the question is asking about. Read those few sentences.

3. Think up YOUR idea of the right answer.

Don't come up with a precise answer. You don't have time. You need only a general sense of what you're after, so you can recognize the correct answer quickly when you read the choices.

4. Scan the answer choices.

Find the one that fits YOUR idea of the right answer. If you don't find one, eliminate wrong choices by checking back to the passage. Rule out choices that are (A) too extreme, (B) go against common sense, and (C) sound reasonable but don't make sense in the context of the passage.

5. Select your answer.

You've eliminated the obvious wrong answers. One of the remaining should match YOUR right answer. If you're left with more than one contender, consider the passage's main idea, then make your best guess.

Q. Which answers do you eliminate if you can't find your ideal answer right away?

(A) Answers that go against common sense or are too extreme

(B) Answers that are too long or too short

(C) Answers that are too funny or not funny enough

(D) Answers that sound so wrong, they must be right

(E) Answers that sound like a deer

Ⓐ Ⓑ Ⓒ Ⓓ Ⓔ   (A)

Big Picture Question Strategy

If you're not clear on the main idea of the passage, do Big Picture questions AFTER Little Picture questions. By doing the Little Picture questions first, you'll have a bunch of clues to the passage's main points.

PAIRED PASSAGES: FIRST THINGS FIRST, SECOND THINGS SECOND

Paired passage questions focus on relationships between two passages. Approach the paired passage as you would a single passage, with a few minor alterations.

1. Skim the **FIRST** passage, looking for the general outline (as you would with a single passage).

2. Do the questions that relate to the **FIRST** passage.

3. Skim the **SECOND** passage, looking for the general outline and thinking about how the second passage relates to the first.

4. Do the questions that relate to the **SECOND** passage.

5. Now you're ready to do the remaining questions, which will ask about the relationship between **BOTH** passages.

Skimming the first passage and answering its questions before doing the same with the second passage is REALLY IMPORTANT if you're short of time. You'll be able to answer at least some of the questions (and get a few extra points) before time runs out.

By the time you've looked at both passages and answered the questions about each passage, you'll have a good sense of how the pair relate. That will help you to answer the questions relating the two. Practice "First Things First/Second Things Second" on the practice passage at the end of the chapter.

RUNNING OUT OF TIME: TWO-MINUTE WARNING

Of course it's better to skim a passage before you hit the questions. But if you only have a few minutes left, you can still score points even while time is running out.

If you have just a couple of minutes remaining, and you haven't read the passage, SKIP READING IT, do its Definition-in-Context questions first, and then its Little Picture questions.

You can answer many Definition-in-Context questions and Little Picture questions without even reading the passage. If the question has a line reference, locate the material you need to find your answer and Read/Locate/Think/Scan/Select. You won't have the main idea of the passage to guide you, but you should be able to at least rule out some answer choices, and then guess from what's left.

CONCLUSION

You now know important skills and strategies that should help you improve your score on the Critical Reading part of the SAT. Apply what you've learned to the following paired passage, and go through the answers and explanations very carefully when you're done.

PRACTICE

Critical Reading Passage

Number of Minutes—15; Number of Questions—13

Questions 1–13 are based on the following passages.

The following passages present two views of the genius of Leonardo da Vinci. Passage 1 emphasizes Leonardo's fundamentally artistic sensibility. Passage 2 offers a defense of his technological achievements.

Passage 1

What a marvelous and celestial creature was Leonardo da Vinci. As a scientist and engineer, his gifts were unparalleled. But his
Line accomplishment in these capacities was
(5) hindered by the fact that he was, before all else, an artist. As one conversant with the perfection of art, and knowing the futility of trying to bring such perfection to the realm of practical application, Leonardo tended
(10) toward variability and inconstancy in his endeavors. His practice of moving compulsively from one project to the next, never bringing any of them to completion, stood in the way of his making any truly
(15) useful technical advances.

When Leonardo was asked to create a memorial for one of his patrons, he designed a bronze horse of such vast proportions that it proved utterly impractical—even
(20) impossible—to produce. Some historians maintain that Leonardo never had any intention of finishing this work in the first place. But it is more likely that he simply became so intoxicated by his grand artistic
(25) conception that he lost sight of the fact that the monument actually had to be cast. Similarly, when Leonardo was commissioned to paint the *Last Supper*, he left the head of Christ unfinished, feeling incapable of
(30) investing it with a sufficiently divine demeanor. Yet, as a work of art rather than science or engineering, it is still worthy of

our greatest veneration, for Leonardo succeeded brilliantly in capturing the acute
(35) anxiety of the Apostles at the most dramatic moment of the Passion narrative.

Such mental restlessness, however, proved more problematic when applied to scientific matters. When he turned his mind to the
(40) natural world, Leonardo would begin by inquiring into the properties of herbs and end up observing the motions of the heavens. In his technical studies and scientific experiments, he would generate an endless
(45) stream of models and drawings, designing complex and unbuildable machines to raise great weights, bore through mountains, or even empty harbors.

It is this enormous intellectual fertility that
(50) has suggested to many that Leonardo can and should be regarded as one of the originators of modern science. But Leonardo was not himself a true scientist. "Science" is not the hundred-odd principles or *pensieri** that have
(55) been pulled out of his *Codici*. Science is comprehensive and methodical thought. Granted, Leonardo always became fascinated by the intricacies of specific technical challenges. He possessed the artist's interest in
(60) detail, which explains his compulsion with observation and problem solving. But such things alone do not constitute science, which requires the working out of a systematic body of knowledge—something Leonardo displayed
(65) little interest in doing.

pensieri: thoughts (Italian)

Passage 2

As varied as Leonardo's interests were, analysis of his writings points to technology as his main concern. There is hardly a field of
Line applied mechanics that Leonardo's searching
(70) mind did not touch upon in his notebooks. Yet some of his biographers have actually expressed regret that such a man, endowed with divine artistic genius, would "waste" precious years of his life on such a "lowly"
(75) pursuit as engineering.

To appreciate Leonardo's contribution to technology, one need only examine his analysis of the main problem of technology— the harnessing of energy to perform useful
(80) work. In Leonardo's time, the main burden of human industry still rested on the muscles of humans and animals. But little attention was given to analyzing this primitive muscle power so that it could be brought to bear
(85) most effectively on the required tasks. Against this background, Leonardo's approach to work was revolutionary. When he searched for the most efficient ways of using human muscle power, the force of every limb was
(90) analyzed and measured.

Consider Leonardo's painstaking building approach to the construction of canals. After extensive analysis of the requirements for a particular canal by hand, he concluded that
(95) the only reasonable solution was to mechanize the whole operation. Then he considered and ultimately discarded numerous schemes to clear excavated material by wheeled vehicles. It was not that
(100) Leonardo underestimated wheeled vehicles. But he realized that a cart is useful only on level ground; on steep terrain the material's weight would nullify the effort of the animal.

Having systematically rejected several
(105) solutions in this way, Leonardo began to examine the feasibility of excavation techniques incorporating a system of cranes. Power was again his main concern. To activate a crane, the only transportable motor
(110) available at the time would have been a treadmill, a machine that converts muscle power into rotary motion. This is not to suggest that Leonardo invented the external treadmill. However, it was Leonardo who first
(115) used the principle of the treadmill rationally and in accordance with sound engineering principles.

Because Leonardo's insights were sometimes so far beyond the standards of his
(120) time, their importance to the development of modern engineering is often underestimated. Many scholars, in fact, still regard his work merely as the isolated accomplishments of a remarkably prophetic dreamer, refusing to
(125) concede that Leonardo was one of our earliest and most significant engineers.

1. The author of Passage 1 seems to regard the "perfection of art" (line 7) as

   (A) a more valuable goal than scientific accomplishment
   (B) achievable only with diligence and constant effort
   (C) applicable to the solving of technical problems
   (D) a model to which scientists should aspire
   (E) unattainable in the fields of science and engineering

2. The author of Passage 1 considers the *Last Supper* ultimately successful as a work of art because it

   (A) is much sought-after by collectors
   (B) emphasizes the role of the Apostles in comforting Christ before his crucifixion
   (C) captures the divinity of Christ on the eve of his death
   (D) depicts a well-known moment in the history of Christianity
   (E) conveys the anxiety felt by Christ's Apostles

3. The word *variability* in line 10 most nearly means

   (A) comprehensiveness
   (B) changeability
   (C) uncertainty
   (D) confusion
   (E) disorder

4. In lines 39–42, the author most likely describes the way Leonardo "turned his mind to the natural world" in order to show that

   (A) Leonardo's mind was constantly leaping from one topic to another
   (B) elements of the natural world are all interconnected
   (C) Leonardo's mind was preoccupied with scientific experiments
   (D) Leonardo preferred artistic pursuits to scientific inquiry
   (E) Leonardo tended to become distracted by his artistic projects

5. The author of Passage 1 is critical of Leonardo's *pensieri* (line 54) primarily because they

   (A) are factually incorrect
   (B) do not constitute a systematic body of thought
   (C) contradict widely accepted scientific principles
   (D) were never thoroughly tested
   (E) are based on intuition rather than observation

6. In the last paragraph of Passage 1, the author's attitude towards modern scientific investigation can best be characterized as

   (A) sentimental
   (B) disparaging
   (C) respectful
   (D) detached
   (E) superficial

7. In lines 71–75, the author is critical of some of Leonardo's biographers primarily because they

   (A) overestimate his artistic genius
   (B) do not adequately recognize his technological contributions
   (C) were careless in their analyses of his writings
   (D) understate the importance of his artistic masterpieces
   (E) ignore the value of science in relation to art and culture

8. The author of Passage 2 considers Leonardo's approach to work "revolutionary" (line 87) principally because he

   (A) attempted to replace humans and animals with machines
   (B) adapted traditional solutions to previously impossible tasks
   (C) studied the mechanics of muscles with unprecedented thoroughness
   (D) proposed technical solutions that most people regarded as impossible to achieve
   (E) shifted the main burden of industry from human to animal power

9. In lines 99–103, the discussion of wheeled vehicles is presented in order to support the author's point about Leonardo's

   (A) thoroughness in examining all possible solutions to a problem
   (B) tendency to let his artistic genius interfere with his effectiveness as an engineer
   (C) ability to arrive immediately at the best way of approaching a technical task
   (D) harmful practice of moving from one idea to the next
   (E) underestimation of traditional technology

10. The word *concede* in line 125 most nearly means

   (A) surrender
   (B) acknowledge
   (C) admit weakness
   (D) resign
   (E) sacrifice

11. Both passages suggest that which of the following is fundamental to scientific inquiry?

   (A) Intuitive genius
   (B) Familiarity with the perfections of art
   (C) An ability to combine knowledge from many different areas
   (D) Meticulous observation and analysis
   (E) Knowledge of the interconnectedness of all phenomena

12. The author of Passage 1 would probably regard the painstaking analysis of canal-building described in Passage 2 as an example of Leonardo's

   (A) revolutionary approach to work
   (B) ability to complete ambitious engineering projects
   (C) artistic fascination with details
   (D) predisposition to lose interest in specific problems
   (E) penchant for designing unbuildable machines

13. How would the author of Passage 2 respond to the implication in Passage 1 that Leonardo's insights did not result in "truly useful technical advances" (lines 14–15)?

   (A) Usefulness is not an appropriate criterion for judging solutions to technical problems.
   (B) Leonardo would have accomplished more had he not been distracted by his artistic endeavors.
   (C) Leonardo's invention of the external treadmill is one of countless useful advances he instigated.
   (D) Leonardo's ideas were so advanced that they often could not be put into practice in his time.
   (E) Leonardo's contributions to modern engineering have been deliberately ignored by many scholars.

Answers and Explanations

The italicized intro reveals the basic contrast between the two passages: Author #1 stresses Leonardo's "artistic sensibility," while Author #2 stresses his "technological achievements." Author #1 argues that Leonardo's artistic mentality interfered with his real accomplishments. He "tended toward variability and inconstancy in his endeavors," he was impractical and restless, and despite his extraordinary inventiveness, he was more of an artist than a true scientist. Author #2 has a diametrically opposite view, arguing that Leonardo was an engineering genius, that his approach to scientific problems was thoroughly systematic. With that basic difference in mind, let's rack up some points.

1. (E)

The overall point of paragraph 1 is that Leonardo's accomplishments as a scientist and engineer were limited by the fact that he approached everything as an artist—he moved compulsively from one engineering project to the next because he realized that "the perfection of art" was not attainable in those fields.

2. (E)

The author's opinion of the *Last Supper* is expressed pretty clearly at the end of paragraph 2—despite its shortcomings, it is "worthy of our greatest veneration" because it "succeeded brilliantly in capturing the acute anxiety of the Apostles."

3. (B)

The author expands on Leonardo's "variability and inconstancy" at the end of the paragraph—we're told that Leonardo made a habit of "moving compulsively from one project to the next." So *variability* means "changeability" in this context.

4. (A)

Leonardo's approach to natural science is scatter-brained; he begins by "inquiring into the properties of herbs," and ends up "observing the motions of the heavens." So the author is describing it as an example of his "mental restlessness . . . when applied to scientific matters."

5. (B)

The author's criticism of the *pensieri* is that while they reflect Leonardo's "compulsion with observation and problem-solving . . . such things alone do not constitute science, which requires the working out of a systematic body of knowledge."

6. (C)

The author presents modern scientific investigation as "the working out of a systematic body of knowledge," implying throughout that Leonardo wasn't sufficiently disciplined in his work to pursue this. Essentially, the author's attitude towards science is respectful.

7. (B)

The author of passage 2 is critical of Leonardo's biographers because they contradict his or her point of view; the author regards Leonardo as an engineer who made great contributions to technology whereas biographers regard Leonardo's interest in engineering as a waste of time.

8. (B)

Leonardo's approach to analyzing human muscle power was "revolutionary" because "little attention" had been given to this area before.

9. (A)

The underlying point of paragraphs 2 and 3 is that Leonardo was exhaustive in his approach to engineering problems. Wheeled vehicles are discussed to show that Leonardo was farsighted enough to realize that they weren't the solution to the problem of mechanizing canals.

10. (B)

The issue in the last paragraph is whether Leonardo was "one of our earliest and most significant engineers"—the author believes that he was, but the scholars refuse to concede this. Essentially, the author is suggesting that scholars are unwilling to admit this fact, so *concede* in this context means "acknowledge."

11. (D)

The last sentence of passage 1 defines science as "the working out of a systematic body of knowledge," suggesting that Leonardo wasn't interested in focusing his abilities. Passage 2 presents a contrasting picture of Leonardo, but suggests something very similar about the nature of scientific inquiry—we're told that Leonardo approached his engineering in a "painstaking" and "systematic" manner. So both authors would agree that "meticulous observation and analysis" was crucial to scientific inquiry.

12. (C)

The overall point of passage 1 is that Leonardo's artistic temperament adversely affected his approach to science and engineering. We're told in the last paragraph that "he possessed an artist's interest in detail, which explains his compulsion with observation and problem-solving." Consequently, the author of passage 1 would probably see Leonardo's painstaking work on canals in this light.

13. (D)

The last paragraph of passage 2 explains why Leonardo's accomplishments as an engineer are so often overlooked. We're told that Leonardo's insights were often "far beyond the standards of his time." And so choice (D)—Leonardo was too advanced—would be the most appropriate response to the first author's criticism.

Building Your Vocabulary

You may understand a Critical Reading passage but get thrown by one tough vocabulary word. You may know the relationship between the stem words in an Analogy, but recognize none of the words in the answer choices. You may know precisely what kind of word to fill in on a Sentence Completion, and then find all of the answer choices resemble the random mumblings of the camera-shy bass player in your favorite retro punk band.

Often, to get a Verbal question correct, you need to at least have a sense of the meaning of a tough word. Sadly, a great vocabulary takes years to build, and years you do not have. Luckily, there are strategies for improving your *SAT vocabulary* that you can use weeks and months before the SAT, and shortcuts you can take when you're pressed for time. We'll discuss both.

STEP 5 PREVIEW

Strategies
Strengthen your vocabulary:
- Learn words strategically (word families)
- Use word roots
- Trust your hunches

Practice
Use it before you lose it (Learn the word families)

STRATEGIES

There are two types of hard SAT words:

1. Unfamiliar words
2. Familiar words with secondary meanings

Some words are hard because you haven't seen them before. The words *scintilla* and *circumlocution*, for instance, are probably not part of your everyday vocabulary. Easy words such as *recognize* and *appreciation* may also trip you up because they have secondary meanings that you aren't used to. Analogies and Critical Reading in particular will throw you familiar words with unfamiliar meanings.

Learn Words Strategically

The most important words for you to learn are those that have appeared on the SAT before, regardless of your familiarity with them. Test writers are not very creative in their choice of words for each test; words that have appeared frequently are good bets to show up again.

The word families that follow group many of these repeated words into common meaning families. For example, *loquacious, verbose,* and *garrulous* all mean "wordy, talkative." *Taciturn, laconic, terse, concise,* and *pithy* all mean "not talkative, not wordy." All of these words appear on the SAT over and over again. By learning them together you get a bunch of words for the price of one definition.

Go through the word families that follow, linking the words that you don't know to the words that you do know. Use the word that you do know in a sentence, write that sentence down, and then replace the known word with the iffy word so you get used to seeing the iffy new words in context. It won't always be a perfect fit, but it should help you get more comfortable with new and/or difficult vocabulary.

Word Families

Talkative

garrulous	glib	loquacious	raconteur
verbose	voluble		

Your sentence: _____

_____

Secret/Hidden

abscond	alias	arcane	clandestine
covert	cryptic	enigma	furtive
incognito	inconspicuous	lurk	obscure
skulk	subterranean	surreptitious	

Your sentence: _____

_____

Not Talkative

concise	curt	laconic	pithy
reticent	succinct	taciturn	

Your sentence: _____

_____

Praise

accolade	adulation	commend	eulogize
exalt	extol	laud	lionize
plaudit	revere		

Your sentence: _____

_____

Criticize/Scold

admonish	berate	castigate	censure
chastise	defame	denigrate	disdain
disparage	excoriate	malign	obloquy
rail	rebuke	reproach	reprimand
reprove	revile	upbraid	vilify

Your sentence: _____

_____

Stubborn

intractable	mulish	obdurate	obstinate
pertinacious	recalcitrant	refractory	tenacious

Your sentence: _____

_____

Lazy/Lacking Energy

indolent	lackadaisical	laggard	languid
lassitude	lethargic	listless	loiter
phlegmatic	sluggard	somnolent	torpid

Your sentence: _____

_____

Cowardly

craven	diffident	pusillanimous	timid
timorous			

Your sentence: _____

_____

Inexperienced

callow	fledgling	infantile	ingenuous
neophyte	novice	tyro	

Your sentence: _____

_____

Obedient

amenable	assent	compliant	deferential
docile	pliant	submissive	tractable

Your sentence: _____

_____

Haughty/Pretentious

affected   aloof   bombastic   grandiloquent

grandiose   magniloquent   mannered   ostentatious

pontificate   supercilious

Your sentence: _____

_____

Friendly

affable   amiable   amicable   bonhomie

convivial   gregarious

Your sentence: _____

_____

Lucky

auspicious   fortuitous   opportune   serendipity

windfall

Your sentence: _____

_____

Soothe

allay   alleviate   anodyne   assuage

liniment   mitigate   mollify   pacify

palliate   placate

Your sentence: _____

_____

Hostility/Hatred

abhor	anathema	animosity	antagonism
antipathy	aversion	contentious	deplore
odious	rancor		

Your sentence: _____

_____

Stupid

buffoon	dolt	dupe	fatuous
imbecile	inane	insipid	obtuse
simpleton	vacuous	vapid	

Your sentence: _____

_____

Subservient

fawn	grovel	obsequious	servile
subjection	sycophant	toady	

Your sentence: _____

_____

Argumentative

adversarial	bellicose	belligerent	fractious
irascible	obstreperous	pugnacious	quibble

Your sentence: _____

_____

Cautious

chary	circumspect	discretion	leery
prudent	wary		

Your sentence: _____

_____

Impermanent

ephemeral	evanescent	fleeting	transient
transitory			

Your sentence: _____

_____

Ability/Intelligence

acumen	adept	adroit	agile
astute	cogent	deft	dexterous
erudite	literate	lithe	lucidity
sagacious	trenchant		

Your sentence: _____

_____

Kind/Generous

altruistic	beneficent	benevolent	bestow
largess	liberal	magnanimous	munificent
philanthropic			

Your sentence: _____

_____

Use Word Roots

Most SAT words are made up of prefixes and roots that can get you at least partway to a definition. Often, that's all you need to get a right answer. Knowing roots can help you in others ways as well. First, instead of learning one word at a time, you can learn a whole group of words that contain a certain root. They'll be related in meaning, so if you remember one, it will be easier for you to remember others. Second, roots can often help you decode an unknown SAT word. If you recognize a familiar root, you could get a good enough idea of the word to answer the question.

Use the root list that follows to pick up the most valuable SAT roots. Target these words in your vocabulary preparation.

Word Roots

A, AN—not, without

amoral, atrophy, asymmetrical, anarchy, anesthetic, anonymity, anomaly

AB, A—from, away, apart

abnormal, abdicate, aberration, abhor, abject, abjure, ablution, abnegate, abortive, abrogate, abscond, absolve, abstemious, abstruse, annul, avert, aversion

AC, ACR—sharp, sour

acid, acerbic, exacerbate, acute, acuity, acumen, acrid, acrimony

AD, A—to, towards

adhere, adjacent, adjunct, admonish, adroit, adumbrate, advent, abeyance, abet, accede, accretion, acquiesce, affluent, aggrandize, aggregate, alleviate, alliteration, allude, allure, ascribe, aspersion, aspire, assail, assonance, attest

ALI, ALTR—another

alias, alienate, inalienable, altruism

AM, AMI—love

amorous, amicable, amiable, amity

AMBI, AMPHI—both

ambiguous, ambivalent, ambidextrous, amphibious

AMBL, AMBUL—walk

amble, ambulatory, perambulator, somnambulist

ANIM—mind, spirit, breath

animal, animosity, unanimous, magnanimous

KAPLAN

ANN, ENN—year
annual, annuity, superannuated, biennial, perennial

ANTE, ANT—before
antecedent, antediluvian, antebellum, antepenultimate, anterior, antiquity, antiquated, anticipate

ANTHROP—human
anthropology, anthropomorphic, misanthrope, philanthropy

ANTI, ANT—against, opposite
antidote, antipathy, antithesis, antacid, antagonist, antonym

AUD—hear
audio, audience, audition, auditory, audible

AUTO—self
autobiography, autocrat, autonomous

BELLI, BELL—war
belligerent, bellicose, antebellum, rebellion

BENE, BEN—good
benevolent, benefactor, beneficent, benign

BI—two
bicycle, bisect, bilateral, bilingual, biped

BIBLIO—book
Bible, bibliography, bibliophile

BIO—life
biography, biology, amphibious, symbiotic, macrobiotics

BURS—money, purse
reimburse, disburse, bursar

CAD, CAS, CID—happen, fall
accident, cadence, cascade, deciduous

CAP, CIP—head
captain, decapitate, capitulate, precipitous, precipitate, recapitulate

CAP, CAPT, CEPT, CIP—take, hold, seize

capable, capacious, captivate, deception, intercept, precept, inception, anticipate, emancipation, incipient, percipient

CARN—flesh

carnal, carnage, carnival, carnivorous, incarnate

CED, CESS—yield, go

cease, cessation, incessant, cede, precede, accede, recede, antecedent, intercede, secede, cession

CHROM—color

chrome, chromatic, monochrome

CHRON—time

chronology, chronic, anachronism

CIDE—murder

suicide, homicide, regicide, patricide

CIRCUM—around

circumference, circumlocution, circumnavigate, circumscribe, circumspect, circumvent

CLIN, CLIV—slope

incline, declivity, proclivity

CLUD, CLUS, CLAUS, CLOIS—shut, close

conclude, reclusive, claustrophobia, cloister, preclude, occlude

CO, COM, CON—with, together

coeducation, coagulate, coalesce, coerce, cogent, cognate, collateral, colloquial, colloquy, commensurate, commodious, compassion, compatriot, complacent, compliant, complicity, compunction, concerto, conciliatory, concord, concur, condone, conflagration, congeal, congenial, congenital, conglomerate, conjugal, conjure, conscientious, consecrate, consensus, consonant, constrained, contentious, contrite, contusion, convalescence, convene, convivial, convoke, convoluted, congress

COGN, GNO—know

recognize, cognition, cognizance, incognito, diagnosis, agnostic, prognosis, gnostic, ignorant

CONTRA—against

controversy, incontrovertible, contravene

CORP—body
corpse, corporeal, corpulence

COSMO, COSM—world
cosmopolitan, cosmos, microcosm, macrocosm

CRAC, CRAT—rule, power
democracy, bureaucracy, theocracy, autocrat, aristocrat, technocrat

CRED—trust, believe
incredible, credulous, credence

CRESC, CRET—grow
crescent, crescendo, accretion

CULP—blame, fault
culprit, culpable, inculpate, exculpate

CURR, CURS—run
current, concur, cursory, precursor, incursion

DE—down, out, apart
depart, debase, debilitate, declivity, decry, deface, defamatory, defunct, delegate, demarcation, demean, demur, deplete, deplore, depravity, deprecate, deride, derivative, desist, detest, devoid

DEC—ten, tenth
decade, decimal, decathlon, decimate

DEMO, DEM—people
democrat, demographics, demagogue, epidemic, pandemic, endemic

DI, DIURN—day
diary, quotidian, diurnal

DIA—across
diagonal, diatribe, diaphanous

DIC, DICT—speak
abdicate, diction, interdict, predict, indict, verdict

DIS, DIF, DI—not, apart, away

disaffected, disband, disbar, disburse, discern, discordant, discredit, discursive, disheveled, disparage, disparate, dispassionate, dispirit, dissemble, disseminate, dissension, dissipate, dissonant, dissuade, distend, differentiate, diffidence, diffuse, digress, divert

DOC, DOCT—teach

docile, doctrine, doctrinaire

DOL—pain

condolence, doleful, dolorous, indolent

DUC, DUCT—lead

seduce, induce, conduct, viaduct, induct

EGO—self

ego, egoist, egocentric

EN, EM—in, into

enter, entice, encumber, endemic, ensconce, enthrall, entreat, embellish, embezzle, embroil, empathy

ERR—wander

erratic, aberration, errant

EU—well, good

eulogy, euphemism, euphony, euphoria, eurhythmics, euthanasia

EX, E—out, out of

exit, exacerbate, excerpt, excommunicate, exculpate, execrable, exhume, exonerate, exorbitant, exorcise, expatriate, expedient, expiate, expunge, expurgate, extenuate, extort, extremity, extricate, extrinsic, exult, evoke, evict, evince, elicit, egress, egregious

FAC, FIC, FECT, FY, FEA—make, do

factory, facility, benefactor, malefactor, fiction, fictive, beneficent, affect, confection, refectory, magnify, unify, rectify, vilify, feasible

FAL, FALS—deceive

infallible, fallacious, false

FERV—boil

fervent, fervid, effervescent

FID—faith, trust
confident, diffidence, perfidious, fidelity

FLU, FLUX—flow
fluent, affluent, confluence, effluvia, superfluous, flux

FORE—before
forecast, foreboding, forestall

FRAG, FRAC—break
fragment, fracture, diffract, fractious, refract

FUS—pour
profuse, infusion, effusive, diffuse

GEN—birth, class, kin
generation, congenital, homogeneous, heterogeneous, ingenious, engender, progenitor, progeny

GRAD, GRESS—step
graduate, gradual, retrograde, centigrade, degrade, gradation, gradient, progress, congress, digress, transgress, ingress, egress

GRAPH, GRAM—writing
biography, bibliography, epigraph, grammar, epigram

GRAT—pleasing
grateful, gratitude, gratis, ingrate, congratulate, gratuitous, gratuity

GRAV, GRIEV—heavy
grave, gravity, aggravate, grieve, aggrieve, grievous

GREG—crowd, flock
segregate, gregarious, egregious, congregate, aggregate

HABIT, HIBIT—have, hold
habit, cohabit, habitat, inhibit

HAP—by chance
happen, haphazard, hapless, mishap

HELIO, HELI—sun
heliocentric, heliotrope, aphelion, perihelion, helium

HETERO—other
heterosexual, heterogeneous, heterodox

HOL—whole
holocaust, catholic, holistic

HOMO—same
homosexual, homogenize, homogeneous, homonym

HOMO—man
homo sapiens, homicide, bonhomie

HYDR—water
hydrant, hydrate, dehydration

HYPER—too much, excess
hyperactive, hyperbole, hyperventilate

HYPO—too little, under
hypodermic, hypothermia, hypochondria, hypothesis, hypothetical

IN, IG, IL, IM, IR—not
incorrigible, indefatigable, indelible, indubitable, inept, inert, inexorable, insatiable, insentient, insolvent, insomnia, interminable, intractable, incessant, inextricable, infallible, infamy, innumerable, inoperable, insipid, intemperate, intrepid, inviolable, ignorant, ignominious, ignoble, illicit, illimitable, immaculate, immutable, impasse, impeccable, impecunious, impertinent, implacable, impotent, impregnable, improvident, impassioned, impervious, irregular

IN, IL, IM, IR—in, on, into
invade, inaugurate, incandescent, incarcerate, incense, indenture, induct, ingratiate, introvert, incarnate, inception, incisive, infer, infusion, ingress, innate, inquest, inscribe, insinuate, inter, illustrate, imbue, immerse, implicate, irrigate, irritate

INTER—between, among
intercede, intercept, interdiction, interject, interlocutor, interloper, intermediary, intermittent, interpolate, interpose, interregnum, interrogate, intersect, intervene

INTRA, INTR—within
intrastate, intravenous, intramural, intrinsic

IT, ITER—between, among
transit, itinerant, transitory, reiterate

JECT, JET—throw
eject, interject, abject, trajectory, jettison

JOUR—day
journal, adjourn, sojourn

JUD—judge
judge, judicious, prejudice, adjudicate

JUNCT, JUG—join
junction, adjunct, injunction, conjugal, subjugate

JUR—swear, law
jury, abjure, adjure, conjure, perjure, jurisprudence

LAT—side
lateral, collateral, unilateral, bilateral, quadrilateral

LAV, LAU, LU—wash
lavatory, laundry, ablution, antediluvian

LEG, LEC, LEX—read, speak
legible, lecture, lexicon

LEV—light
elevate, levitate, levity, alleviate

LIBER—free
liberty, liberal, libertarian, libertine

LIG, LECT—choose, gather
eligible, elect, select

LIG, LI, LY—bind
ligament, oblige, religion, liable, liaison, lien, ally

LING, LANG—tongue
lingo, language, linguistics, bilingual

LITER—letter
literate, alliteration, literal

LITH—stone
monolith, lithograph, megalith

LOQU, LOC, LOG—speech, thought

eloquent, loquacious, colloquial, colloquy, soliloquy, circumlocution, interlocutor, monologue, dialogue, eulogy, philology, neologism

LUC, LUM—light

lucid, elucidate, pellucid, translucent, illuminate

LUD, LUS—play

ludicrous, allude, delusion, allusion, illusory

MACRO—great

macrocosm, macrobiotics

MAG, MAJ, MAS, MAX—great

magnify, magnanimous, magnate, magnitude, majesty, master, maximum

MAL—bad

malady, maladroit, malevolent, malodorous

MAN—hand

manual, manuscript, emancipate, manifest, manumission

MAR—sea

submarine, marine, maritime

MATER, MATR—mother

maternal, matron, matrilineal

MEDI—middle

intermediary, medieval, mediate

MEGA—great

megaphone, megalomania, megaton, megalith

MEM, MEN—remember

memory, memento, memorabilia, reminisce

METER, METR, MENS—measure

meter, thermometer, perimeter, metronome, commensurate

MICRO—small

microscope, microorganism, microcosm, microbe

MIS—wrong, bad, hate
misunderstand, misanthrope, misapprehension, misconstrue, misnomer, mishap

MIT, MISS—send
transmit, emit, missive

MOLL—soft
mollify, emollient, mollusk

MON, MONIT—warn
admonish, monitor, premonition

MONO—one
monologue, monotonous, monogamy, monolith, monochrome

MOR—custom, manner
moral, mores, morose

MOR, MORT—dead
morbid, moribund, mortal, amortize

MORPH—shape
amorphous, anthropomorphic, metamorphosis, morphology

MOV, MOT, MOB, MOM—move
remove, motion, mobile, momentum, momentous

MUT—change
mutate, mutability, immutable, commute

NAT, NASC—born
native, nativity, natal, neonate, innate, cognate, nascent, renascent, renaissance

NAU, NAV—ship, sailor
nautical, nauseous, navy, circumnavigate

NEG—not, deny
negative, abnegate, renege

NEO—new
neoclassical, neophyte, neologism, neonate

NIHIL—none, nothing
annihilation, nihilism

NOM, NYM—name
nominate, nomenclature, nominal, cognomen, misnomer, ignominious, antonym, homonym, pseudonym, synonym, anonymity

NOX, NIC, NEC, NOC—harm
obnoxious, noxious, pernicious, internecine, innocuous

NOV—new
novelty, innovation, novitiate

NUMER—number
numeral, numerous, innumerable, enumerate

OB—against
obstruct, obdurate, obfuscate, obnoxious, obsequious, obstinate, obstreperous, obtrusive

OMNI—all
omnipresent, omnipotent, omniscient, omnivorous

ONER—burden
onerous, exonerate

OPER—work
operate, cooperate, inoperable

PAC—peace
pacify, pacifist, pacific

PALP—feel
palpable, palpitation

PAN—all
panorama, panacea, panegyric, pandemic, panoply

PATER, PATR—father
paternal, paternity, patriot, compatriot, expatriate, patrimony, patricide, patrician

PATH, PASS—feel, suffer
sympathy, antipathy, empathy, apathy, pathos, impassioned

PEC—money
pecuniary, impecunious, peculation

PED, POD—foot
pedestrian, pediment, expedient, biped, quadruped, tripod

PEL, PULS—drive
compel, compelling, expel, propel, compulsion

PEN—almost
peninsula, penultimate, penumbra

PEND, PENS—hang
pendant, pendulous, compendium, suspense, propensity

PER—through, by, for, throughout
perambulator, percipient, perfunctory, permeable, perspicacious, pertinacious, perturbation, perusal, perennial, peregrinate

PER—against, destruction
perfidious, pernicious, perjure

PERI—around
perimeter, periphery, perihelion, peripatetic

PET—seek, go towards
petition, impetus, impetuous, petulant, centripetal

PHIL—love
philosopher, philanderer, philanthropy, bibliophile, philology

PHOB—fear
phobia, claustrophobia, xenophobia

PHON—sound
phonograph, megaphone, euphony, phonetics, phonics

PLAC—calm, please
placate, implacable, placid, complacent

PON, POS—put, place
postpone, proponent, exponent, preposition, posit, interpose, juxtaposition, depose

PORT—carry
portable, deportment, rapport

POT—drink
potion, potable

POT—power
potential, potent, impotent, potentate, omnipotence

PRE—before
precede, precipitate, preclude, precocious, precursor, predilection, predisposition, preponderance, prepossessing, presage, prescient, prejudice, predict, premonition, preposition

PRIM, PRI—first
prime, primary, primal, primeval, primordial, pristine

PRO—ahead, forth
proceed, proclivity, procrastinator, profane, profuse, progenitor, progeny, prognosis, prologue, promontory, propel, proponent, propose, proscribe, protestation, provoke

PROTO—first
prototype, protagonist, protocol

PROX, PROP—near
approximate, propinquity, proximity

PSEUDO—false
pseudoscientific, pseudonym

PYR—fire
pyre, pyrotechnics, pyromania

QUAD, QUAR, QUAT—four
quadrilateral, quadrant, quadruped, quarter, quarantine, quaternary

QUES, QUER, QUIS, QUIR—question
quest, inquest, query, querulous, inquisitive, inquiry

QUIE—quiet
disquiet, acquiesce, quiescent, requiem

QUINT, QUIN—five
quintuplets, quintessence

RADI, RAMI—branch
radius, radiate, radiant, eradicate, ramification

RECT, REG—straight, rule
rectangle, rectitude, rectify, regular

REG—king, rule
regal, regent, interregnum

RETRO—backward
retrospective, retroactive, retrograde

RID, RIS—laugh
ridiculous, deride, derision

ROG—ask
interrogate, derogatory, abrogate, arrogate, arrogant

RUD—rough, crude
rude, erudite, rudimentary

RUPT—break
disrupt, interrupt, rupture

SACR, SANCT—holy
sacred, sacrilege, consecrate, sanctify, sanction, sacrosanct

SCRIB, SCRIPT, SCRIV—write
scribe, ascribe, circumscribe, inscribe, proscribe, script, manuscript, scrivener

SE—apart, away
separate, segregate, secede, sedition

SEC, SECT, SEG—cut
sector, dissect, bisect, intersect, segment, secant

SED, SID—sit
sedate, sedentary, supersede, reside, residence, assiduous, insidious

SEM—seed, sow
seminar, seminal, disseminate

SEN—old
senior, senile, senescent

SENT, SENS—feel, think
sentiment, nonsense, assent, sentient, consensus, sensual

SEQU, SECU—follow
sequence, sequel, subsequent, obsequious, obsequy, non sequitur, consecutive

SIM, SEM—similar, same
similar, verisimilitude, semblance, dissemble

SIGN—mark, sign
signal, designation, assignation

SIN—curve
sine curve, sinuous, insinuate

SOL—sun
solar, parasol, solarium, solstice

SOL—alone
solo, solitude, soliloquy, solipsism

SOMN—sleep
insomnia, somnolent, somnambulist

SON—sound
sonic, consonance, dissonance, assonance, sonorous, resonate

SOPH—wisdom
philosopher, sophistry, sophisticated, sophomoric

SPEC, SPIC—see, look
spectator, circumspect, retrospective, perspective, perspicacious, perspicuous

SPER—hope
prosper, prosperous, despair, desperate

SPERS, SPAR—scatter
disperse, sparse, aspersion, disparate

SPIR—breathe
respire, inspire, spiritual, aspire, transpire

STRICT, STRING—bind
strict, stricture, constrict, stringent, astringent

STRUCT, STRU—build
structure, obstruct, construe

SUB—under
subconscious, subjugate, subliminal, subpoena, subsequent, subterranean, subvert

SUMM—highest
summit, summary, consummate

SUPER, SUR—above
supervise, supercilious, supersede, superannuated, superfluous, insurmountable, surfeit

SURGE, SURRECT—rise
surge, resurgent, insurgent, insurrection

SYN, SYM—together
synthesis, sympathy, synonym, syncopation, synopsis, symposium, symbiosis

TACIT, TIC—silent
tacit, taciturn, reticent

TACT, TAG, TANG—touch
tact, tactile, contagious, tangent, tangential, tangible

TEN, TIN, TAIN—hold, twist
detention, tenable, tenacious, pertinacious, retinue, retain

TEND, TENS, TENT—stretch
intend, distend, tension, tensile, ostensible, contentious

TERM—end
terminal, terminus, terminate, interminable

TERR—earth, land
terrain, terrestrial, extraterrestrial, subterranean

TEST—witness
testify, attest, testimonial, testament, detest, protestation

THE—god
atheist, theology, apotheosis, theocracy

THERM—heat
thermometer, thermal, thermonuclear, hypothermia

TIM—fear, frightened
timid, intimidate, timorous

TOP—place
topic, topography, utopia

TORT—twist
distort, extort, tortuous

TORP—stiff, numb
torpedo, torpid, torpor

TOX—poison
toxic, toxin, intoxication

TRACT—draw
tractor, intractable, protract

TRANS—across, over, through, beyond
transport, transgress, transient, transitory, translucent, transmutation

TREM, TREP—shake
tremble, tremor, tremulous, trepidation, intrepid

TURB—shake
disturb, turbulent, perturbation

UMBR—shadow
umbrella, umbrage, adumbrate, penumbra

UNI, UN—one
unify, unilateral, unanimous

URB—city
urban, suburban, urbane

VAC—empty
vacant, evacuate, vacuous

VAL, VAIL—value, strength
valid, valor, ambivalent, convalescence, avail, prevail, countervail

VEN, VENT—come
convene, contravene, intervene, venue, convention, circumvent, advent, adventitious

VER—true
verify, verity, verisimilitude, veracious, aver, verdict

VERB—word
verbal, verbose, verbiage, verbatim

VERT, VERS—turn
avert, convert, pervert, revert, incontrovertible, divert, subvert, versatile, aversion

VICT, VINC—conquer
victory, conviction, evict, evince, invincible

VID, VIS—see
evident, vision, visage, supervise

VIL—base, mean
vile, vilify, revile

VIV, VIT—life
vivid, vital, convivial, vivacious

VOC, VOK, VOW—call, voice
vocal, equivocate, vociferous, convoke, evoke, invoke, avow

VOL—wish
voluntary, malevolent, benevolent, volition

VOLV, VOLUT—turn, roll

revolve, evolve, convoluted

VOR—eat

devour, carnivore, omnivorous, voracious

Trust Your Hunches

When you come across an unfamiliar word, your first reaction may be: "Gosh dang. Don't know it. Should skip it." No you shouldn't. Vocabulary knowledge on is NOT an all-or-nothing proposition. There are instead many levels of knowledge:

- Some words you know so well you can rattle off their dictionary definitions.
- Some words you sort of know. You understand them when you hear them or see them in context, but you would never use them, for fear of embarrassing yourself.
- Some words are only barely familiar. You've heard them somewhere before, maybe, but that's about it.

Depending on your familiarity level, try the following methods to jog your memory.

Remember where you've heard the word before

If you can recall a phrase in which the word appears, that may be enough to eliminate some answer choices, or even to zero in on the right answer. Let's try a sample question.

> Between the two villages was a deep - - - - through which passage was difficult and hazardous.
>
> (A) precipice
> (B) beachhead
> (C) quagmire
> (D) market
> (E) prairie

To answer this question, it helps to know the word *quagmire*. You may remember *quagmire* from news reports referring to "a foreign policy quagmire" or "a quagmire of financial indebtedness." If you can remember how *quagmire* was used, you'll have a rough idea of what it means, and you'll see it fits.

Important

If you think you recognize a word, go with your hunch.

You may also be reminded of the word *mire*, as in "We got mired in the small details and never got to the larger issue." Sounds something like "stuck," right? You don't need an exact definition. A *quagmire* is a situation that's difficult to get out of, so (C) is correct. (A *quagmire* is a soft, spongy, easy-to-get-stuck-in piece of land.)

Decide if the word has a positive or negative "charge"

Simply knowing that you're dealing with a positive or negative word can earn you points on the SAT. Take the word *cantankerous*. Say it to yourself. Can you guess whether it's positive or negative? Often words that sound harsh have a negative meaning while smooth-sounding words tend to have positive meanings. If *cantankerous* sounded negative to you, you were right. It means "disagreeable" and "difficult to deal with."

You can also use prefixes and roots to help determine a word's charge. *Mal-, de-, dis-, un-, in, im-, a-,* and *mis-* often indicate a negative, while *pro-, ben-,* and *magn-* are often positives.

Not all SAT words sound positive or negative; some sound neutral. But if you can define the charge, you can probably eliminate some answer choices on that basis alone. Try this one:

> He seemed at first to be honest and loyal, but before long it was
> necessary to - - - - him for his - - - - behavior.
>
> (A) admonish . . steadfast
> (B) extol . . conniving
> (C) reprimand . . scrupulous
> (D) exalt . . insidious
> (E) castigate . . perfidious

You don't need an exact definition of the words that go in the blanks. The word *but* tells you that the words for both blanks have to be negative (to contrast with the positive words *honest* and *loyal*). So you scan the answer choices for a choice that contains two clearly negative words. (E) is right. *Castigate* means "punish or scold harshly," and *perfidious* means "disloyal" or "treacherous."

Use your foreign-language skills

Many of the roots you'll encounter in SAT words come from Latin. Spanish, French, and Italian also come from Latin, and have retained much of it in their modern forms. English is also a cousin to German and Greek. So if you don't recognize a word, you should try to remember if you know a similar word in another language.

Look at the word *carnal*. Unfamiliar? What about *carne*, as in chili con carne? *Carn* means "meat" or "flesh," which leads you straight to the meaning of *carnal*: "pertaining to the flesh." You could decode *carnivorous*, or meat eating, in the same way.

When all else fails . . .

Some choices on verbal questions will just sound wrong. If you can eliminate at least one wrong-sounding choice, you improve your chances of a correct guess.

Q. When I come across a word I don't know on the SAT, I should

   (A) remain positive and charge the negative test proctor

   (B) look for word roots, prefixes, foreign words, and phrases that may contain the word to help jog my memory

   (C) skip the question and DO NOT answer it no matter what

   (D) think to myself "What would the camera-shy bass player in my favorite retro punk band do?"

   (E) cry until someone takes my hand and gently leads me away

                                               (B)

PRACTICE

Go back to the list of word families. Every day, get to know one word family like you know the back of your arm. Look up every word in your dictionary and be able to use every definition of the word in a sentence. There are 22 word families, so, if you take weekends off, this will take you about four weeks. At the end of your word family month, you will know a ton of words that are use on the SAT all of the time, and your score should show it.

Section Three

UNDERSTANDING THE MATH SECTION

STEP SIX

Math Section Overview

You should approach the SAT Math section with a definite plan of action. You need to know what to expect beforehand so you are ready with the right strategies. Steps 6–9 show you exactly what to expect from the SAT Math section, and how you can tackle it quickly and correctly.

This step is a little longer than the rest, and it's very important, so take twice as much time on this step as you have been spending on the previous chapters.

STEP 6 PREVIEW

Format

Get comfortable with the SAT Math format:
- Math directions
- Regular Math
- Quantitative Comparisons
- Grid-ins

Strategies

Learn the SAT Math techniques:
- Kaplan's Five-Step Method
- Alternative techniques: picking numbers, backsolving
- Quantitative Comparison techniques
- Grid-in techniques
- When and when not to use your calculator

Practice

Use it before you lose it (Three short practice sets / total of 25 minutes)

FORMAT

There are three scored Math sections on the SAT:

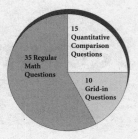

- One 30-minute section with 35 Regular Math questions
- One 30-minute section with a set of 15 Quantitative Comparisons and a set of 10 Grid-ins
- One 15-minute section with 10 Regular Math questions

The SAT Math question sets start off easy and gradually increase in difficulty. ALWAYS be aware of the difficulty level as you go through a question set. The harder the question, the more traps you have to avoid.

The Directions

You'll save time by knowing the directions. The directions are the same for every test, so with a little practice, you can skip the directions and go straight to the first question. (Grid-ins and Quantitative Comparisons have slightly different instructions, which we'll discuss in detail when we get to them.)

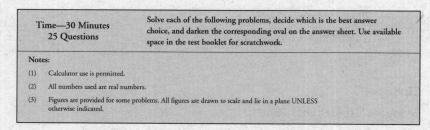

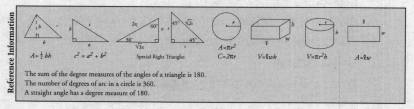

Note (2) means you won't have to deal with imaginary numbers, such as i (the square root of −1).

Note (3) tells you diagrams are drawn to scale, which means you can use these diagrams to estimate measurements. However, if the diagrams are labeled "Figure not drawn to scale," you can't do this.

Saying the figures "lie in a plane" simply means you are dealing with flat figures, like rectangles or circles, unless the question says otherwise.

Read these directions through carefully at least five times. By the day of the test you should know these formulas by heart. If you forget, you know where to find them.

Regular Math

The 35 Regular Math questions count for just over one half of your total math score. Regular Math questions are standard, multiple-choice questions, just like the questions on the Verbal section of the SAT. We have a lot of techniques you can use to attack these questions, which we'll get to soon.

Quantitative Comparisons

The 15 Quantitative Comparison questions count for one fourth of your Math score. The 15 Quantitative Comparisons (QCs) appear in the 30-minute Math section that also contains the 10 Grid-in questions (you'll learn about those in a moment).

Quantitative Comparisons are a special kind of math problem found only on the SAT. In a QC question, you need compare two quantities and figure out if one is greater in value (bigger) than the other, if both quantities are equal, or if the question doesn't provide enough information for you to figure it out. This odd format can make QCs look really hard. However, once you get used to them, QCs can be quicker and easier than the other types of Math questions, and a great way to pile up points.

The QC directions look like this:

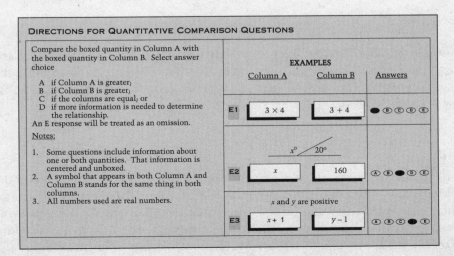

Each question gives two mathematical expressions, one in Column A, the other in Column B. Here's a sample (we'll explain this problem later on in the chapter):

Column A	Column B
$x(x-1)$	$x^2 - x$

Some questions include additional information about one or both of the columns. This information is centered above the two columns. Your job is to compare the quantities in each column. If Column A is bigger, choose (A); if Column B is bigger, choose (B); if they're equal, choose (C); and if you don't have enough information to tell, choose (D).

Important

Choice (E) is NEVER the answer to a QC. Be careful NEVER to mark (E) when you mean (D).

Answer Choice (D)

Choices (A), (B), and (C) all represent relationships between the quantities in Column A and Column B. Choice (D) represents a relationship that cannot be determined. Here are two things to remember about choice (D) that will help you decide when to pick it:

- Choice (D) is NEVER correct if both columns contain only numbers and no variables. The relationship between numbers is unchanging and can ALWAYS be established, but choice (D) means that more than one relationship is possible.

- Choice (D) is correct if you can demonstrate two different relationships between the columns.

Suppose you ran across the following QC:

Column A	Column B
$2x$	$3x$

If x is a positive number, Column B is greater than Column A. If $x = 0$, the columns are equal. If x equals any negative number, Column B is less than Column A. Since more than one relationship is possible, (D) must be correct. In fact, as soon as you find a second possibility, stop working and pick choice (D).

Grid-ins

You get 10 Grid-ins, following the QCs, in one of the Math sections. They count for one sixth of your Math score. The Grid-in section on the SAT is more like math tests at school—you figure out your own answer and fill it in on a special grid. Some Grid-ins have only one correct answer, while others have several correct answers. There is no penalty for wrong answers on the Grid-ins section. Here are the directions for the Grid-ins section:

For each of the questions below (16–25), solve the problem and indicate your answer by darkening the ovals in the special grid. For example:

Answer: 1.25 or $\frac{5}{4}$ or 5/4

Write answer in boxes. →
Grid in result →

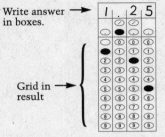

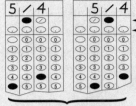

Fraction line

Decimal point

You may start your answers in any column, space permitting. Columns not needed should be left blank.

Either position is correct.

- It is recommended, though not required, that you write your answer in the boxes at the top of the columns. However, you will receive credit only for darkening the ovals correctly.

- Grid only one answer to a question, even though some problems have more than one correct answer.

- Darken no more than one oval in a column.

- No answers are negative.

- Mixed numbers cannot be gridded. For example: the number $1\frac{1}{4}$ must be gridded as 1.25 or 5/4.

  (If ⌷⌷⌷⌷ is gridded, it will be interpreted as $\frac{11}{4}$ not $1\frac{1}{4}$.)

- Decimal Accuracy: Decimal answers must be entered as accurately as possible. For example, if you obtain an answer such as 0.1666..., you should record the result as .166 or .167. **Less accurate values such as .16 or .17 are not acceptable.**

Acceptable ways to grid $\frac{1}{6}$ = .1666...

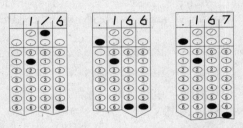

Each Grid-in question provides four boxes and a column of ovals, or "bubbles," to write your answer in. You write your numerical answer in the boxes first, one digit, decimal point, or fraction sign per box. Then you fill in the appropriate bubbles. The numbers in these boxes are there just to help you grid in the bubbles properly, they're not read by the scoring computer.

You CANNOT grid:

- Negative answers
- Answers with variables (*x, y, w,* etc.)
- Answers greater than 9,999
- Answers with commas (write 1000, not 1,000)
- Mixed numbers (such as $2\frac{1}{2}$, which must be gridded as $\frac{5}{2}$ or 2.5)

If you come up with any of these answers to a question, you are wrong.

Q. The SAT Math section has _____ types of questions: _____.

(A) two; Quantitative Comparison, and Regular Math
(B) three; Grid-in, Mixed Number, and Regular Math
(C) three; Quantitative Comparison, Regular Math, and Grid-in
(D) four; Grid-in, Quantitative Comparison, Mixed Number, and Regular Math
(E) four; Grid-in, Quantitative Comparison, Regular Math, and Analogies

(A) (B) (C) (D) (E)   (C)

KAPLAN'S FIVE-STEP MATH METHOD

Now you know the three kinds of questions you'll see on the SAT Math section. To maximize your score on these questions, you need to work systematically. Just like the Verbal questions, the key to working systematically on Math questions is to think about the question before you look for the answer. On basic problems, you may know what to do right away. But on harder problems, a few extra seconds spent looking for traps, thinking about your approach, and deciding whether to work on the problem now or come back to it later is very important.

Kaplan's Five-Step Method is a good system for tackling *all* SAT Math problems. Here it is:

1. Estimate the question's difficulty.
2. Read the question.
3. Skip or do?
4. Look for fastest approach.
5. Make an educated guess.

Consider the following problem:

12. At a certain diner, Joe orders three strips of bacon and a cup of warm water and is charged $2.25. Stella orders two strips of bacon and a cup of warm water and is charged $1.70. What is the price of two strips of bacon?

(A) $0.55
(B) $0.60
(C) $1.10
(D) $1.30
(E) $1.80

1. Estimate the Question's Difficulty.

All SAT Math questions are arranged in order of difficulty. Decide whether the question is basic, medium, or hard. Within a set, the first questions are basic, the middle ones moderately difficult, and the last ones are hard. Question 12 above is a moderately difficult word problem.

On difficult questions, watch out for "Math Traps" (see Step 8). Hard questions are often misleadingly worded to trip you up. Make sure you know what's being asked.

2. Read the Question.

If you try to start solving the problem before reading it all the way through, you may end up doing unnecessary work. Question 12 looks straightforward, but read through it carefully and you'll see a slight twist. You're asked to find the cost of *two* strips of bacon, not one. Many people will find the price of a single bacon strip and forget to double it. Pity these poor people, but don't be one.

3. Skip or Do?

If a problem renders you clueless, circle it in your test booklet and move on. Spend your time on the problems you can solve, then come back to the ones you had trouble on later, if you have time.

4. Look for the Fastest Approach.

On an easy question, all the information you need to solve the problem may be given up front in the question stem or in a diagram. Harder questions often hide the information that will help you solve the problem. Since questions are arranged in order of difficulty, you should be a little wary of question 12. If you get the answer too easily, you may have missed something. (In this case, you're asked to find the price of two strips of bacon, not one.)

Look for shortcuts. Sometimes the obvious way of doing a problem is the long way. If the method you choose involves lots of calculating, look for another route. There's usually a shortcut you can use that won't involve tons of arithmetic.

In question 12, the cost of bacon and warm water could be translated into two distinct equations using the variables b and w. You could find w in terms of b, then plug this into the other equation. But if you think carefully, you'll see there's a quicker way. The difference in price between three bacon strips and a cup of warm water and two bacon strips and a cup of warm water is the price of one bacon strip. So one bacon strip costs $2.25 - $1.70 = $0.55. (Remember, you have to find the price of two strips of bacon. Twice $0.55 is $1.10.)

Step 7 (Tested Math Concepts) will review many strategies for specific problem types that will help you get to the answer fast. You can also use special Kaplan methods, such as **picking numbers** and **backsolving**, which we will get to soon in this step.

5. Make an Educated Guess.

If you've tried solving a problem and are stuck, cut your losses. Eliminate any wrong answer choices you can, make an educated guess, and move on. (Step 9 covers guessing strategies in detail.)

Let's say it's taking too long to solve the bacon and water problem. Can you eliminate any answer choices? The price of two pieces of bacon and a cup of warm water is $1.70. That means the cost of two bacon strips alone can't be $1.80, which eliminates choice (E). Now you can choose between the remaining choices, and your odds of guessing correctly have improved.

Q. When using Kaplan's Five-Step Math Method, you should NEVER

　(A) estimate the difficulty of the question first
　(B) skip the question if you think it's way too hard
　(C) guess at an answer if you can eliminate other answer choices
　(D) spend a lot of time on the question even if you have no idea what any part of it means
　(E) try several different strategies to get the correct answer

　Ⓐ　Ⓑ　Ⓒ　Ⓓ　Ⓔ   (D)

ALTERNATIVE TECHNIQUES

Kaplan's Five-Step Math Method will help you save time and avoid mistakes on the SAT. But the Five-Step Method is not foolproof. Luckily, there are usually a lot of different ways to get to the right answer to a Math problem. On the SAT, there are two techniques in particular that can be useful when you don't see a way to solve the problem: picking numbers and backsolving. Each takes longer than traditional methods, but they're worth trying if you have enough time.

Picking Numbers

Sometimes you get stuck on a Math question just because it's too general or abstract. A good way to bring an abstract question to its knees and make it beg for sweet mercy is to substitute particular numbers for its variables. This "picking numbers" strategy works especially well with even/odd questions.

If a is an odd integer and b is an even integer, which of the following must be odd?

　(A) $2a + b$
　(B) $a + 2b$
　(C) ab
　(D) a^2b
　(E) ab^2

Rather than trying to wrap your brain around abstract variables, simply pick numbers for *a* and *b*. When it comes to adding, subtracting, and multiplying evens and odds, what happens with one pair of numbers generally happens with all similar pairs. Just say, for the time being, that $a = 3$ and $b = 2$. Plug those values into the answer choices, and there's a good chance that only one choice will be odd:

(A) $2a + b = 2(3) + 2 = 8$

(B) $a + 2b = 3 + 2(2) = 7$

(C) $ab = (3)(2) = 6$

(D) $a^2b = (3^2)(2) = 18$

(E) $ab^2 = (3)(2^2) = 12$

Choice (B) is the only odd one for $a = 3$ and $b = 2$, so it must be the one that's odd no matter what odd number *a* and even number *b* actually stand for. The answer is (B).

Another good situation for "picking numbers" is when the answer choices to a percent problem are all percents.

> From 1985 to 1990, the population of Pod *x* increased by 20 percent.
> From 1990 to 1995, the population increased by 30 percent. What was
> the percent increase in the population over the entire ten-year period
> 1985–1995?
>
> (A) 10%
> (B) 25%
> (C) 50%
> (D) 56%
> (E) 60%

Instead of trying to solve this problem in the abstract, pick a number for the original 1985 population and see what happens. There's no need to pick a realistic number. You're better off picking a number that's easy to work with. And in percent problems the number that's easiest to work with is almost always 100.

Say the 1985 population was 100, then what would the 1990 population be? Twenty percent more than 100 is 120. Now, if the 1990 population was 120, what would the 1995 population be? What's 30 percent more than 120? Be careful. Don't just add 30 to 120. You need to find 30 percent of 120 and add that on. Thirty percent of 120 is $(.30)(120) = 36$. Add 36 to 120 and you get a 1995 population of 156. What percent greater is 156 than 100? That's easy— that's why we picked 100 to start with. It's a 56 percent increase. The answer is (D).

A third good situation for "picking numbers" is when the answer choices to a word problem are algebraic expressions.

If n Velcro tabs cost p dollars, then how many dollars would q Velcro tabs cost?

(A) $\dfrac{np}{q}$

(B) $\dfrac{nq}{p}$

(C) $\dfrac{pq}{n}$

(D) $\dfrac{n}{pq}$

(E) $\dfrac{p}{nq}$

The only thing that's hard about this question is that it uses variables instead of numbers. So, make it real. Pick numbers for the variables. Pick numbers that are easy to work with. Say $n = 2$, $p = 4$, and $q = 3$. Then the question becomes: "If two Velcro tabs cost $4.00, how many dollars would three Velcro tabs cost?" That's easy—$6.00. When $n = 2$, $p = 4$, and $q = 3$, the correct answer should equal 6. Plug those values into the answer choices and see which ones yield 6:

(A) $\dfrac{np}{q} = \dfrac{(2)(4)}{3} = \dfrac{8}{3}$

(B) $\dfrac{nq}{q} = \dfrac{(2)(3)}{3} = \dfrac{6}{3} = 2$

(C) $\dfrac{pq}{n} = \dfrac{(4)(3)}{2} = \dfrac{12}{2} = 6$

(D) $\dfrac{n}{pq} = \dfrac{2}{(4)(3)} = \dfrac{2}{12} = \dfrac{1}{6}$

(E) $\dfrac{p}{nq} = \dfrac{4}{(2)(3)} = \dfrac{4}{6} = \dfrac{2}{3}$

Choice (C) is the only one that yields 6, so it must be the correct answer.

When picking numbers for an abstract word problem like this one, try all five answer choices. Sometimes more than one choice will yield the correct result. When that happens, pick another set of numbers to weed out the coincidences. Avoid picking 0 and 1—these often give several "possibly correct" answers.

Backsolving

On some Math questions, when you can't figure out the question, you can try working backwards from the answer choices. Plug the choices back into the question until you find the one that works. Backsolving works best:

- When the question is a complex word problem and the answer choices are numbers
- When the alternative is setting up multiple algebraic equations

Don't backsolve:

- If the answer choices include variables
- On algebra questions or word problems that have ugly answer choices such as radicals and fractions (plugging them in takes too much time)

Complex Question, Simple Answer Choices

Sometimes backsolving is faster than setting up an equation. For example:

> A music club draws 27 patrons. If there are seven more hippies than punks in the club, how many patrons are hippies?
>
> (A)   8
> (B)   10
> (C)   14
> (D)   17
> (E)   20

The five answer choices represent the possible number of hippies in the club, so try them in the question stem. The choice that gives a total of 27 patrons, with seven more hippies than punks, will be the correct answer.

Plugging in choice (C) gives you 14 hippies in the club. Since there are seven more hippies than punks, there are seven punks in the club. But $14 + 7 < 27$. The sum is too small, so there must be more than 14 hippies. Eliminate answer choices (A), (B), and (C).

Either (D) or (E) will be correct. Plugging in (D) gives you 17 hippies in the club and $17 - 7$, or 10 punks. $17 + 10 = 27$ patrons total. Answer choice (D) is correct.

Algebra Problems with Multiple Equations

> If $a + b + c = 110$, $a = 4b$, and $3a = 2c$, then $b =$
>
> (A)   6
> (B)   8
> (C)   9
> (D)   10
> (E)   14

You're looking for b, so plug in the answer choices for b in the question and see what happens. The choice that gives us 110 for the sum $a + b + c$ must be correct.

Start with the midrange number, 9, choice (C):

> If $b = 9$, then $a = 4 \times 9 = 36$.
>
> $2c = 3a = 3 \times 36 = 108$
>
> $c = 54$
>
> $a + b + c = 36 + 9 + 54 = 99$

Since this is a smaller sum than 110, the correct value for b must be greater. Therefore, eliminate answer choices (A), (B), and (C). Now plug in either (D) or (E) and see if it works. If it doesn't, the remaining choice must be correct.

Short on time? Try guessing between (D) and (E). But guess intelligently. Since (C) wasn't far wrong, you want a number just slightly bigger. That's choice (D).

QUANTITATIVE COMPARISON STRATEGIES

The key to QC success is focusing on the relationship between the two columns. QCs rarely test your ability to plug numbers into your calculator. Rather, they test your ability to manipulate quantities so that you can compare them accurately.

QC Strategy 1: Make One Column Look Like the Other

When the quantities in Columns A and B are expressed differently, you can often make the comparison easier by changing one column so it looks like the other. If one column is a percent, and the other a fraction, try converting the fraction to a percent. If the expression under Column A is expressed in hours while that under Column B is expressed in minutes, convert the figure in Column A to minutes.

Column A	Column B
$x(x-1)$	$x^2 - x$

Here Column A has parentheses, and Column B doesn't. To make Column A look more like Column B, get rid of the parentheses. You end up with $x^2 - x$ in both columns, which means they are equal and the answer is (C).

Column A	Column B

The diameter of circle O is d and the area is a.

Column A	Column B
$\dfrac{\pi d^2}{2}$	a

Make Column B look more like Column A by rewriting a, the area of the circle, in terms of the diameter, d. The area of any circle equals πr^2, where r is the radius.

Since the radius is half the diameter, we can plug in for r in the area formula to get $\pi\left(\dfrac{d}{2}\right)^2$ in Column B. Simplifying, we get $\dfrac{\pi d^2}{4}$. Since both columns now contain πd^2 in the numerator, we can get rid of both and simply compare $\dfrac{1}{2}$ with $\dfrac{1}{4}$. Column A is greater, so the answer is choice (A).

QC Strategy 2: Do the Same Thing to Both Columns

Some QC questions become much clearer if you change the values of both columns. Treat them like two sides of an inequality, with the sign temporarily hidden. You can add or subtract the same amount from both columns or multiply or divide by the same positive amount without altering the relationship.

Important

DO NOT multiply or divide both QC columns by a negative number. Be careful with fractions. Remember that negative numbers and fractions behave very differently than positive integers.

What could you do to both columns in this QC question?

Column A	Column B
$4a + 3 = 7b$	
$20a + 10$	$35b - 5$

The terms in the two columns are all multiples of 5, so divide both columns by 5 to simplify. You're left with $4a + 2$ in Column A and $7b - 1$ in Column B. This resembles the equation given in the centered information. In fact, if you add 1 to both columns, you have $4a + 3$ in Column A and $7b$ in Column B. The centered equation tells us they are equal. Choice (C) is correct.

What could you do to both columns here?

Column A	Column B
$y > 0$	
$1 + \dfrac{y}{(1 + y)}$	$1 + \dfrac{1}{(1+y)}$

Solution: First subtract 1 from both sides. That gives you $\dfrac{y}{(1+y)}$ in Column A, and $\dfrac{1}{(1+y)}$ in Column B. Get rid of the identical denominators and you're left comparing y with 1. You know y is greater than 0, but it could be a fraction less than 1, so it could be greater or less than 1. Since you can't say for sure which column is greater, the answer is (D).

QC Strategy 3: Pick Numbers

If a QC involves variables, try picking numbers to make the relationship clearer. Here's how:

1. Pick numbers that are easy to work with.
2. Plug in the numbers and calculate the values. Note the relationship between the columns.
3. Pick another number for each variable and calculate the values again. Is it the same relationship?

Column A	Column B

$$r > s > t > w > 0$$

$$\dfrac{r}{t} \qquad\qquad\qquad \dfrac{s}{w}$$

Try $r = 4$, $s = 3$, $t = 2$, and $w = 1$. Then Column A $= \dfrac{r}{t} = \dfrac{4}{2} = 2$. And Column B $= \dfrac{s}{w} = \dfrac{3}{1} = 3$. So in this case Column B is greater than Column A.

Always Pick More Than One Number and Calculate Again

In the example above, we first found that Column B was bigger. But this doesn't mean that Column B is always bigger and that the answer is (B). It does mean that the answer is not (A) or (C). But the answer could still be (D), not enough information to decide. If time is short, guess between (B) and (D). But whenever you can, pick another set of numbers and calculate again.

Make a special effort to find a second set of numbers that will alter the relationship. Here, try making r a lot larger. Pick $r = 30$ and keep the other variables as they were. Now Column A $= \dfrac{30}{2} = 15$. This time, Column A is greater than Column B, so choice (D) is the correct answer.

Important

If the relationship between Columns A and B changes when you pick other numbers, (D) must be the answer.

Pick Different Kinds of Numbers

Don't assume that all variables represent positive integers. Unless you're told otherwise, variables can represent zero, negative numbers, or fractions. Since different kinds of numbers behave differently, always pick a different kind of number the second time around. In the example above, we plugged in a small positive number the first time and a larger number the second.

QC Strategy 4: Avoid Common QC Traps

To avoid QC traps, always be alert. Don't assume anything. Be especially cautious near the end of the question set.

Trap: Misleading Information

Column A	Column B
Sven is taller than Milla.	
Sven's weight in pounds	Milla's weight in pounds

The test makers hope you'll think, "If Sven is taller, he must weigh more." But there's no guaranteed relationship between height and weight, so you don't have enough information. The answer is (D).

Trap: Assuming Too Much

A common QC mistake is to assume that variables represent positive integers. As we saw in using the number-picking strategy, fractions or negative numbers often show another relationship between the columns.

Column A	Column B
When 1 is added to the square of x the result is 37.	
x	6

It is easy to assume that x must be 6, since the square of x is 36. That would make choice (C) correct. However, it's possible that $x = -6$. Since x could be either 6 or -6, the answer is (D).

Trap: Not Considering Other Possibilities

The following question appears at the end of a QC section.

Column A	Column B

$$
\begin{array}{r}
R \\
S \\
+\ T \\
\hline
1W
\end{array}
$$

In the addition problem above, R, S, and T are different digits that are multiples of 3, and W is a digit.

W	8

Since you're told that R, S, and T are digits and different multiples of 3, most people will think of 3, 6, and 9, which add up to 18. That makes W equal to 8, and Columns A and B equal. But that's too obvious for a QC at the end of the section.

There's another possibility: 0 is also a digit and a multiple of 3. So the three digits could be 0, 3, and 9, or 0, 6, and 9, which give totals of 12 and 15, respectively. That means W could be 8, 2, or 5. Since the columns could be equal, or Column B could be greater, answer choice (D) must be correct.

Trap: Look-Alikes

Column A	Column B
$\sqrt{5} + \sqrt{5}$	$\sqrt{10}$

At first glance, forgetting the rules of radicals, you might think that these quantities are equal and the answer is (C). But use some common sense to see this isn't the case. $\sqrt{5}$ has to be bigger than $\sqrt{4}$ (which is 2), so $\sqrt{5} + \sqrt{5}$ in Column A has to be bigger than 4. Meanwhile, $\sqrt{10}$ in column B is smaller than another familiar number, $\sqrt{16}$, so Column B is less than 4. The answer is (A).

Don't go with what just "looks right" or assume that the first answer you choose is necessarily correct.

GRID-IN STRATEGIES

The Grid-in section is special. Grid-ins have no multiple-choice answers and there is no penalty for wrong answers. You have to figure out your own answer and fill it in on a special grid.

Write Your Answers in the Number Boxes

This doesn't get you points by itself, but you will make fewer mistakes if you write your answers in the number boxes. You may think that gridding directly will save time, but writing first, then gridding, helps ensure accuracy, which means more points.

Always Start Your Answer in the First Column Box

You *can* start in any column, it's a free country, but we recommend you submit happily to the totalitarian dictates of this strategy. If you always start with the first column, even if your answer has only one or two figures, your answers will always fit. Since there is no oval for 0 in the first column, grid an answer of 0 in any other column.

Important

If your answer is .7, don't grid 0.7! You can't grid a 0 in the first column.

In a Fractional Answer, Grid (/) in the Correct Column

The sign (/) separates the numerator from the denominator. It appears only in columns two and three. A fractional answer with four digits—like 31/42—won't fit.

Change Mixed Numbers to Decimals or Fractions Before You Grid

If you try to grid a mixed number, it will be read as a fraction, and be counted wrong. For example, $4\frac{1}{2}$ will be read as the fraction $\frac{41}{2}$, which is $20\frac{1}{2}$. So first change mixed numbers to fractions or decimals, then grid in. In this case:

- Change $4\frac{1}{2}$ to $\frac{9}{2}$ and grid in the fraction; or

- Change $4\frac{1}{2}$ to 4.5 and grid in the decimal.

Watch Where You Put Your Decimal Points

A few pointers:

- For a decimal less than 1, such as .127, enter the decimal point in the first box.
- Only put a zero before the decimal point if it's part of the answer, as in 20.5—don't put one there (if your answer is, say, .5) just to make your answer look more accurate.
- Never grid a decimal point in the last column.

With Long or Repeating Decimals . . .

. . . grid the first three digits only and plug in the decimal point where it belongs. For example: Say three answers are .45454545, 82.452312, and 1.428743. Grid .454, 82.4, and 1.42, respectively.

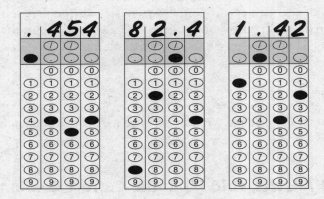

You could round 1.428743 up to the nearest hundredth (1.43). Since it's not required, though, don't bother rounding. You could make a mistake. Note that rounding to an even shorter answer—1.4—would be incorrect.

More than One Right Answer? Choose One and Enter It

Say you're asked for a two-digit integer that is a multiple of 2, 3, and 5. You might answer 30, 60, or 90. Whichever you grid would be right.

Some Grid-ins Have a Range of Possible Answers

Suppose you're asked to grid a value of m where $1 - 2m < m$ and $5m - 2 < m$. Solving for m in the first inequality, you find that $\frac{1}{3} < m$. Solving for m in the second inequality, you find that $m < \frac{1}{2}$. So $\frac{1}{3} < m < \frac{1}{2}$. Grid in any value between $\frac{1}{3}$ and $\frac{1}{2}$. (Gridding in $\frac{1}{3}$ or $\frac{1}{2}$ would be wrong.) When the answer is a range of values, it's often easier to work with decimals: $.333 < m < .5$. Then you can quickly grid .4 (or .35 or .45, etc.) as your answer.

USING YOUR CALCULATOR (OR NOT)

Thank you for slogging through all of these SAT Math techniques. Now we've gotten to the question most students really care about:

What about my calculator?

You're allowed to use a calculator on the SAT. But that's not all good. Yes, you can do computations faster. But you may be tempted to waste time using a calculator on questions that shouldn't involve lengthy computation. Remember, you never *need* a calculator to solve an SAT problem. If you ever find yourself doing extensive calculations—elaborate division or long drawn-out multiplication—stop. You probably missed a shortcut.

Should I Just Leave It at Home?

No. Bring it. By zeroing in on the parts of problems that need calculation, you can increase your score and save yourself time on the SAT by using your calculator.

What Kind of Calculator Should I Bring?

One that you're comfortable with. If you don't have a calculator now, buy one right away, and practice using it between now and test day. You can use just about any small calculator *except*:

- Calculators that print out your calculations
- Handheld minicomputers or laptop computers
- Any calculators with a typewriter keypad
- Calculators with an angled readout screen
- Calculators that require a wall outlet

When Should I Use My Calculator?

Calculators help the most on Grid-ins and the least on QCs. The reason for this is that QCs are designed to be done very quickly, and rarely involve much computation; if you think you need a calculator on them, you're probably missing something. Both Grid-ins and Regular Math will sometimes involve computation—never as the most important part of the question, but often as a final step.

Since Grid-ins don't give you answer choices to choose from, it's especially important to be sure of your work. Calculators can help you check your work and avoid careless errors.

Remember, a calculator can be useful when used selectively and strategically. Not all parts of a problem will necessarily be easier with a calculator. Consider this problem:

> If four grams of cadmium yellow pigment can make 3 kilograms of cadmium yellow oil paint, how many kilograms of paint could be produced from 86 grams of pigment?

This word problem has two steps. Step one is to set up the following proportion:

$$\frac{4 \text{ gm}}{3 \text{ kg}} = \frac{86 \text{ gm}}{x \text{ kg}}$$

A little algebraic engineering tells you that:

$$x \text{ kg} = \frac{3 \text{ kg} \times 86 \text{ gm}}{4 \text{gm}}$$

Here's where you whip out that calculator. This problem has now been reduced down to pure calculation: $(3 \times 86) \div 4 = 64.5$.

Important

Calculators help most on Grid-ins and least on Quantitative Comparisons.

When Should I Avoid My Calculator Like the Plague?

You may be tempted to use your calculator on every problem, but many questions will be easier without it. That's particularly true of QCs. Consider this problem:

Column A	Column B

The ratio of b:7 is equal to the ratio of 143:188.

b	7

Sure, you could set up the proportion $\frac{b}{7} = \frac{143}{188}$, grab your calculator, and cross multiply to find that $b = 5.324468085$. But why bother doing the calculation? Once you've set up the proportion, you can make a quick comparison without any further calculation. Your task is to compare b to 7. If $b = 7$, then $\frac{b}{7} = 1$. However, $\frac{b}{7}$ must be less than 1 since $\frac{143}{188} < 1$. Therefore, $b < 7$. Column B must be greater.

Common Calculator Mistake #1: Calculating Before You Think

On the Grid-in problem below, how should (and shouldn't) you use your calculator?

> The sum of all the integers from 1 to 44, inclusive, is subtracted from the sum of all the integers from 7 to 50, inclusive. What is the result?

The Wrong Approach

1. Grab calculator.
2. Punch in all the numbers.
3. Put down answer and hope you didn't hit any wrong buttons.

You might be tempted to punch in all the numbers from 1 to 44, find their sum, then do the same for the numbers 7 through 50, and subtract the first sum from the second. But doing that means punching 252 keys. The odds are you'll hit the wrong key somewhere and get the wrong answer. Even if you don't, punching in all those numbers takes too much time.

The Kaplan Approach

1. Think first.
2. Decide on the best way to solve the problem.
3. Only then, use your calculator.

The right approach is to *think first*. The amount of computation involved in directly solving this tells you that there must be an easier way. You'll see this if you realize that both sums contain the same number of consecutive integers. Each integer in the first sum has a corresponding integer 6 greater than it in the second sum:

$$
\begin{array}{ll}
1 & 7 \\
+2 & +8 \\
+3 & +9 \\
\cdot & \cdot \\
\cdot & \cdot \\
\cdot & \cdot \\
+42 & +48 \\
+43 & +49 \\
+44 & +50 \\
= & =
\end{array}
$$

As you'll see in the Math Traps step, the way to find the number of integers in a consecutive series is to subtract the smallest from the largest and add 1 ($44 - 1 = 43$; $43 + 1 = 44$ OR $50 - 7 = 43$; $43 + 1 = 44$). So there are 44 pairs of integers that are 6 apart.

Therefore, the total difference between the two sums will be the difference between each pair of integers times the number of pairs. Now take out your calculator, punch "$6 \times 44 =$," and get the correct answer of 264, with little or no time wasted.

Important

If you're just punching keys instead of thinking, you're approaching the problem the wrong way.

Common Calculator Mistake #2: Forgetting the Order of Operations

Even when you use your calculator, you can't just enter numbers in the order they appear on the page—you've got to follow the order of operations. This is a very simple error, but it can cost you lots of points. The order of operations is "PEMDAS," which stands for:

- **Parentheses** first, then deal with
- **Exponents**, then
- **Multiplication** and
- **Division**, and finally
- **Addition** and
- **Subtraction**

That means you do whatever is in parentheses first, then deal with exponents, then multiplication and division (from left to right), and finally addition and subtraction (from left to right). For example, say you want to find the value of the expression $\frac{x^2 + 1}{x + 3}$ when $x = 7$.

If you just punched in "$7 \times 7 + 1 \div 7 + 3 =$" you would get the wrong answer.

The correct way to work it out is:

$$(7^2 + 1) \div (7 + 3) = (7 \times 7 + 1) \div (7 + 3) = (49 + 1) \div 10 = 50 \div 10 = 5$$

Combining a calculator with an understanding of when and how to use it can help you boost your score.

PRACTICE

Following are three separate practice sets. Approach the Regular Math, Quantitative Comparisons, and Grid-ins as you would if they were questions taken straight from the SAT. Follow the time limit instructions for each practice set, and use the strategies we covered in this step.

Regular Math

Number of Minutes—12; Number of Questions—6

1. A certain pump can drain a full 375-gallon tank in 15 minutes. At this rate, how many more minutes would it take to drain a full 600-gallon tank?

   (A) 9
   (B) 15
   (C) 18
   (D) 24
   (E) 25

2. A gardener plants flowers in the following order: carnations, daffodils, larkspurs, tiger lilies, and zinnias. If the gardener planted 47 flowers, what kind of flower did he plant last?

   (A) Carnations
   (B) Daffodils
   (C) Larkspurs
   (D) Tiger lilies
   (E) Zinnias

3. How many different positive two-digit integers are there such that the tens' digit is greater than 5 and the units' digit is odd?

   (A) 10
   (B) 12
   (C) 15
   (D) 20
   (E) 25

4. If a and b are positive integers, what is a percent of b percent of 200?

    (A) $\dfrac{ab}{100}$

    (B) $\dfrac{ab}{50}$

    (C) ab

    (D) $50ab$

    (E) $100ab$

5. A $7\frac{1}{2}$ liter mixture of water and molasses is 60 percent molasses. If $1\frac{1}{2}$ liters of water are added, approximately what percent of the new mixture is molasses?

    (A) 40%

    (B) 50%

    (C) 63%

    (D) 64%

    (E) 68%

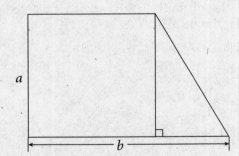

6. The figure above is formed from a square and a right triangle. What is its area?

    (A) $\dfrac{a(a+b)}{2}$

    (B) $\dfrac{a^2+b^2}{2}$

    (C) $\dfrac{a(b-a)}{2}$

    (D) a^2+b^2

    (E) $a^2+\dfrac{ab}{2}$

Answers and Explanations

1. (A)

Basic Question

You're given that a pump can drain a 375-gallon tank in 15 minutes. Therefore, the **rate** of the pump is $\dfrac{375 \text{ gallons}}{15 \text{ minutes}}$, or 25 gallons per minute. At this rate, the pump will drain a 600-gallon tank in $\dfrac{600}{25}$, or 24, minutes. So it will take $24 - 15$, or 9 more minutes to drain the 600-gallon tank.

2. (B)

Basic Question

You're looking for the 47th flower in a repeating pattern. Since there are five different flowers in the pattern, the last flower in the pattern corresponds to a multiple of 5. So the 5th, 10th, . . . , and 45th flowers will be zinnias. But there will also be two **remainders**, and so the 46th will be the first flower in the pattern and the 47th will be the second flower, which is a daffodil.

3. (D)

Medium Question

Simply count all the possibilities. If the numbers must have a tens' digit greater than 5, they must be 60 or greater. Since they are two-digit numbers, they must be less than 100. Since the units' digit is odd, they must be odd. So you need to count all the odd numbers between 60 and 100. Well, there are five such numbers with a tens' digit of 6: 61, 63, 65, 67 and 69. Similarly there will be five more numbers with a tens' digit of 7, five more with a tens' digit of 8, and another five with a tens' digit of 9. That's $5 + 5 + 5 + 5$, or 20 such numbers.

4. (B)

Medium Question

In this percent word problem, since *percent* means *hundredths*, a percent $= \dfrac{a}{100}$ and b percent $= \dfrac{b}{100}$. So a percent of b percent of $200 = \dfrac{a}{100} \times \dfrac{b}{100} \times 200 = \dfrac{200ab}{10,000} = \dfrac{ab}{50}$.

5. (B)

Hard Question

First find the amount of molasses in the original mixture. There are 7.5 liters of the mixture, of which 60% is molasses so there are $\frac{60}{100} \times 7.5 = 4.5$ liters of molasses. An additional 1.5 liters of water is added, so now the mixture is $7.5 + 1.5 = 9$ liters, of which 4.5 liters is molasses. Percent = $\frac{\text{Part}}{\text{Whole}} \times 100\%$, so in this case, $\frac{4.5}{9} \times 100\% = .5 \times 100\% = 50\%$.

6. (A)

Hard Question

To find the area, add the dimensions of the square and the triangle. First re-label the diagram as follows:

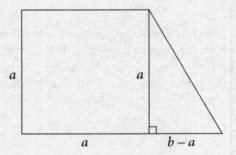

The area of a square is the length of a side squared, so the area of this square is a^2. The area of this right triangle is $\frac{1}{2}(\text{leg}_1 \times \text{leg}_2) = \frac{1}{2}(a)(b-a) = \frac{ab}{2} - \frac{a^2}{2}$. So the combined area is:

$$a^2 + \frac{ab}{2} - \frac{a^2}{2} = \frac{2a^2}{2} - \frac{a^2}{2} + \frac{ab}{2}$$

$$= \frac{a^2}{2} + \frac{ab}{2}$$

$$= \frac{a^2 + ab}{2}$$

$$= \frac{a(a + b)}{2}$$

Quantitative Comparisons

Number of Minutes—8; Number of Questions—6

Compare the quantity in Column A with the quantity in Column B. Select answer choice

    A   if Column A is greater

    B   if Column B is greater

    C   if the columns are equal

    D   if more information is needed to determine the relationship

1.

Column A	Column B
The amount of change from a ten-dollar bill with a $6.75 purchase	The amount of change from a ten-dollar bill with a $7.65 purchase

2.

    Column A   Column B

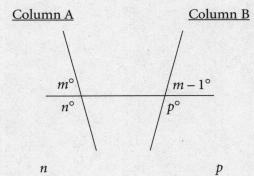

3.

Column A	Column B

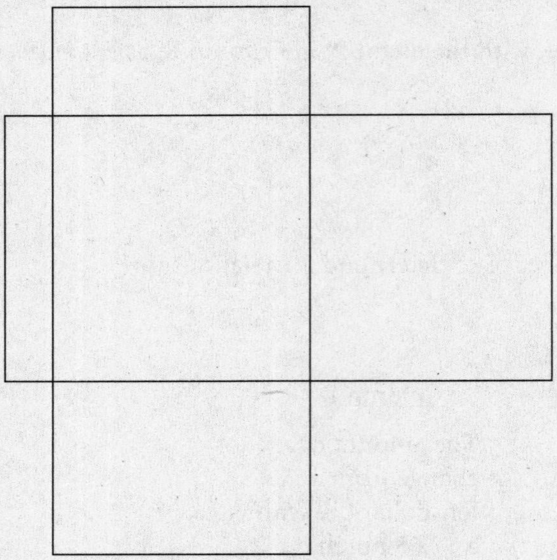

Two boards with dimensions 2 meters by 4 meters overlap to form the figure above. All the angles shown measure 90°.

The area of the figure, in square meters	16

4.

Column A	Column B
$\sqrt{102} \times \sqrt{83}$	$\sqrt{8000}$

5.

Column A	Column B

$$k > 60$$

50% of k	35

6.

Column A	Column B

$$75\% \text{ of } 80 > 25\% \text{ of } x$$

x	200

Answers and Explanations

1. (A)

Basic Question

It's not necessary to spend time calculating the exact amount of change in each column. $6.75 is less than $7.65, so the change from the $6.75 purchase will be greater.

2. (B)

Basic Question

Angle m must be greater than angle $m - 1$, so redraw the diagram to exaggerate this difference:

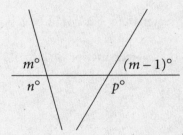

Now you can see that angle p in Column B must be greater than angle n in Column A.

3. (B)

Medium Question

Since all the angles shown measure 90 degrees, the two boards and all of the other quadrilaterals in the diagram are **rectangles**. The area of the figure is equal to the areas of the two boards minus the area of the part where the two boards overlap. The two boards are each 2-meter by 4-meter rectangles, so they each have an area of 2 times 4, or 8 square meters. Together they have a total area of 16 square meters. The area of the figure must be less than 16, since you still have to subtract the area of the overlap. Since Column A is less than 16 and Column B equals 16, Column B must be greater.

4. (A)

Medium Question

Change one column to make it look more like the other. Simplify the radical expression in Column B by rewriting it as $\sqrt{80}$ times $\sqrt{100}$. Since 102 > 100 and 83 > 80, the product in Column A must be greater than that in Column B. This method is faster than using your calculator.

5. (D)

Hard Question

Try picking different values of k. If $k = 70$, Column A is 35 and the columns are equal; if k is any number greater than 70, Column A would be greater than 35 and therefore greater than Column B. Since more than one relationship is possible, the answer is (D).

6. (D)

Hard Question

Seventy-five percent of 80 is the same as $\frac{3}{4}$ of 80, or 60. Twenty-five percent is the same as $\frac{1}{4}$, so 25% of x is $\frac{1}{4}$ of x. If 60 is greater than $\frac{1}{4}$ of x then 4 times 60, or 240, is greater than 4 times $\frac{1}{4}$ of x, or x. If 240 is greater than x, x could be less than 200, but it could also be greater than or equal to 200, so the correct answer is (D).

Grid-ins

Number of Minutes—2.5; Number of Questions—5

1. If $r = 8$, then $(r + 4)^2 =$

2. Bill bought 3 books at $14.50 each. If the tax was already included in the cost, how much change did he receive from a $50 bill? (Disregard the $ sign when gridding your answer.)

3. If two points on a certain line in a coordinate plane have coordinates (2, 6) and (4, 9), what is the slope of the line?

4. Nuala baked 64 cookies for a party. After each party guest ate n cookies, there were 9 cookies left uneaten. If there were more than 9 guests at the party, and if n is an integer greater than 1, what is the value of n?

5. At a certain company, the number of production employees was increased from 300 to 390. The number of clerical employees was increased by twice the percent increase of the production employees. If the final number of clerical employees was 192, what was the original number of clerical employees?

Answers and Explanations

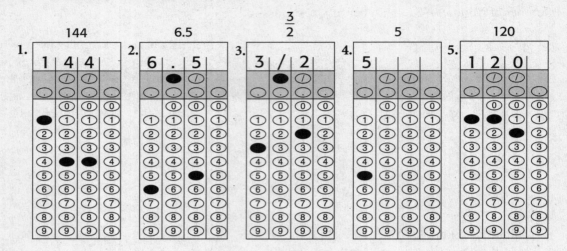

1. 144

Just substitute 8 for r in the equation. $(8 + 4)^2 = (12)^2 = 144$

2. 6.5 or $\frac{13}{2}$

Three books at 14.50 = 3($14.50) = $43.50. If Bill paid with a $50.00 bill, he would receive $50.00 − $43.50 = $6.50 in change.

3. $\frac{3}{2}$

Here you just have to know that slope is equal to $\frac{\text{rise}}{\text{run}}$, or, in mathematical terms $\frac{y_2 - y_1}{x_2 - x_1}$. So here the slope equals $\frac{9 - 6}{4 - 2} = \frac{3}{2}$.

4. 5

Start by figuring out how many cookies were eaten. Nuala started with 64, and 9 were left: 64 − 9 = 55. You need to pick a number of guests, a number greater than 9. Pick 11, since it's a factor of 55. If 11 guests ate 5 cookies each, you'd be left with 9 cookies, which makes 5 the right answer.

5. 120

If the number of production employees rises from 300 to 390, that's an increase of $\frac{90}{300} = \frac{30}{100} = 30\%$. The number of clerical workers increases by twice that percent, or $2 \times 30\% = 60\%$, resulting in a total of 192 clerical workers. The question asks you to solve for the original number of clerical workers, which you can call x. You aren't told how many of the 192 are new employees, but you know that this total of 192 is equal to the original number plus 60% of the original number. Since percent × whole = part, then $160\% \times x = 192$, or $1.6 \times x = 192$. So $x = 120$.

Tested Math Concepts

There are a handful of math skills tested OVER AND OVER AGAIN on the SAT. When you are confident that you understand these basic math concepts, the SAT Math section gets a whole lot easier. Step 7 is designed to introduce you to these basic math concepts and show you how the SAT tests them. Our techniques for solving these problems work with all three types of SAT Math questions: Regular Math, Quantitative Comparisons, and Grid-ins.

Of course there are many other math concepts related to these that the SAT also covers. After you finish Step 7, turn to Appendix A: SAT Math in a Nutshell. Go through the 100 concepts listed there and circle the ones you are unsure of. Learn four of those concepts a day, and you should know them all well within a month.

Here's your outline for Step 7:

STEP 7 PREVIEW

Math Concepts
Know the concepts most commonly tested on the SAT:
- Remainders
- Averages
- Ratios
- Rates
- Percents
- Simultaneous Equations
- Symbols
- Special Triangles
- Multiple and Strange Figures

Practice
Use it before you lose it (18 questions / no time limit)

REMAINDERS

Remainder questions can be easier than they look. Lots of people think you have to solve for a certain value in a remainder question, but that's usually not the case. Take this example:

> When n is divided by 7, the remainder is 4. What is the remainder when $2n$ is divided by 7?
>
> (A) 0
> (B) 1
> (C) 2
> (D) 3
> (E) 4

This question doesn't depend on knowing the value of n. In fact, n has an infinite number of possible values. The easy way to solve this kind of problem is to pick a number for n. Since the remainder when n is divided by 7 is 4, pick any multiple of 7 and add 4. The easiest multiple to work with is 7. So, $7 + 4 = 11$. Plug 11 in for n and see what happens:

> What is the remainder when $2n$ is divided by 7?
>
> ... the remainder when $2(11)$ is divided by 7?
>
> ... the remainder when 22 is divided by 7?
>
> ... $\frac{22}{7} = 3$ remainder 1

The remainder is 1 when $n = 11$. So the answer is (B). The remainder will also be 1 when $n = 18, 25,$ or 46.

AVERAGES

Instead of giving you a list of values to plug into the average formula $\left(\dfrac{\text{Sum of Terms}}{\text{Number of Terms}} \right)$, SAT average questions often put a spin on the problem, like so:

> The average weight of five amplifiers in a guitar shop is 32 pounds. If four of the amplifiers weigh 25, 27, 19, and 35 pounds, what is the weight of the fifth amplifier?
>
> (A) 28 pounds
> (B) 32 pounds
> (C) 49 pounds
> (D) 54 pounds
> (E) 69 pounds

This problem tells you the average of a group of terms and asks you to find the value of a missing term. To get the answer, you need to work with the sum. Let x = the weight of the fifth amplifier. Plug this into the average for formula:

$$\text{Average} = \frac{\text{Sum of Terms}}{\text{Number of Terms}}$$

$$32 = \frac{25 + 27 + 19 + 35 + x}{5}$$

$$32 \times 5 = 25 + 27 + 19 + 35 + x$$

The average weight of the amplifiers times the number of amplifiers equals the total weight of the amplifiers. The new formula is:

$$\text{Average} \times \text{Number of Terms} = \text{Sum of Terms}$$

Remember this version of the average formula so you can find the total sum whenever you know the average of a group of terms and the number of terms. Now you can solve for the weight of the fifth amplifier:

$$32 \times 5 = 25 + 27 + 19 + 35 + x$$
$$160 = 106 + x$$
$$54 = x$$

So the weight of the fifth amplifier is 54 pounds, choice (D). Rock on.

RATIOS

SAT test writers often try to get you to set up the wrong ratio in a ratio question. Don't be angry with them. Understand that they can't help themselves, and calmly work around their tricks.

Out of every 50 CDs produced in a certain factory, 20 are scratched. What is the ratio of nondefective CDs produced to scratched CDs produced?

(A) 2:5
(B) 3:5
(C) 2:3
(D) 3:2
(E) 5:2

You need to find the parts and the whole in the problem. In this case the total number of CDs is the whole, and the number of nondefective CDs and the number of scratched CDs are the parts that make up this whole. You're given a part-to-whole ratio (the ratio of scratched CDs to all CDs) and asked to find a part-to-part ratio (the ratio of nondefective CDs to scratched CDs).

If 20 CDs out of every 50 are scratched, the remaining 30 CDs must be OK. So the part-to-part ratio of good to scratched CDs is $\frac{30}{20}$, or $\frac{3}{2}$, which is equivalent to 3:2, choice (D). If you hadn't identified the part and the whole first it would be easy to get confused and compare a part to the whole, like the ratios in answer choices (A), (B), and (E).

This approach also works for ratio questions where you need to find actual quantities. Here's an example.

> Out of every 5 CDs produced in a certain factory, 2 are scratched. If 2,200 CDs were produced, how many were scratched?

Here you need to find a quantity: the number of defective CDs. If you're looking for the actual quantities in a ratio, set up and solve a proportion. You're given a part-to-whole ratio (the ratio of scratched CDs to all CDs), and total CDs produced. You can find the answer by setting up and solving a proportion:

$$\frac{\text{Number of scratched CDs}}{\text{Total number of CDs}} = \frac{2}{5} = \frac{x}{2,200}$$

$$x = \text{number of scratched CDs}$$

$$5x = 4,400 \left(\text{by cross-multiplying } \frac{2}{5} = \frac{x}{2,200} \right)$$

$$x = 880 \text{ (by dividing both sides by 5)}$$

Remember that ratios compare only relative size; they don't tell you the actual quantities involved. Distinguish clearly between the parts and the whole in ratio problems.

RATES

A rate is a ratio that compares quantities measured in different units. In the following problem, the units are dollars and headphones.

> If 8 headphones cost a dollars, b headphones would cost how many dollars?
>
> (A) $8ab$
>
> (B) $\frac{8a}{b}$
>
> (C) $\frac{8}{ab}$
>
> (D) $\frac{a}{8b}$
>
> (E) $\frac{ab}{8}$

What makes this rate problem difficult is the variables. It's hard to get a clear picture of the relationship between the units. You need to pick numbers for the variables to make the relationship between the units clearer.

Pick numbers for a and b that will be easy for you to work with in the problem. Let $a = 16$. Then 8 headphones cost \$16. So the cost per headphone at this rate $= \dfrac{\$16}{8 \text{ headphones}} = \$2$ per headphone.

Let $b = 5$. So the cost of 5 headphones at this rate is 5 headphones $\times$ \$2 per headphone $= \$10$. Now plug in $a = 16$ and $b = 5$ into the answer choices to see which one gives you a value of 10.

Choice (A): $8 \times 16 \times 5 = 640$. Eliminate.

Choice (B): $\dfrac{8 \times 16}{5} = \dfrac{128}{5}$. Eliminate.

Choice (C): $\dfrac{8}{16 \times 5} = \dfrac{1}{10}$. Eliminate.

Choice (D): $\dfrac{16}{8 \times 5} = \dfrac{2}{5}$. Eliminate.

Choice (E): $\dfrac{16 \times 5}{8} = 10$.

Since (E) is the only one that gives the correct value, it is correct, and those are some cheap headphones.

PERCENTS

In percent problems, you're usually given two pieces of information and asked to find the third, like so:

> Last year Aunt Edna's annual salary was \$20,000. This year's raise brings her to an annual salary of \$25,000. If she gets a raise of the same percentage every year, what will her salary be next year?

(A) \$27,500

(B) \$30,000

(C) \$31,250

(D) \$32,500

(E) \$35,000

When you see a percent problem, remember the following formulas.

If you are solving for a percent: $\dfrac{\text{Part}}{\text{Whole}} = \text{Percent}$

If you need to solve for a part: Percent × Whole = Part

This problem asks for Aunt Edna's projected salary for next year—that is, her current salary plus her next raise. You know last year's salary ($20,000) and you know this year's salary ($25,000), so you can find the difference between the two salaries:

$25,000 – $20,000 = $5,000 = her raise

Now find the percent this raise represents by using the formula Percent = $\frac{Part}{Whole}$. Since Aunt Edna's raise was calculated on last year's salary, divide by $20,000. Be sure you know which whole to plug in. Here you're looking for a percentage of $20,000, not of $25,000.

$$\text{Percent} = \frac{\$5,000}{\$20,000} = \frac{1}{4} = 25\%$$

You know Aunt Edna will get the same percent raise next year, so solve for the part. Use the formula Percent × Whole = Part. Make sure you change the percent to either a fraction or a decimal before beginning calculations.

Her raise next year will be 25% × $25,000 = $\frac{1}{4}$ × 25,000 = $6,250. Add that amount to this year's salary and you have her projected salary:

$25,000 + $6,250 = $31,250, or answer choice (C).

Aunt Edna must be doing something right.

SIMULTANEOUS EQUATIONS

In order to get a numerical value for each variable in a simultaneous equation, you need as many different equations as there are variables to solve for. So, if you have two variables, you need two distinct equations.

If $p + 2q = 14$ and $3p + q = 12$, then $p =$
(Note: This is a Grid-in, so there are no answer choices.)

You could tackle this problem by solving for one variable in terms of the other, and then plugging this expression into the other equation. But the simultaneous equations that appear on the SAT can usually be handled in an easier way. Combine the equations, by adding or subtracting them, to cancel out all but one of the variables. You can't eliminate p or q by adding or subtracting the equations in their present forms. But if you multiply the second equation by 2:

$$2(3p + q) = 2(12)$$
$$6p + 2q = 24$$

Now when you subtract the first equation from the second, the qs will cancel out so you can solve for p:

$$6p + 2q = 24$$
$$\underline{-[p + 2q = 14]}$$
$$5p + 0 = 10$$

If $5p = 10$, $p = 2$. On the answer sheet, you would grid in the answer 2.

SYMBOLISM

You should be quite familiar with the arithmetic symbols $+, -, \times, \div$, and %. Finding the value of $10 + 2$, $18 - 4$, 4×9, or $96 \div 16$ is easy.

However, on the SAT, you may come across bizarre symbols. You may even be asked to find the value of $10 \bigstar 2$, $5 \text{❄} 7$, $10 \text{✳} 6$, or $65 \text{♥} 2$.

The SAT test makers put strange symbols in questions to confuse or unnerve you. Don't let them. The question stem always tells you what the strange symbol means. Although this type of question may look difficult, it is really an exercise in plugging in. Look at the following example:

> If $a \bigstar b = \sqrt{a + b}$ for all non-negative numbers, what is the value of $10 \bigstar 6$?
>
> (A)   0
> (B)   2
> (C)   4
> (D)   8
> (E)   16

To solve, just plug in 10 for a and 6 for b into the expression $\sqrt{a + b}$. That equals $\sqrt{10 + 6}$ or $\sqrt{16}$ or 4, choice (C).

Don't freak out, plug in the numbers, and you'll be fine.

SPECIAL TRIANGLES

Look for the special triangles in geometry problems. Special triangles contain a lot of information. For instance, if you know the length of one side of a 30-60-90 triangle, you can easily work out the lengths of the others. Special triangles allow you to transfer one piece of information around the whole figure.

The following are the special triangles you should look for on the SAT. You don't have to memorize the ratios (they're listed in the instructions), but you should be familiar enough with them to recognize them when you see them.

Equilateral Triangles

All interior angles are 60° and all sides have equal length.

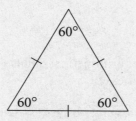

Isosceles Triangles

Two sides have equal length, and the angles facing these sides are equal.

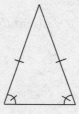

Right Triangles

These contain a 90° angle. The sides are related by the Pythagorean theorem: $a^2 + b^2 = c^2$ where a and b are the legs and c is the hypotenuse.

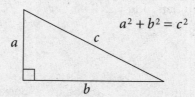

The "Special" Right Triangles

Many triangle problems contain "special" right triangles, whose side lengths always come in predefined ratios. If you recognize them, you won't have to use the Pythagorean theorem to find the value of a missing side length.

The 3-4-5 Right Triangle

(Be on the lookout for multiples of 3-4-5 as well.)

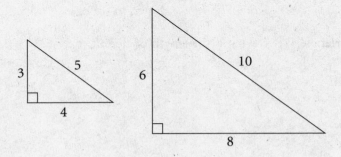

The Isosceles Right Triangle

(Note the side ratio: 1 to 1 to $\sqrt{2}$.)

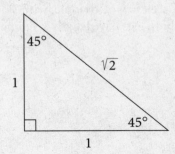

The 30-60-90 Right Triangle

(Note the side ratio: 1 to $\sqrt{3}$ to 2, and which side is opposite which angle.)

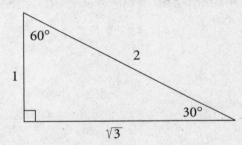

Now that we've gone through all the special triangles, try this problem.

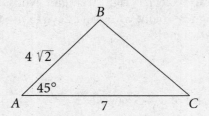

Note: Figure not drawn to scale.

In the triangle above, what is the length of side *BC* ?

(A) 4
(B) 5
(C) 4√2
(D) 6
(E) 5√2

You can drop a vertical line from *B* to line *AC*. This divides the triangle into two right triangles.

That means you know two of the angles in the triangle on the left: 90° and 45°. The third angle must also be 45°, so this is an isosceles right triangle, with sides in the ratio of 1 to 1 to √2. The hypotenuse here is 4√2, so both legs have length 4. Filling this in, you have the following:

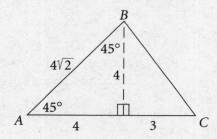

Now you can see that the legs of the smaller triangle on the right must be 4 and 3, making this a 3-4-5 right triangle, and the length of hypotenuse *BC* is 5. So choice (B) is correct.

Basic Math Tips

Averages—Work with the sum.

Ratios—Identify the parts and the whole.

Rates—Pick numbers for the variables to make the relationship between units clear.

Percents—Make sure you know which whole to plug in.

Simultaneous Equations—Combine equations by adding or subtracting them to cancel out all but one variable.

Special Triangles—Look for special triangles in geometry problems.

MULTIPLE AND STRANGE FIGURES

In a problem that combines figures, you have to look for the relationship between the figures. Look for pieces the figures have in common. For instance, if two figures share a side, information about that side will probably be the key.

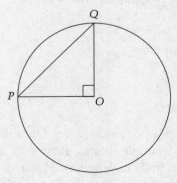

In the figure above, if the area of the circle with center O is 9π, what is the area of triangle POQ?

(A) 4.5
(B) 6
(C) 9
(D) 3.5π
(E) 4.5π

In this case the figures don't share a side, but the triangle's legs are important features of the circle—they are radii. You can see that $PO = OQ =$ the radius of circle O. The area of the circle is 9π. The area of a circle is πr^2, where $r =$ the radius. So $9\pi = \pi r^2$, $9 = r^2$, and the radius $= 3$. The area of a triangle is $\frac{1}{2}$ base times height. Therefore, the area of ΔPOQ is $\frac{1}{2}$ (leg$_1$ × leg$_2$) $= \frac{1}{2}$ (3 × 3) $= \frac{9}{2} = 4.5$, answer choice (A).

But what if, instead of a number of familiar shapes, you are given something like this?

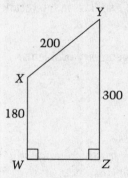

What is the perimeter of quadrilateral $WXYZ$?

(A)   680
(B)   760
(C)   840
(D)   920
(E) 1,000

Try breaking the unfamiliar shape into familiar ones. Once this is done, you can use the same techniques that you would for multiple figures. Perimeter is the sum of the lengths of the sides of a figure, so you need to find the length of WZ. Drawing a perpendicular line from point X to side YZ will divide the figure into a right triangle and a rectangle. Call the point of intersection A.

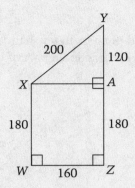

Opposite sides of a rectangle have equal length, so $WZ = XA$ and $WX = ZA$. WX is labeled as 180, so $ZA = 180$. Since YZ measures 300, AY is $300 - 180 = 120$. In right triangle XYA, hypotenuse $XY = 200$ and leg $AY = 120$; you should recognize this as a multiple of a 3-4-5 right triangle. The hypotenuse is 5×40, one leg is 3×40, so XA must be 4×40 or 160. (If you didn't recognize this special right triangle you could have used the Pythagorean theorem to find the length of XA.) Since $WZ = XA = 160$, the perimeter of the figure is $180 + 200 + 300 + 160 = 840$, answer choice (C).

CONCLUSION

Do the practice set that follows, then remember to turn to Appendix A: Math in a Nutshell. Carefully read through the 100 concepts listed there and circle the ones you are unsure of. Learn four of those concepts a day, and you should know them all well within a month.

PRACTICE

We have labeled the following questions by the math concept they test. If you get stumped, go back to the appropriate part of this step and refresh your memory on how to solve that kind of problem. These questions are organized in ascending order of difficulty, just like on the SAT. There is no time limit for this practice set.

Remainders

1. When z is divided by 8, the remainder is 5. What is the remainder when $4z$ is divided by 8?

   (A) 1
   (B) 3
   (C) 4
   (D) 5
   (E) 7

Ratios

2. The ratio of right-handed pitchers to left-handed pitchers in a certain baseball league is 11:7. What fractional part of the pitchers in the league are left-handed?

   (A) $\dfrac{6}{7}$

   (B) $\dfrac{6}{11}$

   (C) $\dfrac{7}{11}$

   (D) $\dfrac{7}{18}$

   (E) $\dfrac{11}{18}$

Percents

Column A	Column B
3. 5% of 3% of 45	6.75

Simultaneous Equations

4. If $x + y = 8$ and $y - x = -2$, then $y =$

   (A) −2
   (B) 3
   (C) 5
   (D) 8
   (E) 10

Special Triangles

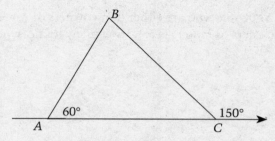

Note: Figure not drawn to scale.

5. In triangle *ABC* above, if *AB* = 4, then *AC* =

   (A) 10
   (B)   9
   (C)   8
   (D)   7
   (E)   6

Remainders

Column A	Column B

   When *x* is divided by 6 the remainder is 3.

   When *y* is divided by 6 the remainder is 4.

6.   *x*   *y*

Averages

7. Bart needs to buy five gifts with $80. If two of the gifts cost a total of $35, what is the average (arithmetic mean) amount Bart can spend on each of the remaining three gifts?

   (A) $45
   (B) $17
   (C) $16
   (D) $15
   (E) $10

Ratios

8. In a group of 24 people who are either homeowners or renters, the ratio of homeowners to renters is 5:3. How many homeowners are in the group?

    (A) 15
    (B) 14
    (C) 12
    (D)   9
    (E)   8

Rates

9. Bill has to type a paper that is p pages long, with each page containing w words. If Bill types an average of x words per minute, how many hours will it take him to finish the paper?

    (A) $60wpx$

    (B) $\dfrac{wx}{60p}$

    (C) $\dfrac{60wp}{x}$

    (D) $\dfrac{wpx}{60}$

    (E) $\dfrac{wp}{60x}$

Percents

10. Eighty-five percent of the members of a student organization registered to attend a certain field trip. If 16 of the members who registered were unable to attend, resulting in only 65 percent of the members making the trip, how many members are in the organization?

Simultaneous Equations

11. If $4a + 3b = 19$ and $a + 2b = 6$, then $a + b =$

Special Triangles

    <u>Column A</u>   <u>Column B</u>

In the coordinate plane, point R has coordinates $(0, 0)$ and point S has coordinates $(9, 12)$.

12.   The distance from   16
      R to S

Multiple and Strange Figures

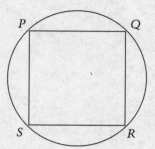

13. In the figure above, square *PQRS* is inscribed in a circle. If the area of square *PQRS* is 4, what is the radius of the circle?

    (A) 1
    (B) $\sqrt{2}$
    (C) 2
    (D) $2\sqrt{2}$
    (E) $4\sqrt{2}$

Averages

14. The average (arithmetic mean) of five numbers is 8. If the average of two of these numbers is −6, what is the sum of the other three numbers?

    (A) 28
    (B) 34
    (C) 46
    (D) 52
    (E) 60

Rates

15. If Seymour drove 120 miles in *x* hours at constant speed, how many miles did he travel in the first 20 minutes of his trip?

    (A) $60x$
    (B) $3x$
    (C) $\dfrac{120}{x}$
    (D) $\dfrac{40}{x}$
    (E) $\dfrac{6}{x}$

Symbolism

$$c \star d = \frac{(c-d)}{c}, \text{ where } c \neq 0.$$

16. $12 \star 3 =$

 (A) -3

 (B) $\frac{1}{4}$

 (C) $\frac{2}{3}$

 (D) $\frac{3}{4}$

 (E) 3

Multiple and Strange Figures

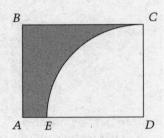

Note: Figure not drawn to scale.

17. In the figure above, the quarter circle with center D has a radius of 4 and rectangle $ABCD$ has a perimeter of 20. What is the perimeter of the shaded region?

 (A) $20 - 8\pi$

 (B) $10 + 2\pi$

 (C) $12 + 2\pi$

 (D) $12 + 4\pi$

 (E) $4 + 8\pi$

Symbolism

18. If $9 \star 4 = 15 \star k$, then $k =$

 (A) 3

 (B) 6

 (C) $\frac{20}{3}$

 (D) $\frac{25}{3}$

 (E) 9

Answers and Explanations

Remainders

1. (C)

Let $z = 13$ and plug in $4z = 4(13) = 52$, which leaves a remainder of 4 when divided by 8.

Ratios

2. (D)

The parts are the number of right-handed (11) and the number of left-handed pitchers (7). The whole is the total number of pitchers (right-handed + left-handed), which is $11 + 7$, or 18. So:

$$\frac{\text{part}}{\text{whole}} = \frac{\text{left-handed}}{\text{total}} = \frac{7}{11 + 7} = \frac{7}{18}$$

Percents

3. (B)

Percent $\times$ Whole = Part. Five percent of (3 percent of 45) = $.05 \times (.03 \times 45) = .05 \times 1.35 = .0675$, which is less than 6.75 in Column B.

Simultaneous Equations

4. (B)

When you add the two equations, the xs cancel out and you find that $2y = 6$, so $y = 3$.

Special Triangles

5. (C)

Angle *BCA* is supplementary to the angle marked 150°, so angle $BCA = 180° - 150° = 30°$. Since the sum of interior angles of a triangle is 180°, angle A + angle B + angle $BCA = 180°$, so angle $B = 180° - 60° - 30° = 90°$. So triangle *ABC* is a 30-60-90 right triangle, and its sides are in the ratio $1 : \sqrt{3} : 2$. The side opposite the 30°, *AB*, which we know has length 4, must be half the length of the hypotenuse, *AC*. Therefore $AC = 8$, and that's answer choice (C).

Remainders

6. (D)

We determine that x can be any of the integers 3, 9, 15, 21, ..., and y can be any of the integers 4, 10, 16, 22, ... Since x could be greater than or less than y, the correct answer must be choice (D).

Averages

7. (D)

Bart has $80 and spent $35 on two gifts; therefore he has $45 left to spend on the remaining three. So,

$$x = \frac{\$45}{3}$$

$$x = \$15$$

Ratios

8. (A)

The parts are the number of homeowners (5) and the number of renters (3). The whole is the total (homeowners + renters). So:

$$\frac{\text{part}}{\text{whole}} = \frac{\text{homeowners}}{\text{homeowners} + \text{renters}} = \frac{5}{5+3} = \frac{5}{8}$$

Rates

9. (E)

Pick numbers for p, w, and x that work well in the problem. Let $p = 3$ and let $w = 100$. So there are three pages with 100 words per page, or 300 words total. Say he types five words a minute, so $x = 5$. So he types 5×60, or 300 words an hour. Therefore, it takes him one hour to type the paper. The only answer choice that equals 1 when $p = 3$, $w = 100$, and $x = 5$ is choice (E).

Percents

10. (80)

You need to solve for the Whole, so identify the Part and the Percent. If 85 percent planned to attend and only 65 percent did, 20 percent failed to attend, and you know that 16 students failed to attend.

$$\text{Percent} \times \text{Whole} = \text{Part}$$

$$\frac{20}{100} \times \text{Whole} = 16$$

$$\text{Whole} = 16 \times \frac{100}{20}$$

$$\text{Whole} = 80$$

Simultaneous Equations

11. (5)

Adding the two equations, you find that $5a + 5b = 25$. Dividing by 5 shows that $a + b = 5$.

Special Triangles

12. (B)

Draw a diagram. Since *RS* isn't parallel to either axis, the way to compute its length is to create a right triangle with legs that are parallel to the axes, so their lengths are easy to find. If the triangle formed is not a special triangle, we can then use the Pythagorean theorem to find the length of *RS*.

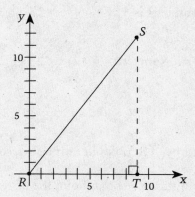

Since *S* has a *y*-coordinate of 12, it's 12 units above the x-axis, so the length of *ST* must be 12. And since *T* is the same number of units to the right of the *y*-axis as *S*, given by the *x*-coordinate of 9, the distance from the origin to *T* must be 9. So we have a right triangle with legs of 9 and 12. You should recognize this as a multiple of the 3-4-5 triangle. $9 = 3 \times 3$; $12 = 3 \times 4$; so the hypotenuse *RS* must be 3×5, or 15. That's the value of Column A, so Column B is greater.

Multiple and Strange Figures

13. (B)

Draw in diagonal *QS* and you will notice that it is also a diameter of the circle.

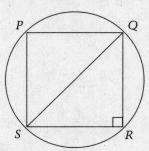

Since the area of the square is 4 its sides must each be 2. Think of the diagonal as dividing the square into two isosceles right triangles. Therefore, the diagonal $= 2\sqrt{2} =$ the diameter; the radius is half this amount, or $\sqrt{2}$.

Averages

14. (D)

Average × Number of Terms = Sum of Terms

The sum of all five numbers is

$8 \times 5 = 40$

The sum of two of these numbers is

$(-6) \times 2 = -12$

So, the difference of these two sums, $40 - (-12) = 52$, is the sum of the other numbers.

Rates

15. (D)

Let $x = 4$. That means that he drove 120 miles in four hours, so his speed was $\dfrac{120 \text{ miles}}{4 \text{ hours}}$, or

30 miles per hour. Since 20 minutes $= \dfrac{1}{3}$ of an hour, the distance he traveled in the first 20

minutes is $\dfrac{1}{3}$ hours × 30 miles per hour = 10 miles. The only answer choice that equals 10

when $x = 4$ is choice (D).

Symbolism

16. (D)

Plug in 12 for c and 3 for d: $\dfrac{12 - 3}{12} = \dfrac{9}{12} = \dfrac{3}{4}$.

Multiple and Strange Figures

17. (C)

The perimeter of the shaded region is $BC + AB + AE +$ arc EC. The quarter circle has its center at D, and point C lies on the circle, so side DC is a radius of the circle and equals 4.

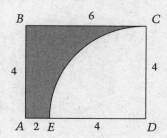

Opposite sides of a rectangle are equal, so AB is also 4. The perimeter of the rectangle is 20, and since the two short sides account for 8, the two longer sides must account for 12, making BC and AD each 6. To find AE, subtract the length of ED, another radius of length 4, from the length of AD, which is 6; $AE = 2$.

Since arc EC is a quarter circle, the length of the arc EC is $\frac{1}{4}$ of the circumference of a whole circle with radius 4: $\frac{1}{4} \times 2\pi r = \frac{1}{4} \times 8\pi = 2\pi$.

So the perimeter of the shaded region is $6 + 4 + 2 + 2\pi = 12 + 2\pi$.

Symbolism

18. (C)

Plug in on both sides of the equation:

$$\frac{9-4}{9} = \frac{15-k}{15}$$

$$\frac{5}{9} = \frac{15-k}{15}$$

Cross-multiply and solve for k:

$$75 = 135 - 9k$$

$$-60 = -9k$$

$$\frac{-60}{-9} = k$$

$$\frac{20}{3} = k$$

STEP EIGHT

Math Traps

As we've mentioned at least twenty-three times, SAT problem sets are arranged in order of difficulty with the easiest problems coming first and the hardest problems coming last. Knowing this causes you, the test taker, to treat question #3 differently than question #14. This is where SAT Math traps come into play.

If you arrive at an answer choice to a late (hard) Math problem without too much effort, THAT ANSWER IS PROBABLY A TRAP. Learning how to recognize and avoid common SAT Math traps will help you do better on hard math questions. There are 10 common Math traps on the SAT. We'll show you the trap, the wrong answer it's trying to trick you into choosing, how to avoid it, and how to solve the problem quickly and correctly.

STEP 8 PREVIEW

SAT Math Traps
Learn how to spot the test writers' favorite traps:

- Trap 1: Percent Increase/Decrease
- Trap 2: Weighted Averages
- Trap 3: Ratio:Ratio:Ratio
- Trap 4: Unspecified Order
- Trap 5: Length:Area Ratios
- Trap 6: Hidden Instructions
- Trap 7: Average Rates
- Trap 8: Counting Numbers
- Trap 9: Expressions That Look Equal—But Aren't
- Trap 10: Not All Numbers Are Positive Integers

Practice
Use it before you lose it (17 questions / no time limit)

TRAP 1: PERCENT INCREASE/DECREASE

Sylvester Stallone purchased a new car in 1990. Three years later he sold it to a dealer for 40 percent less than he paid for it in 1990. The dealer then added 20 percent onto the price she paid and resold it to another customer. The price the final customer paid for the car was what percent of the original price Sylvester Stallone paid in 1990?

(A) 40%
(B) 60%
(C) 72%
(D) 80%
(E) 88%

The Wrong Answer

The increase/decrease percentage problem usually appears at the end of a section and invariably contains a trap. Most students will figure that taking away 40 percent and then adding 20 percent will give them an overall loss of 20 percent, and they'll pick choice (D), 80 percent, as the correct answer. Most students will be wrong.

The Trap

When a quantity is increased or decreased by a percentage more than once, you can't simply add and subtract the percents to get the answer. In this kind of percent problem, the first percent change is a percent of the starting amount, but the second change is a percent of the new amount.

Avoiding the Trap

Don't blindly add and subtract percents. Percents can be added and subtracted only when they are percents of the same amount.

Finding the Right Answer

We know:

- The "40 percent less" that Mr. Stallone got for the car is 40 percent of his original price.
- The 20 percent the dealer adds on is 20 percent of what the dealer paid, a much smaller amount.
- Adding on 20 percent of that smaller amount is *not* the same thing as adding back 20 percent of the original price.

Solving the Problem Fast

Use 100 for a starting quantity, whether or not it's plausible in the real situation. The problem asks for the relative amount of change. So you can take any starting number, and compare it with the final result. Because you're dealing with percents, 100 is the easiest number to work with.

- If Stallone paid $100 for the car, what is 40 percent less?
- In the case of $100, each percent equals $1, so 100 − 40 = 60. Sylvester Stallone sold the car for $60.
- If the dealer charges 20 percent more than his purchase price, she's raising the price by 20 percent of $60, which is $60 × 0.20 = $12 (not 20 percent of $100, which would be $20!).
- Therefore, the dealer sold the car again for $60 + $12, or $72.
- Finally, what percent of the starting price ($100) is $72? It's 72%. So the correct answer here is choice (C).

TRAP 2: WEIGHTED AVERAGES

In a class of 27 plumbers, the average (arithmetic mean) score of the male plumbers on the final exam was 83. If the average score of the 15 female plumbers in the class was 92, what was the average of the whole class?

(A) 86.2
(B) 87.0
(C) 87.5
(D) 88.0
(E) 88.2

The Wrong Answer

Some students will rush in and simply average 83 and 92 to come up with 87.5 as the class average. Some students will be as disappointed as an *American Idol* wannabe.

The Trap

You cannot combine averages of different quantities by taking the average of those averages. In an averages problem, if one value occurs more frequently than others it is "weighted" more. Remember that the average formula calls for the sum of all the terms, divided by the total number of terms.

Avoiding the Trap

Don't just take the average of the averages. Work with the sums, not the averages.

Finding the Right Answer

If 15 of the 27 plumbers are girls, the remaining 12 must be boys. We can't just add 83 to 92 and divide by two. In this class there are more females than males, and therefore the girls' test scores are "weighted" more—they contribute more to the class average. So the answer must be either (D) or (E).

To find each sum, multiply each average by the number of terms it represents. After you have found the sums of the different terms, find the combined average by plugging them into the average formula.

$$\text{Total class average} = \frac{\text{Sum of girls' scores} + \text{sum of boys' scores}}{\text{Total number of students}}$$

$$= \frac{(\# \text{ of girls} \times \text{girls' average score}) + (\# \text{ of boys} \times \text{boys' average score})}{\text{Total } \# \text{ of students}}$$

$$= \frac{15(92) + 12(83)}{27} = \frac{1{,}380 + 996}{27} = 88$$

So the class average is 88, answer choice (D).

Important

Notice how using a calculator helps in this problem.

TRAP 3: RATIO:RATIO:RATIO

Peter Jennings's coin collection consists of quarters, dimes, and nickels. If the ratio of the number of quarters to the number of dimes is 5 to 2, and the ratio of the number of dimes to the number of nickels is 3 to 4, what is the ratio of the number of quarters to the number of nickels?

(A) 5 to 4
(B) 7 to 5
(C) 10 to 6
(D) 12 to 7
(E) 15 to 8

The Wrong Answer

If you chose 5 to 4 as the correct answer, you fell for the classic ratio trap. If Peter Jennings finds out, he will likely announce it on *World News Tonight*.

The Trap

Parts of different ratios don't always refer to the same whole. In the classic ratio trap, two different ratios each share a common part that is represented by two different numbers. The two ratios do not refer to the same whole, however, so they are not in proportion to each other.

To solve this type of problem, restate both ratios so that the numbers representing the common part (in this case "dimes") are the same. Then all the parts will be in proportion and can be compared to each other.

Avoiding the Trap

Restate ratios so that the same number refers to the same quantity. Make sure the common quantity in both ratios has the same number in both.

Finding the Right Answer

To find the ratio of quarters to nickels, restate both ratios so that the number of dimes is the same in both. You are given two ratios:

Quarters to Dimes = 5 to 2   Dimes to Nickels = 3 to 4

- The number corresponding to dimes in the first ratio is 2.
- The number corresponding to dimes in the second ratio is 3.
- To restate the ratios, find the least common multiple of 2 and 3.
- The least common multiple of 2 and 3 is 2×3, or 6.

Restate the ratios with the number of dimes as 6:

Quarters to Dimes = 15 to 6 (which is the same as 5 to 2)

Dimes to Nickels = 6 to 8 (which is the same as 3 to 4)

The ratios are still in their original proportions, but now they can be compared easily, since dimes are represented by the same number in both. The ratio of quarters to dimes to nickels is 15 to 6 to 8, so the ratio of quarters to nickels is 15 to 8, which is answer choice (E).

TRAP 4: UNSPECIFIED ORDER

Column A	Column B

A, B, and C are points on a line such that point A is 12 units away from point B and point B is 4 units away from point C.

The distance from point A to point C	16

The Wrong Answer

In problems about distances on a line, you should always draw a diagram to help you visualize the relationship between the points.

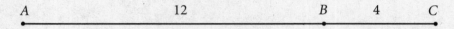

In this diagram, the distance from A to C is 16, which is the same as Column B. But choice (C)—the columns are not equal—is not the right answer.

The Trap

Don't assume that there is only one possible arrangement of the points. In this case, there's no reason to believe that the points lie in alphabetical order. We are not told what the relationship between A and C is. In fact, C could lie to the left of B, as in the following diagram.

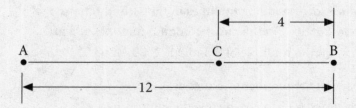

Avoiding the Trap

Don't assume points lie in the order they are given or in alphabetical order—look for alternatives. NEVER assume that there is only one way to draw a diagram.

Finding the Right Answer

In this second case, the distance from A to C is 8, which is less than Column B. Since we have two possible relationships between the columns, the answer must be (D)—you can't be certain from the data given.

TRAP 5: LENGTH:AREA RATIOS

Column A	Column B
The area of a square with a perimeter of 14	Twice the area of a square with a perimeter of 7

The Wrong Answer

Twice the perimeter doesn't mean twice the area. Choice (C)—the columns are equal—is wrong.

The Trap

In proportional figures, the ratio of the areas is not the same as the ratio of the lengths.

Avoiding the Trap

Understand that the ratio of the areas of proportional figures is the square of the ratio of corresponding linear measures. Remember that in proportional figures, the ratio of areas is not the same as the ratio of lengths.

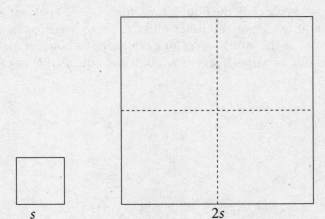

Finding the Right Answer

One way to solve this QC would be to actually compute the respective areas.

A square of perimeter 14 has side length $\frac{14}{4} = 3.5$. Its area then is $(3.5)^2 = 12.25$. On the other hand, the area of the square in Column B is $\left(\frac{7}{4}\right)^2 = (1.75)^2 = 3.0625$. Even twice that area is still less than the 12.25 in Column A. The answer is (A).

But this method takes too much time. A quicker and more clever way to dodge this trap is to understand the relationship between the linear ratio and the area ratio of proportional figures. In proportional figures, the area ratio is the square of the linear ratio.

In the example above, we are given two squares with sides in a ratio of 14:7 or 2:1. Using the rule above, we square the linear 2:1 ratio. The areas of the two figures will be in a 4:1 ratio.

The same goes for circles:

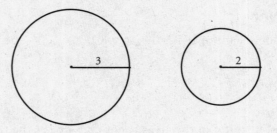

In the figure above, we are given two circles with radii in a 3:2 ratio. Using the rule above, we square the linear 3:2 ratio to get $3^2:2^2$, or 9:4. The areas of the two circles will be in a 9:4 ratio.

TRAP 6: HIDDEN INSTRUCTIONS

At a certain dance club, the hourly wage for a DJ is 20 percent greater than the hourly wage for an usher, and the hourly wage for an usher is half as much as the hourly wage for a bouncer. If a bouncer earns $8.50 an hour, how much less than a bouncer does a DJ earn each hour?

(A) $2.55
(B) $3.40
(C) $4.25
(D) $5.10
(E) $5.95

The Wrong Answer

To solve this problem, you must find the hourly wage of the usher.

- The bouncer earns $8.50 an hour.
- The usher earns half that, or $4.25 an hour.
- The DJ earns 20 percent more than this: $4.25 × 1.2 = $5.10.

So the DJ earns $5.10 an hour, and you might reach automatically to fill in answer choice (D). But (D) is the wrong answer.

The Trap

A small step, easily overlooked, can mean the difference between a right and wrong answer. In this case the word is *less*. After spending all this time finding the DJ's hourly wage, many students skip right over the vital last step. They overlook the fact that the question asks not what the DJ earns, but how much *less* than the bouncer the DJ earns.

Avoiding the Trap

Watch for hidden instructions. MAKE SURE you answer the question that's being asked.

Finding the Right Answer

You have figured out that the DJ earns $5.10 an hour and the bouncer earns $8.50 an hour. To find out how much less than the bouncer the usher earns, subtract the DJ's hourly wage from the bouncer's hourly wage. The correct answer is (B), $3.40.

TRAP 7: AVERAGE RATES

An unusually fast camel traveled from *A* to *B* at an average rate of 40 miles per hour and then immediately traveled back from *B* to *A* at an average speed of 60 miles per hour. What was the camel's average speed for the round trip, in miles per hour?

(A) 45
(B) 48
(C) 50
(D) 52
(E) 54

The Wrong Answer

Do you see which answer choice looks too good to be true? The temptation is simply to average 40 and 60. The answer is "obviously" (C), 50. But 50 is wrong.

The Trap

To get an average rate, you can't just average the rates. Why is the average speed not 50 mph? Because the camel spent more time traveling at 40 mph than at 60 mph. Each leg of the round trip was the same distance, but the first leg, at the slower speed, took more time.

Avoiding the Trap

You can solve almost any Average Rate problem if you apply this general formula:

$$\text{Average Rate} = \frac{\text{Total Distance}}{\text{Total Time}}$$

Use the given information to figure out the total distance and the total time. But how can you do that when many problems don't specify the distances?

Finding the Right Answer

In our sample above, we are told that a fast camel went "from *A* to *B* at 40 miles per hour and back from *B* to *A* at 60 miles per hour." In other words, it went half the total distance at 40 mph and half the total distance at 60 mph.

How do you use the formula, $\text{Average Rate} = \dfrac{\text{Total Time}}{\text{Total Distance}}$, if you don't know the total distance? Why, by picking any number you want for the total distance.

Pick a number. Divide that total distance into half-distances. Calculate the time needed to travel each half-distance at the different rates.

Important

When plugging numbers into the Average Rate formula, pick numbers that are easy to work with.

A good number to pick here would be 240 miles for the total distance, because you can easily figure in your head the times for two 120-mile legs at 40 mph and 60 mph:

A to *B*: $\dfrac{120 \text{ miles}}{40 \text{ miles per hour}} = 3$ hours

B to *A*: $\dfrac{120 \text{ miles}}{60 \text{ miles per hour}} = 2$ hours

Total Time = 5 hours

"Total Distance = 240 miles," so "Total Time = 5 hours" can be plugged into the general formula:

$$\text{Average Rate} = \frac{\text{Total Time}}{\text{Total Distance}}$$

$$= \frac{240 \text{ miles}}{5 \text{ hours}}$$

$$= 48 \text{ miles per hour}$$

Correct answer choice: (B).

TRAP 8: COUNTING NUMBERS

The tickets for a helmet raffle are consecutively numbered. If Louis sold the tickets numbered from 75 to 148 inclusive, how many helmet raffle tickets did he sell?

(Note: This is a Grid-in, so there are no answer choices.)

The Wrong Answer

Many people would subtract 75 from 148 to get 73 as their answer. But that is not correct, and so these people DO NOT deserve a shiny new helmet.

The Trap

Subtracting the first and last integers in a range will give you the difference between the two numbers. It won't give you the number of integers in that range.

Avoiding the Trap

To count the number of integers in a range, subtract the endpoints and then add 1. If this doesn't seem logical to you, test the rule by picking two small numbers that are close together, such as 1 and 4. Obviously, there are four integers from 1 to 4, inclusive. But if you had subtracted 1 from 4, you would have gotten 3. In the diagram below, you can see that 3 is actually the distance between the integers, if the integers were on a number line or a ruler.

> **Important**
>
> To count the number of integers in an inclusive range, subtract the endpoints and then add 1.

Finding the Right Answer

In the problem above, subtract 75 from 148. The result is 73. Add 1 to this difference to get the number of integers.

That gives you 74. This is the number you would grid in on your answer sheet.

The word "inclusive" tells you to include the first and last numbers given. So "the integers from 5 to 15 inclusive" include 5 and 15. Questions always make it clear whether you should include the outer numbers or not, since the correct answer hinges on this point.

TRAP 9: EXPRESSIONS THAT LOOK EQUAL—BUT AREN'T

<u>Column A</u>   <u>Column B</u>

$$p > q > 1$$

$p^2 - q^2$ $(p - q)^2$

The Wrong Answer

If you said the expressions were equal, you'd be wrong, wrong, wrong.

The Trap

At first glance the expressions look like they're equal—but they're not. This common SAT trap happens most often in QCs. Problems like this trap students who are too hasty, who answer on the basis of appearance, without considering the mathematical rules involved.

Avoiding the Trap

If two quantities seem obviously equal, double-check your answer, using your math knowledge and the QC techniques discussed in Step 6. This is a PRIME EXAMPLE of the general rule that whenever an answer to a question late in a section looks obviously correct, it probably isn't.

Finding the Right Answer

In this case you can use the make-one-column-look-more-like-the-other technique discussed in Step 6. Factor Column A and rewrite Column B:

<u>Column A</u>   <u>Column B</u>

$(p - q)(p + q)$ $(p - q)(p - q)$

Now use the do-the-same-thing-to-both-columns technique. Both columns contain $(p - q)$. You know than $p > q$, so $p - q$ is a positive number. Therefore, you can divide both columns by $p - q$:

<u>Column A</u>   <u>Column B</u>

$(p + q)$ $(p - q)$

Since q is positive, adding q in Column A will get you more than subtracting q in Column B. Column A is greater, so the answer is (A). This trap does not apply only to quadratics. Below are some other quantities that the hasty student might mistake as equal. Go through this list and make sure you can tell why these expressions are not equal except for special cases.

- $(x + y)^2$ does NOT equal $x^2 + y^2$
- $(2x)^2$ does NOT equal $2x^2$
- $x^{20} - x^{18}$ does NOT equal x^2
- $x^3 + x^3$ does NOT equal x^6
- $\sqrt{x} + \sqrt{x}$ does NOT equal $\sqrt{2x}$
- $\sqrt{x} - \sqrt{y}$ does NOT equal $\sqrt{x - y}$
- $\frac{1}{x} + \frac{1}{y}$ does NOT equal $\frac{1}{x + y}$

You could prove that any of these quantities need not be equal using the Picking Numbers technique from Step 6.

TRAP 10: NOT ALL NUMBERS ARE POSITIVE INTEGERS

If $n \neq 0$, then which of the following must be true?

I. $n^2 > n$

II. $2n > n$

III. $n + 1 > n$

(A) I only
(B) II only
(C) III only
(D) I and III only
(E) I, II, and III

The Wrong Answer

In the example above, if you considered only positive integers greater than 1 for the value of n, you would assume that all three statements are true. However, of course, that is not the case.

The Trap

Not all numbers are positive integers. Don't forget there are negative numbers and fractions as well. This is important because negative numbers and fractions between 0 and 1 behave very differently from positive integers.

Important

This trap appears most often in QC problems.

Avoiding the Trap

When picking numbers for variables, consider fractions and negative numbers.

Finding the Right Answer

Looking at statement I, you may assume that when you square a number, you end up with a larger number as a result. For example, $4^2 = 16$, or $10^2 = 100$. However, when you square a fraction between 0 and 1, the result is quite different: $\left(\dfrac{1}{2}\right)^2 = \dfrac{1}{4} \cdot \left(\dfrac{1}{10}\right)^2 = \dfrac{1}{100}$, so you get a smaller number.

In statement II, what happens when you multiply a number by 2? $7 \times 2 = 14$; $25 \times 2 = 50$. Multiplying any positive number by 2 doubles that number, so you get a larger result. However, if you multiply a negative number by 2, your result is smaller than the original number. For example, $-3 \times 2 = -6$.

Finally, look at statement III. What happens when you add 1 to any number? Adding 1 to any number gives you a larger number as a result. For example, $5 + 1 = 6$; $\dfrac{1}{2} + 1 = 1\dfrac{1}{2}$; and $-7 + 1 = -6$.

Therefore, only statement III must be true, so choice (C) is correct. If you didn't consider fractions or negative numbers, you would have fallen into the trap and answered the question incorrectly.

PRACTICE

Math Traps

Number of Questions—17

Try to identify the trap in each problem. There's no time limit.

Column A	Column B
A car traveled the first half of a 100-kilometer distance at an average speed of 120 kilometers per hour, and it traveled the remaining distance at an average speed of 80 kilometers per hour.	

1. The car's average speed, in kilometers per hour, for the 100 kilometers   100

| Column A | Column B |

The ratio of $\frac{1}{4}$ to $\frac{2}{5}$ is equal to the ratio of $\frac{2}{5}$ to x.

2. x $\frac{3}{5}$

....

3. $14 - 6$ $\sqrt{14^2 - 6^2}$

....

4. $\dfrac{a + b}{3}$ $a + b$

....

John buys 34 books at $6.00 each, and 17 at $12.00 each.

5. The average price $9.00
   John pays per book

....

On a certain highway Town X lies 50 miles away from Town Y, and Town Z lies 80 miles from Town X.

6. The number of minutes   30
   a car traveling at an average
   speed of 60 miles per hour
   takes to travel from Town Y
   to Town Z

....

a, b, and c are positive numbers; $b < c$

7. $(a + b)^2$ $a^2 + c^2$

....

8. The area of a circle   The sum of the areas
   with a diameter of 3   of three circles each
                            with a diameter of 1

....

Jane invests her savings in a fund that adds 10 percent interest to her savings at the end of every year.

9. The percent by which her   31 percent
   money has increased after
   three years

....

	Column A	Column B

$$x > 1$$

10. $7^{2x} - 7^x$ $7x$

....

11. Pump 1 can drain a 400-gallon water tank in 1.2 hours. Pump 2 can drain the same tank in 1.8 hours. How many minutes longer than pump 1 would it take pump 2 to drain a 100-gallon tank?

    (A) 0.15
    (B) 1.2
    (C) 6
    (D) 9
    (E) 18

....

12. Volumes 12 through 30 of a certain encyclopedia are located on the bottom shelf of a bookcase. If the volumes of the encyclopedia are numbered consecutively, how many volumes of the encyclopedia are on the bottom shelf?

    (A) 17
    (B) 18
    (C) 19
    (D) 29
    (E) 30

....

13. A reservoir is at full capacity at the beginning of summer. By the first day of fall, the level in the reservoir is 30 percent below full capacity. Then during the fall a period of heavy rains raises the level by 30 percent. After the rains, the reservoir is at what percent of its full capacity?

    (A) 100 percent
    (B)   95 percent
    (C)   91 percent
    (D)   85 percent
    (E)   60 percent

14. Two classes, one with 50 students, the other with 30, take the same exam. The combined average of both classes is 84.5. If the larger class averages 80, what is the average of the smaller class?

    (A) 87.2
    (B) 89.0
    (C) 92.0
    (D) 93.3
    (E) 94.5

15. In a pet shop, the ratio of puppies to kittens is 7:6 and the ratio of kittens to guinea pigs is 5:3. What is the ratio of puppies to guinea pigs?

    (A) 7:3
    (B) 6:5
    (C) 13:8
    (D) 21:11
    (E) 35:18

16. A typist typed the first n pages of a book, where $n > 0$, at an average rate of 12 pages per hour and typed the remaining n pages at an average rate of 20 pages per hour. What was the typist's average rate, in pages per hour, for the entire book?

    (A) $14\frac{2}{3}$
    (B) 15
    (C) 16
    (D) 17
    (E) 18

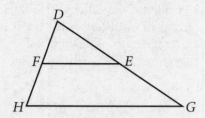

17. In triangle *DGH* above, *DE* = *EG*, *EF* ‖ *GH*, and the area of triangle *DGH* is 30. What is the area of triangle *DEF*?

    (A) 7.5

    (B) 15

    (C) 22.5

    (D) 60

    (E) It cannot be determined from the information given.

Did You Fall for the Traps?

How did you do on the practice questions? Did you spot the trap in each problem? Use the answers below to see what your weaknesses are. Each wrong answer represents one trap you need to work on. Go back and reread the section on that trap. Then look at the practice set's problem again. Do you see the trap now?

1. (B) Trap 7: Average rates
2. (A) Trap 3: Ratio:ratio:ratio
3. (B) Trap 9: Expressions that look equal—but aren't
4. (D) Trap 10: Not all numbers are positive integers
5. (B) Trap 2: Weighted averages
6. (D) Trap 4: Unspecified order
7. (D) Trap 9: Expressions that look equal—but aren't
8. (A) Trap 5: Length:area ratio
9. (A) Trap 1: Percent increase/decrease
10. (A) Trap 9: Expressions that look equal—but aren't
11. (D) Trap 6: Hidden instructions
12. (C) Trap 8: Counting numbers
13. (C) Trap 1: Percent increase/decrease
14. (C) Trap 2: Weighted averages
15. (E) Trap 3: Ratio:ratio:ratio
16. (B) Trap 7: Average rates
17. (A) Trap 5: Length:area ratios

STEP NINE

The Educated Guesser

The SAT's Regular Math and QC sections, like its Verbal sections, are scored to discourage random guessing. For every question that you get right you earn a whole point. For every question you get wrong, you lose a fraction of a point. So if you guess at random on a number of questions, the points you gain from correct guesses should be canceled out by the points you lose on incorrect guesses.

But you CAN and SHOULD make *educated* guesses. If you can eliminate one or more wrong answer choices, it raises your odds of guessing correctly, so the fractional points you lose no longer cancel out all the whole points you gain. This raises your score. We'll show you how.

STEP 9 PREVIEW

Guessing on SAT Math
Learn how to eliminate wrong answers quickly and effectively:

- Master the five strategies for making educated guesses
- See when to eliminate unreasonable or obvious choices
- Practice eyeballing geometry diagrams
- Learn to guess with confidence on Grid-ins

Practice
Use it before you lose it (practice guessing strategies on the test in this book)

THE FIVE STRATEGIES OF EDUCATED GUESSING

To make an educated guess, you need to eliminate answer choices that you know are wrong, and guess from what's left. The more answer choices you can eliminate, the better chance you have of guessing the correct answer from what's left over. You do this by:

1. Eliminating unreasonable answer choices
2. Eliminating the obvious on hard questions
3. Eyeballing lengths, angles, and areas
4. Eliminating choice (D) on some QCs
5. Finding the range on Grid-ins

1. Eliminate Unreasonable Answer Choices

Before you guess, think about the problem and decide which answers don't make sense.

> The ratio of celebrities to nobodies in a certain room is 13:11. If there are 429 celebrities in the room, how many nobodies are there?
>
> (A) 143
> (B) 363
> (C) 433
> (D) 507
> (E) 792

Solution:
- The ratio of celebrities to nobodies is 13:11, so there are more celebrities than nobodies.
- Since there are 429 celebrities, there must be fewer than 429 nobodies.
- So you can eliminate choices (C), (D), and (E).
- The answer must be either (A) or (B), so guess. The correct answer is (B).

2. Eliminate the Obvious on Hard Questions

On the hard questions late in a set, obvious answers are usually wrong. So eliminate them when you guess. This DOES NOT hold true for early, easy questions, when the obvious answer could be right. In the following difficult problem, found late in a question set, which obvious answer would you eliminate?

A number x is increased by 30 percent and then the result is decreased by 20 percent. What is the final result of these changes?

(A) x is increased by 10 percent

(B) x is increased by 6 percent

(C) x is increased by 4 percent

(D) x is decreased by 5 percent

(E) x is decreased by 10 percent

If you picked (A) as the obvious choice to eliminate, you'd be right. Most people would combine the decrease of 20 percent with the increase of 30 percent, getting a net increase of 10 percent. That's the easy, obvious answer, but not the correct answer. If you must guess, avoid (A). The correct answer is (C).

3. Eyeball Lengths, Angles, and Areas on Geometry Problems

Use diagrams that accompany geometry problems to help you eliminate wrong answer choices. First make sure that the diagram is drawn to scale. Diagrams are always drawn to scale UNLESS there's a note like this: "Note: Figure not drawn to scale." If it's not drawn to scale, DO NOT use this strategy. If it is, estimate quantities or eyeball the diagram, then eliminate answer choices that are way too large or too small.

Length

When a geometry question asks for a length, use the given lengths to estimate the unknown length. Measure off the given length by making a nick in your pencil with your thumbnail. Then hold the pencil against the unknown length on the diagram to see how the lengths compare. Try it.

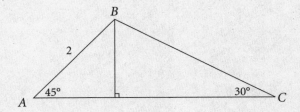

In the figure above, what is the length of *BC* ?

(A) $\sqrt{2}$

(B) 2

(C) $2\sqrt{2}$

(D) 4

(E) $4\sqrt{2}$

Solution:

- *AB* is 2, so measure off this length on your pencil.
- Compare *BC* with this length.
- *BC* appears almost twice as long as AB, so BC is about 4.
- Since $\sqrt{2}$ is about 1.4, and *BC* is clearly longer than *AB*, choices (A) and (B) are too small.
- Choice (E) is much greater than 4, so eliminate that.
- Now guess between (C) and (D). The correct answer is (C).

Angles

You can also eyeball angles. To eyeball an angle, compare the angle with a familiar angle, such as a straight angle (180°), a right angle (90°), or half a right angle (45°). The corner of a piece of paper is a right angle, so use that to see if an angle is greater or less than 90°.

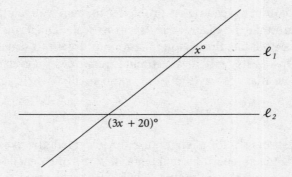

In the figure above, if $\ell_1 \| \ell_2$, what is the value of *x* ?

- (A) 130
- (B) 100
- (C) 80
- (D) 50
- (E) 40

Solution:

- You see that *x* is less than 90 degrees, so eliminate choices (A) and (B).
- Since *x* appears to be much less than 90 degrees, eliminate choice (C).
- Now pick between (D) and (E). In fact, the correct answer is (E).

Areas

Eyeballing an area is similar to eyeballing a length. You compare an unknown area in a diagram to an area that you do know.

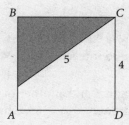

In square *ABCD* above, what is the area of the shaded region?

(A) 10
(B)   9
(C)   8
(D)   6
(E)   4

Solution:

- Since *ABCD* is a square, it has area 4^2, or 16.
- The shaded area is less than one half the size of the square, so its area must be less than 8.
- Eliminate answer choices (A), (B), and (C). The correct answer is (D).

4. Eliminate Choice (D) on Some QCs

If both columns of a QC contain only concrete numbers, choice (D)—"the relationship cannot be determined"—CANNOT be right. With no variables in either column, there must be one consistent relationship, even if you can't find it. If you don't know the answer, eliminate (D) as unreasonable and guess.

Column A	Column B
The largest prime factor of 1,224	18

Each column contains only numbers—so eliminate choice (D) and guess. If you were extra clever, you may also have seen that since 18 isn't prime, and Column A contains a prime number, the answer cannot be (C) either. The correct answer is (B).

5. Find the Range on Grid-ins—Then Guess

On Grid-ins, there are no answer choices to eliminate, but you won't lose points for guessing. So if you are stuck, try to estimate the general range of the answer, and guess. Here are examples of hard Grid-in questions.

1. If the three-digit number 11Q is a prime number, what digit is represented by Q ?
2. The sum of five consecutive odd integers is 425. What is the greatest of these integers?
3. A triangle has one side of length 3 and another of length 7. If the length of the third side is a solution to the equation $x^2 - 2x = 63$, what is the length of the third side?

Solutions:

1. Since Q is a digit, it must be one of the integers 0 through 9. Eliminate all the even digits, since they are divisible by 2. And eliminate 5, since any number ending with 5 is divisible by 5. You can also eliminate 1 and 7, because they are divisible by 3 (the digits add up to a multiple of 3). You are left with 3 and 9 to pick between. The correct answer is 3.

2. Since the integers are consecutive, they are all about the same size. So the number we are looking for is an odd number around 425 ÷ 5, which is 85. The right answer is 89.

3. Even if you can't solve that quadratic, you know that one side of a triangle has to be less than the sum and greater than the difference of the other two sides. So the third side is less than 7 + 3, or 10, and greater than 7 − 3, or 4. Since solutions to SAT quadratics are usually integers, pick an integer from 5 to 9. If you picked 9, you'd be right.

PRACTICE

Use these guessing techniques when you take the practice SAT in the back of this book. When you take the test, write the letter "G" on the test next to each question that you made an educated guess on. When you score your test, count how many guesses you got right, and how many guesses you got wrong.

Right Guesses: _____   _____

Wrong Guesses: _____ × 0.25

Multiply how many you got wrong by 0.25 and subtract that number from the number of right guesses. This is how many raw points you gained from educated guessing.

Section Four

FINAL PREPARATIONS

CHAPTER TEN

Beating Test Stress

You can beat anxiety the same way you can beat the SAT—by knowing what to expect beforehand and developing strategies to deal with it. You have completed nine steps specifically designed to help you with every nook and cranny of the SAT. This step helps you with every nook and cranny of YOUR BRAIN.

STEP 10 PREVIEW

Beating Test Stress

Learn how to relieve stress and mentally prepare for the SAT:

- Identifying sources of stress
- Identifying strengths and weaknesses
- Visualizing success
- Exercising away anxiety
- Eating right
- Doing isometric exercise
- Having a stress-free test day

Practice

Use if before you lose it (Practice these strategies regularly)

SOURCES OF STRESS

In the space provided, write down your sources of test-related stress. The idea is to pin down any sources of anxiety so you can deal with them one by one. We have provided common examples—feel free to use them and any others you think of.

- I always freeze up on tests.
- I'm nervous about the math (or the grammar, the reading comp, etc.).
- I need a good/great score to get into my first choice college.
- My older brother/sister/best friend/girlfriend/boyfriend did really well. I must match their scores or do better.
- My parents, who are paying for school, will be quite disappointed if I don't do well.
- I'm afraid of losing my focus and concentration.
- I'm afraid I'm not spending enough time preparing.
- I study like crazy but nothing seems to stick in my mind.
- I always run out of time and get panicky.
- The simple act of thinking, for me, is like wading through refrigerated honey.

My Sources of Stress

_____

_____

_____

_____

_____

_____

Read through the list. Cross out things or add things. Now rewrite the list in order of most disturbing to least disturbing.

My Sources of Stress, In Order

_____

_____

_____

_____

_____

_____

Chances are, the top of the list is a fairly accurate description of exactly how you react to test anxiety, both physically and mentally. The later items usually describe your fears (disappointing mom and dad, looking bad, etc.). Taking care of the major items from the top of the list should go a long way towards relieving overall test anxiety. That's what we'll do next.

STRENGTHS AND WEAKNESSES

Take 60 seconds to list the areas of the SAT or any other test that you are good at. They can be general ("math") or specific ("addition of even numbers"). Put down as many as you can think of, and if possible, time yourself. Write for the entire time; don't stop writing until you've reached the one-minute stopping point. Go.

Strong Test Subjects

_____

_____

_____

_____

_____

_____

Now take one minute to list areas of the test you're not so good at, just plain bad at, have failed at, or keep failing at. Again, keep it to one minute, and continue writing until you reach the cutoff. Go.

Weak Test Subjects

_____

_____

_____

_____

_____

Taking stock of your assets and liabilities lets you know the areas you don't have to worry about, and the ones that will demand extra attention and effort. It helps a lot to find out where you need to spend extra effort. We mostly fear what we don't know and are probably afraid to face. You can't help feeling more confident when you know you're actively strengthening your chances of earning a higher overall score.

Now, go back to the "good" list, and expand on it for two minutes. Take the general items on that first list and make them more specific; take the specific items and expand them into more general conclusions. Naturally, if anything new comes to mind, jot it down. Focus all of your attention and effort on your strengths. Don't underestimate yourself or your abilities. Give yourself full credit. At the same time, don't list strengths you don't really have; you'll only be fooling yourself.

Expanding from general to specific might go as follows. If you listed "world history" as a broad topic you feel strong in, you would then narrow your focus to include areas of this subject about which you are particularly knowledgeable. Your areas of strength might include modern European history, the events leading up to World War I, the Bolshevik revolution, etc.

Whatever you know well goes on your "good" list. OK. Check your starting time. Go.

Strong Test Subjects: An Expanded List

_____

_____

_____

_____

_____

_____

After you've stopped, check your time. Did you find yourself going beyond the two minutes allotted? Did you write down more things than you thought you knew? Is it possible you know more than you've given yourself credit for? Could that mean you've found a number of areas in which you feel strong?

You just took an active step towards helping yourself. Enjoy your increased feelings of confidence, and use them when you take the SAT.

VISUALIZE YOURSELF SUCCEEDING

This next little group of activities is a follow-up to the "good at" and "bad at" lists. Sit in a comfortable chair in a quiet setting. If you wear glasses, take them off. Close your eyes and breathe in a deep, satisfying breath of air. Really fill your lungs until your rib cage is fully expanded and you can't take in any more. Then, exhale the air completely. Imagine you're blowing out a candle with your last little puff of air. Do this two or three more times, filling your lungs to their maximum and emptying them totally. Keep your eyes closed, comfortably but not tightly. Let your body sink deeper into the chair as you become even more comfortable.

With your eyes shut you can notice something very interesting. You're no longer dealing with the worrisome stuff going on in the world outside of you. Now you can concentrate on what happens inside you. The more you recognize your own physical reactions to stress and anxiety, the more you can do about them. You may not realize it, but you've begun to regain a sense of being in control.

Let images begin to form on TV screens on the back of your eyelids. Allow the images to come easily and naturally; don't force them. Visualize a relaxing situation. It might be in a special place you've visited before or one you've read about. It can be a fictional location that you create in your imagination, but a real-life memory of a place or situation you know is usually better. Make it as detailed as possible and notice as much as you can.

Stay focused on the images as you sink farther into your chair. Breathe easily and naturally. You might have the sensations of any stress or tension draining from your muscles and flowing downward, out your feet and away from you.

Take a moment to check how you're feeling. Notice how comfortable you've become. Imagine how much easier it would be if you could take the test feeling this relaxed and in this state of ease. You've coupled the images of your special place with sensations of comfort and relaxation. You've also found a way to become relaxed simply by visualizing your own safe, special place.

Close your eyes and start remembering a real-life situation in which you did well on a test. If you can't come up with one, remember a situation in which you did something that you were really proud of—a genuine accomplishment. Make the memory as detailed as possible. Think about the sights, the sounds, the smells, even the tastes associated with this remembered experience. Remember how confident you felt as you accomplished your goal. Now start thinking about the SAT. Keep your thoughts and feelings in line with that prior, successful experience. Don't make comparisons between them. Just imagine taking the upcoming test with the same feelings of confidence and relaxed control.

This exercise is a great way to bring the test down to earth. You should practice this exercise often, especially when you feel burned out on SAT preparation. The more you practice it, the more effective the exercise will be for you.

EXERCISE AWAY YOUR ANXIETY

Whether it's jogging, walking, biking, mild aerobics, pushups, or a pickup basketball game, physical exercise is a very effective way to stimulate both your mind and body and to improve your ability to think and concentrate. Lots of students get out of the habit of regular exercise when they're prepping for the exam. Also, sedentary people get less oxygen to the blood, and hence to the brain, than active people. You can watch TV fine with a little less oxygen; you just can't think as well.

Any big test is a bit like a race. Finishing the race strong is just as important as being quick early on. If you can't sustain your energy level in the last sections of the exam, you could blow it. Along with a good diet and adequate sleep, exercise is an important part of keeping yourself in fighting shape and thinking clearly for the long haul.

There's another thing that happens when students don't make exercise an integral part of their test preparation. Like any organism in nature, you operate best if all your "energy systems" are in balance. Studying uses a lot of energy, but it's all mental. When you take a study break, do something active. Take a five- to ten-minute exercise break for every 50 or 60 minutes that you study. The physical exertion helps keep your mind and body in sync. This way, when you finish studying for the night and go to bed, you won't lie there unable to sleep because your head is wasted while your body wants to run a marathon.

One warning about exercise: It's not a good idea to exercise vigorously right before you go to bed. This could easily cause sleep-onset problems. For the same reason, it's also not a good idea to study right up to bedtime. Make time for a "buffer period" before you go to bed. Take 30 to 60 minutes to take a long hot shower, to meditate, or to watch any show on the Food channel except the one starring that Emeril fellow.

SAY NO TO DOING DRUGS, YES TO EATING RIGHT

Using drugs to prepare for or take a big test is not a good idea. Don't take uppers to stay alert. Amphetamines make it hard to retain information. Mild stimulants, such as coffee, cola, or over-the-counter caffeine pills can help you study longer since they keep you awake, but they can also lead to agitation, restlessness, and insomnia. Some people can drink a pot of coffee sludge and sleep like a baby. Others have one cup and start to vibrate. It all depends on your tolerance for caffeine. Remember, a little anxiety is a good thing. The adrenaline that gets pumped into your bloodstream helps you stay alert and think more clearly.

You can also rely on your brain's own endorphins. Endorphins have no side effects and they're free. It just takes some exercise to release them. Running, bicycling, swimming, aerobics, and power walking all cause endorphins to occupy the happy spots in your brain's neural synapses. In addition, exercise develops your mental stamina and increases the oxygen transfer to your brain.

To reduce stress you should eat fruits and vegetables (raw is best, or just lightly steamed or nuked), low-fat protein such as fish, skinless poultry, beans, and legumes (like lentils), or whole grains such as brown rice, whole wheat bread and pastas (no bleached flour). Don't eat sweet, high-fat snacks. Simple carbohydrates like sugar make stress worse, and fatty foods lower your immunity. Don't eat salty foods either. They can deplete potassium, which you need for nerve functions. You can go back to your Combos-and-Dew diet after the SAT.

ISOMETRIC EXERCISE

Here's another natural route to relaxation and invigoration. You can do it whenever you get stressed out, including during the test. Close your eyes. Starting with your eyes and—without holding your breath—gradually tighten every muscle in your body (but not to the point of pain) in the following sequence:

- Close your eyes tightly.
- Squeeze your nose and mouth together so that your whole face is scrunched up. (If it makes you self-conscious to do this in the test room, skip the face-scrunching part.)
- Pull your chin into your chest, and pull your shoulders together.
- Tighten your arms to your body, then clench your fists.
- Pull in your stomach.
- Squeeze your thighs and buttocks together, and tighten your calves.
- Stretch your feet, then curl your toes (watch out for cramping in this part).

At this point, every muscle should be tightened. Now, relax your body, one part at a time, in reverse order, starting with your toes. Let the tension drop out of each muscle. The entire process might take five minutes from start to finish (maybe a couple of minutes during the test). This clenching and unclenching exercise will feel silly at first, especially the buttocks part, but if you get good at it, you will feel very relaxed.

HAVE A STRESS-FREE TEST DAY

As the test gets closer, you may find your anxiety is on the rise. To calm any pretest jitters you may have, let's go over a few strategies for the couple of days before and after the test.

Three Days Before the Test

Take a full-length practice test under timed conditions. Try to use all of the techniques and tips you've learned in this book. Approach the test strategically, actively, and confidently.

WARNING: DO NOT take a full practice SAT if you have fewer than 48 hours left before the test. Doing so will probably exhaust you, hurting your score on the actual test. You wouldn't run a marathon the day before the real thing.

Two Days Before the Test

Go over the results of your practice test. Don't worry too much about your score or whether you got a specific question right or wrong. The practice test doesn't count, remember. But do examine your performance on specific questions with an eye to how you might get through each one faster and with greater accuracy on the actual test to come.

The Night Before the Test: Don't Study

Get together an "SAT survival kit" containing the following items:

- A calculator with fresh batteries
- A watch
- A few No. 2 pencils (pencils with slightly dull points fill the ovals better)
- Erasers
- Photo ID card
- Your admission ticket from ETS
- A snack—there are two breaks, and you'll probably get hungry

Know exactly where you're going, exactly how you're getting there, and exactly how long it takes to get there. It's probably a good idea to visit your test center sometime before the day of the test, so that you know what to expect—what the rooms are like, how the desks are set up, and so on.

Relax the night before the test. Read a good book, take a long hot shower, watch TV (remember, no Emeril). Get a good night's sleep. Go to bed early and leave yourself extra time in the morning.

The Morning of the Test

First, wake up. After that:

- Eat breakfast. Make it something substantial, but not anything too heavy or greasy.
- Don't drink a lot of coffee if you're not used to it; bathroom breaks cut into your time, and too much caffeine is a bad idea.
- Dress in layers so that you can adjust to the temperature of the test room.
- Read something. Warm up your brain with a newspaper or a magazine. You shouldn't let the SAT be the first thing you read that day.
- Be sure to get there early. Allow yourself extra time for traffic, mass transit delays, and/or detours around people who might only add to your stress level if you stopped to talk to them.

During the Test

Don't be shaken. If you find your confidence slipping, remind yourself how well you've prepared. You know the structure of the test; you know the instructions; you've had practice with—and have learned strategies for—every question type.

Even if something goes really wrong, don't panic. If the test booklet is defective—two pages are stuck together or the ink has run—try to stay calm. Raise your hand and tell the proctor you need a new book. If you accidentally misgrid your answer page or put the answers in the wrong section, again, don't panic. Raise your hand and tell the proctor. He or she might be able to arrange for you to regrid your test after it's over, when it won't cost you any time.

Don't think about which section is experimental. Remember, you never know for sure which section won't count. Besides, you can't work on any other section during that section's designated time slot.

After the Test

You might walk out of the SAT thinking that you blew it. This is a normal reaction. Lots of people—even the highest scorers—feel that way. You tend to remember the questions that stumped you, not the ones that you knew. You can always call ETS within 24 hours to find out about canceling your score, but there's usually no good reason to do so. Remember, colleges typically accept your highest SAT score. And no test experience is going to be perfect. If you were distracted by a particularly attractive test proctor this time around, next time you may be even more distracted by construction noise, or a cold, or a particularly unattractive proctor. (Most likely the latter.)

If you don't plan to take the test again, you can destroy this book and resume normal everyday activities.

PRACTICE

If you have a week or more left before the test, practice each of the following at least once:
- Visualization
- Isometric exercise
- Physical exercise
- Eating right

Section Five

TAKE THE PRACTICE TEST

Practice Test

HOW TO TAKE THIS PRACTICE TEST

Before taking this practice test, find a quiet room where you can work uninterrupted for two and a half hours. Make sure you have a comfortable desk, your calculator, and several No. 2 pencils.

Use the answer sheet provided to record your answers. (You can cut it out or photocopy it.)

Once you start this practice test, don't stop until you've finished. Remember—you can review any questions within a section, but you may not go back or forward a section.

You'll find an answer key, score conversion charts, and explanations following the test.

Good luck.

ANSWER SHEET

Remove (or photocopy) this answer sheet and use it to complete the practice test. (See answer key following the test when finished.)

Start with number 1 for each section. If a section has fewer questions than answer spaces, leave the extra spaces blank.

SECTION 1

1 (A) (B) (C) (D) (E)   11 (A) (B) (C) (D) (E)   21 (A) (B) (C) (D) (E)   31 (A) (B) (C) (D) (E)

2 (A) (B) (C) (D) (E)   12 (A) (B) (C) (D) (E)   22 (A) (B) (C) (D) (E)   32 (A) (B) (C) (D) (E)

3 (A) (B) (C) (D) (E)   13 (A) (B) (C) (D) (E)   23 (A) (B) (C) (D) (E)   33 (A) (B) (C) (D) (E)

4 (A) (B) (C) (D) (E)   14 (A) (B) (C) (D) (E)   24 (A) (B) (C) (D) (E)   34 (A) (B) (C) (D) (E)

5 (A) (B) (C) (D) (E)   15 (A) (B) (C) (D) (E)   25 (A) (B) (C) (D) (E)   35 (A) (B) (C) (D) (E)

6 (A) (B) (C) (D) (E)   16 (A) (B) (C) (D) (E)   26 (A) (B) (C) (D) (E)   36 (A) (B) (C) (D) (E)

7 (A) (B) (C) (D) (E)   17 (A) (B) (C) (D) (E)   27 (A) (B) (C) (D) (E)   37 (A) (B) (C) (D) (E)

8 (A) (B) (C) (D) (E)   18 (A) (B) (C) (D) (E)   28 (A) (B) (C) (D) (E)   38 (A) (B) (C) (D) (E)

9 (A) (B) (C) (D) (E)   19 (A) (B) (C) (D) (E)   29 (A) (B) (C) (D) (E)   39 (A) (B) (C) (D) (E)

10 (A) (B) (C) (D) (E)   20 (A) (B) (C) (D) (E)   30 (A) (B) (C) (D) (E)   40 (A) (B) (C) (D) (E)

[ ] # right in section 1   [ ] # wrong in section 1

SECTION 2

1 (A) (B) (C) (D) (E)   11 (A) (B) (C) (D) (E)   21 (A) (B) (C) (D) (E)   31 (A) (B) (C) (D) (E)

2 (A) (B) (C) (D) (E)   12 (A) (B) (C) (D) (E)   22 (A) (B) (C) (D) (E)   32 (A) (B) (C) (D) (E)

3 (A) (B) (C) (D) (E)   13 (A) (B) (C) (D) (E)   23 (A) (B) (C) (D) (E)   33 (A) (B) (C) (D) (E)

4 (A) (B) (C) (D) (E)   14 (A) (B) (C) (D) (E)   24 (A) (B) (C) (D) (E)   34 (A) (B) (C) (D) (E)

5 (A) (B) (C) (D) (E)   15 (A) (B) (C) (D) (E)   25 (A) (B) (C) (D) (E)   35 (A) (B) (C) (D) (E)

6 (A) (B) (C) (D) (E)   16 (A) (B) (C) (D) (E)   26 (A) (B) (C) (D) (E)   36 (A) (B) (C) (D) (E)

7 (A) (B) (C) (D) (E)   17 (A) (B) (C) (D) (E)   27 (A) (B) (C) (D) (E)   37 (A) (B) (C) (D) (E)

8 (A) (B) (C) (D) (E)   18 (A) (B) (C) (D) (E)   28 (A) (B) (C) (D) (E)   38 (A) (B) (C) (D) (E)

9 (A) (B) (C) (D) (E)   19 (A) (B) (C) (D) (E)   29 (A) (B) (C) (D) (E)   39 (A) (B) (C) (D) (E)

10 (A) (B) (C) (D) (E)   20 (A) (B) (C) (D) (E)   30 (A) (B) (C) (D) (E)   40 (A) (B) (C) (D) (E)

[ ] # right in section 2   [ ] # wrong in section 2

Remove (or photocopy) this answer sheet and use it to complete the practice test.

Start with number 1 for each section. If a section has fewer questions than answer spaces, leave the extra spaces blank.

SECTION 3

1 Ⓐ Ⓑ Ⓒ Ⓓ Ⓔ 11 Ⓐ Ⓑ Ⓒ Ⓓ Ⓔ 21 Ⓐ Ⓑ Ⓒ Ⓓ Ⓔ 31 Ⓐ Ⓑ Ⓒ Ⓓ Ⓔ
2 Ⓐ Ⓑ Ⓒ Ⓓ Ⓔ 12 Ⓐ Ⓑ Ⓒ Ⓓ Ⓔ 22 Ⓐ Ⓑ Ⓒ Ⓓ Ⓔ 32 Ⓐ Ⓑ Ⓒ Ⓓ Ⓔ
3 Ⓐ Ⓑ Ⓒ Ⓓ Ⓔ 13 Ⓐ Ⓑ Ⓒ Ⓓ Ⓔ 23 Ⓐ Ⓑ Ⓒ Ⓓ Ⓔ 33 Ⓐ Ⓑ Ⓒ Ⓓ Ⓔ
4 Ⓐ Ⓑ Ⓒ Ⓓ Ⓔ 14 Ⓐ Ⓑ Ⓒ Ⓓ Ⓔ 24 Ⓐ Ⓑ Ⓒ Ⓓ Ⓔ 34 Ⓐ Ⓑ Ⓒ Ⓓ Ⓔ
5 Ⓐ Ⓑ Ⓒ Ⓓ Ⓔ 15 Ⓐ Ⓑ Ⓒ Ⓓ Ⓔ 25 Ⓐ Ⓑ Ⓒ Ⓓ Ⓔ 35 Ⓐ Ⓑ Ⓒ Ⓓ Ⓔ
6 Ⓐ Ⓑ Ⓒ Ⓓ Ⓔ 16 Ⓐ Ⓑ Ⓒ Ⓓ Ⓔ 26 Ⓐ Ⓑ Ⓒ Ⓓ Ⓔ 36 Ⓐ Ⓑ Ⓒ Ⓓ Ⓔ
7 Ⓐ Ⓑ Ⓒ Ⓓ Ⓔ 17 Ⓐ Ⓑ Ⓒ Ⓓ Ⓔ 27 Ⓐ Ⓑ Ⓒ Ⓓ Ⓔ 37 Ⓐ Ⓑ Ⓒ Ⓓ Ⓔ
8 Ⓐ Ⓑ Ⓒ Ⓓ Ⓔ 18 Ⓐ Ⓑ Ⓒ Ⓓ Ⓔ 28 Ⓐ Ⓑ Ⓒ Ⓓ Ⓔ 38 Ⓐ Ⓑ Ⓒ Ⓓ Ⓔ
9 Ⓐ Ⓑ Ⓒ Ⓓ Ⓔ 19 Ⓐ Ⓑ Ⓒ Ⓓ Ⓔ 29 Ⓐ Ⓑ Ⓒ Ⓓ Ⓔ 39 Ⓐ Ⓑ Ⓒ Ⓓ Ⓔ
10 Ⓐ Ⓑ Ⓒ Ⓓ Ⓔ 20 Ⓐ Ⓑ Ⓒ Ⓓ Ⓔ 30 Ⓐ Ⓑ Ⓒ Ⓓ Ⓔ 40 Ⓐ Ⓑ Ⓒ Ⓓ Ⓔ

☐ # right in section 3   ☐ # wrong in section 3

If section 3 of your test book contains math questions that are not multiple choice, continue to item 16 below. Otherwise, continue to item 16 above.

16   17   18   19   20   21   22   23   24   25

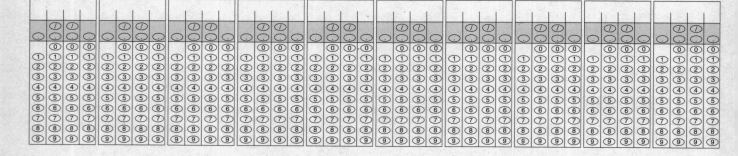

SECTION 4

1 Ⓐ Ⓑ Ⓒ Ⓓ Ⓔ 11 Ⓐ Ⓑ Ⓒ Ⓓ Ⓔ 21 Ⓐ Ⓑ Ⓒ Ⓓ Ⓔ 31 Ⓐ Ⓑ Ⓒ Ⓓ Ⓔ
2 Ⓐ Ⓑ Ⓒ Ⓓ Ⓔ 12 Ⓐ Ⓑ Ⓒ Ⓓ Ⓔ 22 Ⓐ Ⓑ Ⓒ Ⓓ Ⓔ 32 Ⓐ Ⓑ Ⓒ Ⓓ Ⓔ
3 Ⓐ Ⓑ Ⓒ Ⓓ Ⓔ 13 Ⓐ Ⓑ Ⓒ Ⓓ Ⓔ 23 Ⓐ Ⓑ Ⓒ Ⓓ Ⓔ 33 Ⓐ Ⓑ Ⓒ Ⓓ Ⓔ
4 Ⓐ Ⓑ Ⓒ Ⓓ Ⓔ 14 Ⓐ Ⓑ Ⓒ Ⓓ Ⓔ 24 Ⓐ Ⓑ Ⓒ Ⓓ Ⓔ 34 Ⓐ Ⓑ Ⓒ Ⓓ Ⓔ
5 Ⓐ Ⓑ Ⓒ Ⓓ Ⓔ 15 Ⓐ Ⓑ Ⓒ Ⓓ Ⓔ 25 Ⓐ Ⓑ Ⓒ Ⓓ Ⓔ 35 Ⓐ Ⓑ Ⓒ Ⓓ Ⓔ
6 Ⓐ Ⓑ Ⓒ Ⓓ Ⓔ 16 Ⓐ Ⓑ Ⓒ Ⓓ Ⓔ 26 Ⓐ Ⓑ Ⓒ Ⓓ Ⓔ 36 Ⓐ Ⓑ Ⓒ Ⓓ Ⓔ
7 Ⓐ Ⓑ Ⓒ Ⓓ Ⓔ 17 Ⓐ Ⓑ Ⓒ Ⓓ Ⓔ 27 Ⓐ Ⓑ Ⓒ Ⓓ Ⓔ 37 Ⓐ Ⓑ Ⓒ Ⓓ Ⓔ
8 Ⓐ Ⓑ Ⓒ Ⓓ Ⓔ 18 Ⓐ Ⓑ Ⓒ Ⓓ Ⓔ 28 Ⓐ Ⓑ Ⓒ Ⓓ Ⓔ 38 Ⓐ Ⓑ Ⓒ Ⓓ Ⓔ
9 Ⓐ Ⓑ Ⓒ Ⓓ Ⓔ 19 Ⓐ Ⓑ Ⓒ Ⓓ Ⓔ 29 Ⓐ Ⓑ Ⓒ Ⓓ Ⓔ 39 Ⓐ Ⓑ Ⓒ Ⓓ Ⓔ
10 Ⓐ Ⓑ Ⓒ Ⓓ Ⓔ 20 Ⓐ Ⓑ Ⓒ Ⓓ Ⓔ 30 Ⓐ Ⓑ Ⓒ Ⓓ Ⓔ 40 Ⓐ Ⓑ Ⓒ Ⓓ Ⓔ

☐ # right in section 4   ☐ # wrong in section 4

Remove (or photocopy) this answer sheet and use it to complete the practice test.

Start with number 1 for each section. If a section has fewer questions than answer spaces, leave the extra spaces blank.

SECTION 5

1 (A) (B) (C) (D) (E)   11 (A) (B) (C) (D) (E)   21 (A) (B) (C) (D) (E)   31 (A) (B) (C) (D) (E)
2 (A) (B) (C) (D) (E)   12 (A) (B) (C) (D) (E)   22 (A) (B) (C) (D) (E)   32 (A) (B) (C) (D) (E)
3 (A) (B) (C) (D) (E)   13 (A) (B) (C) (D) (E)   23 (A) (B) (C) (D) (E)   33 (A) (B) (C) (D) (E)
4 (A) (B) (C) (D) (E)   14 (A) (B) (C) (D) (E)   24 (A) (B) (C) (D) (E)   34 (A) (B) (C) (D) (E)
5 (A) (B) (C) (D) (E)   15 (A) (B) (C) (D) (E)   25 (A) (B) (C) (D) (E)   35 (A) (B) (C) (D) (E)
6 (A) (B) (C) (D) (E)   16 (A) (B) (C) (D) (E)   26 (A) (B) (C) (D) (E)   36 (A) (B) (C) (D) (E)
7 (A) (B) (C) (D) (E)   17 (A) (B) (C) (D) (E)   27 (A) (B) (C) (D) (E)   37 (A) (B) (C) (D) (E)
8 (A) (B) (C) (D) (E)   18 (A) (B) (C) (D) (E)   28 (A) (B) (C) (D) (E)   38 (A) (B) (C) (D) (E)
9 (A) (B) (C) (D) (E)   19 (A) (B) (C) (D) (E)   29 (A) (B) (C) (D) (E)   39 (A) (B) (C) (D) (E)
10 (A) (B) (C) (D) (E)   20 (A) (B) (C) (D) (E)   30 (A) (B) (C) (D) (E)   40 (A) (B) (C) (D) (E)

[ ] # right in section 5   [ ] # wrong in section 5

SECTION 6

1 (A) (B) (C) (D) (E)   11 (A) (B) (C) (D) (E)   21 (A) (B) (C) (D) (E)   31 (A) (B) (C) (D) (E)
2 (A) (B) (C) (D) (E)   12 (A) (B) (C) (D) (E)   22 (A) (B) (C) (D) (E)   32 (A) (B) (C) (D) (E)
3 (A) (B) (C) (D) (E)   13 (A) (B) (C) (D) (E)   23 (A) (B) (C) (D) (E)   33 (A) (B) (C) (D) (E)
4 (A) (B) (C) (D) (E)   14 (A) (B) (C) (D) (E)   24 (A) (B) (C) (D) (E)   34 (A) (B) (C) (D) (E)
5 (A) (B) (C) (D) (E)   15 (A) (B) (C) (D) (E)   25 (A) (B) (C) (D) (E)   35 (A) (B) (C) (D) (E)
6 (A) (B) (C) (D) (E)   16 (A) (B) (C) (D) (E)   26 (A) (B) (C) (D) (E)   36 (A) (B) (C) (D) (E)
7 (A) (B) (C) (D) (E)   17 (A) (B) (C) (D) (E)   27 (A) (B) (C) (D) (E)   37 (A) (B) (C) (D) (E)
8 (A) (B) (C) (D) (E)   18 (A) (B) (C) (D) (E)   28 (A) (B) (C) (D) (E)   38 (A) (B) (C) (D) (E)
9 (A) (B) (C) (D) (E)   19 (A) (B) (C) (D) (E)   29 (A) (B) (C) (D) (E)   39 (A) (B) (C) (D) (E)
10 (A) (B) (C) (D) (E)   20 (A) (B) (C) (D) (E)   30 (A) (B) (C) (D) (E)   40 (A) (B) (C) (D) (E)

[ ] # right in section 6   [ ] # wrong in section 6

Time—30 Minutes
25 Questions

Solve each of the following problems, decide which is the best answer choice, and darken the corresponding oval on the answer sheet. Use available space in the test booklet for scratchwork.*

Notes:

(1) Calculator use is permitted.

(2) All numbers used are real numbers.

(3) Figures are provided for some problems. All figures are drawn to scale and lie in a plane UNLESS otherwise indicated.

Reference Information

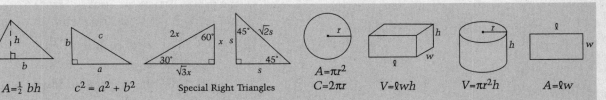

$A = \frac{1}{2} bh$ $c^2 = a^2 + b^2$ Special Right Triangles $A = \pi r^2$ $C = 2\pi r$ $V = \ell w h$ $V = \pi r^2 h$ $A = \ell w$

The sum of the degree measures of the angles of a triangle is 180.
The number of degrees of arc in a circle is 360.
A straight angle has a degree measure of 180.

1. $\left(\frac{1}{5} + \frac{1}{3} \right) \div \frac{1}{2} =$

    (A) $\frac{1}{8}$

    (B) $\frac{1}{4}$

    (C) $\frac{4}{15}$

    (D) $\frac{1}{2}$

    (E) $\frac{16}{15}$

2. What is the value of $x^2 - 2x$ when $x = -2$?

    (A) −8
    (B) −4
    (C) 0
    (D) 4
    (E) 8

3. Vito read 96 pages in 2 hours and 40 minutes. What was Vito's average rate of pages per hour?

    (A) 24
    (B) 30
    (C) 36
    (D) 42
    (E) 48

4. For how many integer values of x will $\frac{7}{x}$ be greater than $\frac{1}{4}$ and less than $\frac{1}{3}$?

    (A) 6
    (B) 7
    (C) 12
    (D) 28
    (E) Infinitely many

*The directions on the actual SAT will vary slightly.

5. What is the average (arithmetic mean) of $2x + 5$, $5x - 6$, and $-4x + 2$?

   (A) $x + \dfrac{1}{3}$

   (B) $x + 1$

   (C) $3x + \dfrac{1}{3}$

   (D) $3x + 3$

   (E) $3x + 3\dfrac{1}{3}$

6. In a group of 25 students, 16 are female. What percent of the group is female?

   (A) 16%

   (B) 40%

   (C) 60%

   (D) 64%

   (E) 75%

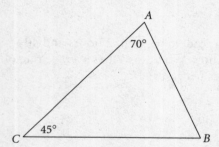

7. In the triangle above, what is the degree measure of angle B ?

   (A) 45

   (B) 60

   (C) 65

   (D) 75

   (E) 80

8. For all $x \neq 0$, $\dfrac{x^2 + x^2 + x^2}{x^2} =$

   (A) 3

   (B) $3x$

   (C) x^2

   (D) x^3

   (E) x^4

9. The equation $x^2 = 5x - 4$ has how many distinct real solutions?

   (A) 0

   (B) 1

   (C) 2

   (D) 3

   (E) Infinitely many

10. Which of the following sets of numbers has the property that the sum of any two numbers in the set is also a number in the set?

    I.   The set of even integers

    II. The set of odd integers

    III. The set of prime numbers

    (A) I only

    (B) III only

    (C) I and II only

    (D) I and III only

    (E) I, II, and III

11. Martin's average (arithmetic mean) score after 4 tests is 89. What score on the 5th test would bring Martin's average up to exactly 90?

    (A) 90

    (B) 91

    (C) 92

    (D) 93

    (E) 94

12. The price s of a sweater is reduced by 25% for a sale. After the sale, the reduced price is increased by 20%. Which of the following represents the final price of the sweater?

    (A) $1.05s$

    (B) $.95s$

    (C) $.90s$

    (D) $.85s$

    (E) $.80s$

GO ON TO THE NEXT PAGE

13. How many distinct prime factors does the number 36 have?

    (A) 2
    (B) 3
    (C) 4
    (D) 5
    (E) 6

14. If the area of a triangle is 36 and its base is 9, what is the length of the altitude to that base?

    (A) 2
    (B) 4
    (C) 6
    (D) 8
    (E) 12

15. Let $a\clubsuit$ be defined for all positive integers a by the equation $a\clubsuit = \dfrac{a}{4} - \dfrac{a}{6}$. If $x\clubsuit = 3$, what is the value of x?

    (A) 18
    (B) 28
    (C) 36
    (D) 40
    (E) 54

16. Joan has q quarters, d dimes, n nickels, and no other coins in her pocket. Which of the following represents the total number of coins in Joan's pocket?

    (A) $q + d + n$
    (B) $5q + 2d + n$
    (C) $.25q + .10d + .05n$
    (D) $(25 + 10 + 5)(q + d + n)$
    (E) $25q + 10d + 5n$

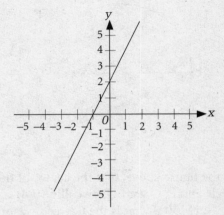

17. Which of the following is an equation for the graph above?

    (A) $y = -2x + 1$
    (B) $y = x + 1$
    (C) $y = x + 2$
    (D) $y = 2x + 1$
    (E) $y = 2x + 2$

18. If an integer is divisible by 6 and by 9, then the integer must be divisible by which of the following?

    I. 12
    II. 18
    III. 36

    (A) I only
    (B) II only
    (C) I and II only
    (D) II and III only
    (E) I, II, and III

GO ON TO THE NEXT PAGE

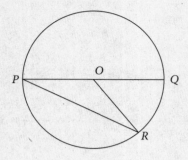

19. In the figure above, O is the center of the circle and P, O, and Q are collinear. If ∠ROQ measures 50°, what is the degree measure of ∠RPQ ?

    (A) 20
    (B) 25
    (C) 30
    (D) 35
    (E) 40

20. A wooden cube with volume 64 is sliced in half horizontally. The two halves are then glued together to form a rectangular solid which is not a cube. What is the surface area of this new solid?

    (A) 128
    (B) 112
    (C) 96
    (D) 56
    (E) 48

21. A drawer contains 6 blue socks, 12 black socks, and 14 white socks. If one sock is chosen at random, what is the probability that it will be black?

    (A) $\frac{1}{4}$

    (B) $\frac{1}{3}$

    (C) $\frac{3}{8}$

    (D) $\frac{1}{2}$

    (E) $\frac{5}{8}$

22. Danielle drives from her home to the store at an average speed of 40 miles per hour. She returns home along the same route at an average speed of 60 miles per hour. What is her average speed, in miles per hour, for her entire trip?

    (A) 45
    (B) 48
    (C) 50
    (D) 52
    (E) 55

23. What is the area of a right triangle if the length of one leg is a and the length of the hypotenuse is c ?

    (A) $\frac{ac}{2}$

    (B) $\frac{ac - a^2}{2}$

    (C) $\frac{ac + c^2}{2}$

    (D) $\frac{a\sqrt{c^2 - a^2}}{2}$

    (E) $\sqrt{a^2 + c^2}$

GO ON TO THE NEXT PAGE

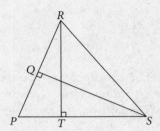

24. In ΔPRS above, RT is the altitude to side PS and QS is the altitude to side PR. If RT = 7, PR = 8, and QS = 9, what is the length of PS?

    (A) $5\frac{1}{7}$

    (B) $6\frac{2}{9}$

    (C) $7\frac{7}{8}$

    (D) $10\frac{2}{7}$

    (E) $13\frac{4}{9}$

25. There are 3 routes from Bay City to Riverville. There are 4 routes from Riverville to Straitstown. There are 3 routes from Straitstown to Frog Pond. If a driver must pass through Riverville and Straitstown exactly once, how many possible ways are there to go from Bay City to Frog Pond?

    (A) 6
    (B) 10
    (C) 12
    (D) 24
    (E) 36

If you finish before time is called, you may check your work on this section only. Do not turn to any other section in the test.

STOP

Time—30 Minutes
35 Questions

For each of the following questions, choose the best answer and darken the corresponding oval on the answer sheet.*

Select the lettered word or set of words that best completes the sentence.

Example:

Today's small, portable computers contrast markedly with the earliest electronic computers, which were ----.
(A) effective
(B) invented
(C) useful
(D) destructive
(E) enormous

1. Finding an old movie poster that is still ---- usually proves difficult because such posters were meant to be used and then ----.

    (A) recognizable . . returned
    (B) relevant . . discarded
    (C) intact . . destroyed
    (D) immaculate . . restored
    (E) displayed . . maintained

2. The Kemp's Ridley turtle, long considered one of the most ---- creatures of the sea, finally appears to be making some headway in its battle against extinction.

    (A) elusive
    (B) prevalent
    (C) combative
    (D) voracious
    (E) imperiled

3. Before the invention of the tape recorder, quotes from an interview were rarely ---- ; journalists usually paraphrased the words of their subject.

    (A) verbatim
    (B) misconstrued
    (C) pragmatic
    (D) extensive
    (E) plagiarized

4. Batchelor's reputation as ---- novelist encouraged hopes that his political thriller would offer more ---- characterizations than are usually found in the genre.

    (A) a serious . . subtle
    (B) a maturing . . sweeping
    (C) a prolific . . accurate
    (D) an accomplished . . fictional
    (E) a reclusive . . authentic

5. The governor commented on the disadvantages of political ----, saying that after his extended tenure in office the voters had grown used to blaming him for everything.

    (A) acumen
    (B) savvy
    (C) longevity
    (D) decorum
    (E) celebrity

* The directions on the actual SAT will vary slightly.

GO ON TO THE NEXT PAGE

6. Although normally ---- , the researcher was ---- by the news that her work had not been accepted for publication.

   (A) introverted . . devastated
   (B) imperious . . incensed
   (C) melodramatic . . electrified
   (D) buoyant . . subdued
   (E) reserved . . bewildered

7. The agency's failure to ---- policies that it has acknowledged are flawed is a potent demonstration of its ---- approach to correcting its problems.

   (A) support . . ambiguous
   (B) institute . . earnest
   (C) rescind . . lackadaisical
   (D) amend . . devoted
   (E) chasten . . meticulous

8. The inconsistency of the educational policies adopted by various schools across the state has been greatly ---- by the rapid turnover of school superintendents.

   (A) counteracted
   (B) stabilized
   (C) criticized
   (D) exacerbated
   (E) understated

9. The journalist's claim of ---- is belied by her record of contributing to the campaign funds of only one party's candidates.

   (A) innocence
   (B) corruption
   (C) impartiality
   (D) affluence
   (E) loyalty

10. The repeated breakdown of negotiations only ---- the view that the two sides were not truly committed to the goal of ---- a military confrontation.

    (A) established . . escalating
    (B) undermined . . avoiding
    (C) distorted . . financing
    (D) strengthened . . initiating
    (E) reinforced . . averting

11. These are times of national budgetary ---- now that a long era of sustained growth has been succeeded by a period of painful ---- .

    (A) turmoil . . acquisition
    (B) stringency . . decline
    (C) expansion . . stagnation
    (D) indecision . . renewal
    (E) prudence . . development

12. To the ---- of those who in bygone years tiptoed their way past poinsettia displays for fear of causing leaves to fall, breeders have developed more ---- versions of the flower.

    (A) consternation . . amorphous
    (B) dismay . . fragrant
    (C) surprise . . alluring
    (D) disappointment . . diversified
    (E) relief . . durable

13. Aristotle espoused a ---- biological model in which all extant species are unchanging and eternal and no new species ever come into existence.

    (A) paradoxical
    (B) morbid
    (C) static
    (D) holistic
    (E) homogeneous

GO ON TO THE NEXT PAGE

Choose the lettered pair of words that is related in the same way as the pair in capital letters.

Example:
FLAKE : SNOW ::
(A) storm : hail
(B) drop : rain
(C) field : wheat
(D) stack : hay
(E) cloud : fog

14. LABORATORY : EXPERIMENT ::

(A) garage : repair
(B) beach : sunbathe
(C) statement : formulate
(D) graveyard : inter
(E) invention : create

15. EXONERATE : BLAME ::

(A) disinfect : contamination
(B) divert : stream
(C) indict : guilt
(D) obey : order
(E) absolve : ministry

16. LOOK : SCRUTINIZE ::

(A) amble : scurry
(B) deliberate : propose
(C) read : peruse
(D) importune : plead
(E) flicker : shine

17. GULLIBLE : DUPE ::

(A) fallible : err
(B) foolhardy : confuse
(C) dejected : dishearten
(D) headstrong : coax
(E) submissive : control

18. CONVERSATION : INTERLOCUTOR ::

(A) speech : orator
(B) hearing : prosecutor
(C) game : player
(D) novel : publisher
(E) diagnosis : doctor

19. ENTOMOLOGY : INSECTS ::

(A) agriculture : cows
(B) pedagogy : education
(C) astronomy : telescope
(D) literature : character
(E) evolution : man

20. SKIRMISH : BATTLE ::

(A) misdemeanor : crime
(B) desertion : divorce
(C) fledgling : expert
(D) faculty : instructor
(E) estimate : measurement

21. FORENSIC : LITIGATION ::

(A) maritime : sea
(B) euphoria : feeling
(C) conjugal : bliss
(D) exemplary : example
(E) illusory : magic

22. FEIGN : IMPRESSION ::

(A) adapt : evolution
(B) perjure : testimony
(C) play : role
(D) impersonate : celebrity
(E) slander : reputation

23. POLEMIC : IMPARTIAL ::

(A) antidote : curative
(B) discipline : harsh
(C) heretic : persecuted
(D) defendant : guilty
(E) extrovert : retiring

GO ON TO THE NEXT PAGE

Answer the questions below based on the information in the accompanying passage.

Questions 24–35 are based on the following passage.

The following passage is an excerpt from a book about wolves, written by a self-taught naturalist who studied them in the wild.

My precautions against disturbing the wolves were superfluous. It had required me a week to get their measure, but they must
Line
have taken mine at our first meeting; and
(05) while there was nothing disdainful in their evident assessment of me, they managed to ignore my presence, and indeed my very existence, with a thoroughness which was somehow disconcerting.

(10) Quite by accident I had pitched my tent within ten yards of one of the major paths used by the wolves when they were going to, or coming from, their hunting paths to the westward; and only a few hours after I had
(15) taken up my residence one of the wolves came back from a trip and discovered me and my tent.

He was at the end of a hard night's work and was clearly tired and anxious to go home
(20) to bed. He came over a small rise fifty yards from me with his head down, his eyes half-closed, and a preoccupied air about him. Far from being the preternaturally alert and suspicious beast of fiction, this wolf was so
(25) self-engrossed that he came straight on to within fifteen yards of me, and might have gone right past the tent without seeing it at all, had I not banged an elbow against the teakettle, making a resounding clank. The
(30) wolf's head came up and his eyes opened wide, but he did not stop or falter in his pace. One brief, sidelong glance was all he vouchsafed to me as he continued on his way.

(35) By the time this happened, I had learned a great deal about my wolfish neighbors, and one of the facts which had emerged was that they were not nomadic roamers, as is almost universally believed, but were settled beasts
(40) and the possessors of a large permanent estate with very definite boundaries. The territory owned by my wolf family comprised more than a hundred square miles, bounded on one side by a river but
(45) otherwise not delimited by geographical features. Nevertheless there were boundaries, clearly indicated in wolfish fashion.

Once a week, more or less, the clan made the rounds of the family lands and freshened
(50) up the boundary markers—a sort of lupine* beating of the bounds. This careful attention to property rights was perhaps made necessary by the presence of two other wolf families whose lands abutted on ours,
(55) although I never discovered any evidence of bickering or disagreements between the owners of the various adjoining estates. I suspect, therefore, that it was more of a ritual activity.

(60) In any event, once I had become aware of this strong feeling of property among the wolves, I decided to use this knowledge to make them at least recognize my existence. One evening, after they had gone off for their
(65) regular nightly hunt, I staked out a property claim of my own, embracing perhaps three acres, with the tent at the middle, and including a hundred yard long section of the wolves' path. This took most of the night and
(70) required frequent returns to the tent to consume copious quantities of tea; but before dawn brought the hunters home the task was done and I retired, somewhat exhausted, to observe the results.

(75) I had not long to wait. At 0814 hours, according to my wolf log, the leading male of the clan appeared over the ridge behind me, padding homeward with his usual air of preoccupation. As usual, he did not deign to

(80) look at the tent; but when he reached the point where my property line intersected the trail, he stopped as abruptly as if he had run into an invisible wall. His attitude of fatigue vanished and was replaced by one of

(85) bewilderment. Cautiously he extended his nose and sniffed at one of my marked bushes. After a minute of complete indecision he backed away a few yards and sat down. And then, finally, he looked

(90) directly at the tent and me. It was a long, considering sort of look.

Having achieved my object—that of forcing at least one of the wolves to take cognizance of my existence—I now began to

(95) wonder if, in my ignorance, I had transgressed some unknown wolf law of major importance and would have to pay for my temerity. I found myself regretting the absence of a weapon as the look I was getting

(100) became longer, more thoughtful, and still more intent. In an effort to break the impasse I loudly cleared my throat and turned my back on the wolf to indicate as clearly as possible that I found his continued

(105) scrutiny impolite, if not actually offensive.

He appeared to take the hint. Briskly, and with an air of decision, he turned his attention away from me and began a systematic tour of the area, sniffing each

(110) boundary marker once or twice, and carefully placing his mark on the outside of each clump of grass or stone. In fifteen minutes he rejoined the path at the point where it left my property and trotted off

(115) towards his home, leaving me with a good deal to occupy my thoughts.

lupine: relating to wolves

24. According to the author, why were his precautions against disturbing the wolves "superfluous" (line 2)?

   (A) It was several weeks before he encountered his first wolf.
   (B) Other wild animals posed a greater threat to his safety.
   (C) The wolves noticed him, but were not interested in harming him.
   (D) He was not bothered by the wolves until he started interfering with them.
   (E) The wolves were unable to detect him due to their poor eyesight.

25. The author mentions the wolves' "assessment" of him (line 6) in order to

   (A) account for their strange behavior towards him
   (B) convey his initial fear of being attacked
   (C) emphasize his ignorance on first encountering them
   (D) indicate the need for precautions against disturbing them
   (E) suggest his courage in an unfamiliar situation

26. In the third paragraph, the author is primarily surprised to find that the wolf

   (A) is traveling alone
   (B) lacks the energy to respond
   (C) is hunting at night
   (D) is not more on its guard
   (E) does not attack him

GO ON TO THE NEXT PAGE

27. In line 19, the word *anxious* most nearly means

    (A) distressed
    (B) afraid
    (C) eager
    (D) uneasy
    (E) worried

28. In line 39, the word *settled* most nearly means

    (A) decided
    (B) resolute
    (C) stable
    (D) inflexible
    (E) confident

29. Lines 35–41 provide

    (A) a contradiction of popular myth
    (B) an explanation of a paradox
    (C) a rebuttal of established facts
    (D) an exception to a general rule
    (E) a summary of conclusions

30. The author suggests that boundary marking was a "ritual activity" (lines 59–60) because

    (A) the wolves marked their boundaries at regular intervals
    (B) no disputes over territory ever seemed to occur
    (C) the boundaries were marked by geographical features
    (D) the boundaries were marked at the same time each week
    (E) the whole family of wolves participated in the activity

31. Which of the following discoveries would most weaken the author's thesis concerning the wolves' "strong feeling of property" (line 62)?

    (A) Disputes over boundaries are a frequent occurrence.
    (B) Wolf territories are typically around one hundred square miles in area.
    (C) Wolf families often wander from place to place to find food.
    (D) Territorial conflicts between wolves and human beings are rare.
    (E) Wolves are generally alert when encountering other animals.

32. The author most likely mentions an "invisible wall" (line 83) in order to emphasize

    (A) his delight in attracting the wolf's attention
    (B) the wolf's annoyance at encountering a challenge
    (C) the high speed at which the wolf was traveling
    (D) the sudden manner in which the wolf stopped
    (E) the wolf's exhaustion after a night of hunting

33. The wolf's first reaction on encountering the author's property marking is one of

    (A) combativeness
    (B) confusion
    (C) anxiety
    (D) wariness
    (E) dread

34. In line 99, *temerity* means

    (A) discourtesy
    (B) rashness
    (C) courage
    (D) anger
    (E) discretion

35. The author turns his back on the wolf
    (lines 104–106) primarily in order to

    (A) demonstrate his power over the wolf
    (B) bring about some change in the
        situation
    (C) compel the wolf to recognize his
        existence
    (D) look for a suitable weapon
    (E) avoid the wolf's hypnotic gaze

If you finish before time is called, you may check your work on this
section only. Do not turn to any other section in the test.

STOP

Time—30 Minutes
25 Questions

Solve each of the following problems, decide which is the best answer choice, and darken the corresponding oval on the answer sheet. Use available space in the test booklet for scratchwork.*

Notes:

(1) Calculator use is permitted.

(2) All numbers used are real numbers.

(3) Figures are provided for some problems. All figures are drawn to scale and lie in a plane UNLESS otherwise indicated.

Reference Information

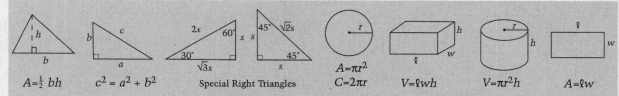

$A=\frac{1}{2}bh$ $\quad$ $c^2=a^2+b^2$ $\quad$ Special Right Triangles $\quad$ $A=\pi r^2$ $\quad$ $V=\ell wh$ $\quad$ $V=\pi r^2 h$ $\quad$ $A=\ell w$

$\quad$ $\quad$ $\quad$ $\quad$ $C=2\pi r$

The sum of the degree measures of the angles of a triangle is 180.
The number of degrees of arc in a circle is 360.
A straight angle has a degree measure of 180.

Directions for Quantitative Comparison Questions

Compare the boxed quantity in Column A with the boxed quantity in Column B. Select answer choice

  A   if Column A is greater;
  B   if Column B is greater;
  C   if the columns are equal; or
  D   if more information is needed to determine the relationship.

An E response will be treated as an omission.

Notes:

1. Some questions include information about one or both quantities. That information is centered and unboxed.
2. A symbol that appears in both Column A and Column B stands for the same thing in both columns.
3. All numbers used are real numbers.

EXAMPLES

	Column A	Column B	Answers
E1	3×4	$3 + 4$	Ⓐ Ⓑ Ⓒ Ⓓ
E2	x	160	Ⓐ Ⓑ Ⓒ Ⓓ
E3	$x + 1$	$y - 1$	Ⓐ Ⓑ Ⓒ Ⓓ

E2: *(figure showing angles $x°$ and $20°$ on a line)*

E3: *x and y are positive*

	Column A	Column B
1.	$\dfrac{1}{8} + \dfrac{1}{10}$	$\dfrac{1}{9} + \dfrac{1}{11}$

$$x < 1$$

	Column A	Column B
2.	x	$\dfrac{1}{x}$

| 3. | 52% of 34 | 17 |

| 4. | $3(x-2)$ | $3x - 4$ |

The product of two integers is 10.

| 5. | 6 | The sum of the integers |

x and y are nonzero integers.

| 6. | $\dfrac{x^2}{y^2}$ | $x^2 y^2$ |

Column A   Column B

A B C D

$$AC = BD$$

| 7. | AB | BC |

$$x > 0$$
$$y > 1$$

| 8. | x | xy |

$$x > 1$$

| 9. | x^5 | $(x^3)^2$ |

$$y \neq 0$$

| 10. | $\dfrac{1}{y}$ | $\dfrac{y^2}{y}$ |

GO ON TO THE NEXT PAGE

	Column A	**Column B**
11.	The number of square units in the area of a square with side 6	The number of units in the perimeter of a square with side 9

Wildredo's math test scores are the following:
88, 82, 94, 93, 85, 90, 93, 98

	Column A	**Column B**
12.	Wilfredo's mode test score	Wilfredo's median test score

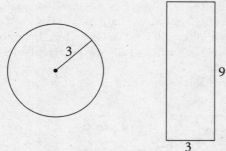

	Column A	**Column B**
13.	The area of the circle	The area of the rectangle

Column A　　　　**Column B**

$$y > 0$$

	Column A	**Column B**
14.	$1 - \dfrac{y}{1 + y}$	$1 - \dfrac{1}{1 + y}$

ABCD is a rectangle with perimeter 32.
$AB > BC$

	Column A	**Column B**
15.	The area of *ABCD*	The area of a square with perimeter 32

GO ON TO THE NEXT PAGE

Directions for Student-Produced Response Questions

For each of the questions below (16–25), solve the problem and indicate your answer by darkening the ovals in the special grid. For example:

Answer: 1.25 or $\frac{5}{4}$ or 5/4

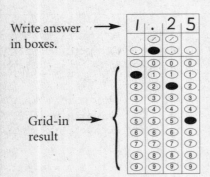

Write answer in boxes. →

Grid-in → result

Either position is correct.

Fraction → line

Decimal → point

You may start your answers in any column, space permitting. Columns not needed should be left blank.

- It is recommended, though not required, that you write your answer in the boxes at the top of the columns. However, you will receive credit only for darkening the ovals correctly.

- Grid only one answer to a question, even though some problems have more than one correct answer.

- Darken no more than one oval in a column.

- No answers are negative.

- Mixed numbers cannot be gridded. For example: the number $1\frac{1}{4}$ must be gridded as 1.25 or 5/4.

(If [1 1 / 4] is gridded, it will be interpreted as $\frac{11}{4}$, not $1\frac{1}{4}$.)

- Decimal Accuracy: Decimal answers must be entered as accurately as possible. For example, if you obtain an answer such as 0.1666..., you should record the result as .166 or .167. **Less accurate values such as .16 or .17 are not acceptable.**

Acceptable ways to grid $\frac{1}{6}$ = .1666...

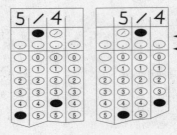

16. In the figure above, if line p is parellel to line q, what is the value of y ?

17. What is $\frac{1}{4}$ percent of 16?

GO ON TO THE NEXT PAGE

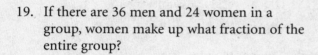

18. Each of the fractions above is in its simplest reduced form and *a* is an integer greater than 1 and less than 50. Grid in one possible value of *a* .

19. If there are 36 men and 24 women in a group, women make up what fraction of the entire group?

20. What is the value of $\dfrac{3s + 5}{4}$ when $s = 9$?

21. If the positive integer *x* leaves a remainder of 2 when divided by 6, what will the remainder be when $x + 8$ is divided by 6 ?

22. Pat deposited 15% of last week's take-home pay into a savings account. If she deposited $37.50, what was last week's take-home pay?

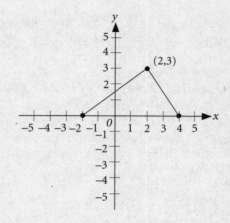

23. What is the area of the triangle in the figure above?

24. A square is divided in half to form two congruent rectangles, each with perimeter 24. What is the area of the original square?

25. The formula for converting a Fahrenheit temperature reading to a Celsius temperature reading is $C = \dfrac{5}{9}(F - 32)$, where *C* is the reading in degrees Celsius and *F* is the reading in degrees Fahrenheit. What is the Fahrenheit equivalent to a reading of 95° Celsius?

If you finish before time is called, you may check your work on this section only. Do not turn to any other section in the test.

STOP

Time—30 Minutes
31 Questions

For each of the following questions, choose the best answer and darken the corresponding oval on the answer sheet.

Select the lettered word or set of words that best completes the sentence.

Example:

Today's small, portable computers contrast markedly with the earliest electronic computers, which were ----.
(A) effective
(B) invented
(C) useful
(D) destructive
(E) enormous

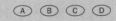

1. The band has courted controversy before in order to get attention, and the ---- lyrics on their new album demonstrate that they found the strategy ---- .

   (A) sedate . . plausible
   (B) vacuous . . rewarding
   (C) belligerent . . counterproductive
   (D) scandalous . . effective
   (E) provocative . . comparable

2. James Joyce regarded ---- as central to the creative process, which is evident in the numerous scribbled edits that cover even his supposedly final drafts.

   (A) contrivance
   (B) revision
   (C) inspiration
   (D) obsession
   (E) disavowal

3. Fans who believe that the players' motivations are not ---- would be ---- to learn that they now charge for their signatures.

   (A) self-serving . . vindicated
   (B) venal . . chagrined
   (C) altruistic . . unsurprised
   (D) atypical . . disillusioned
   (E) tainted . . gratified

4. Though the film ostensibly deals with the theme of ---- , the director seems to have been more interested in its absence—in isolation and the longing for connection.

   (A) reliance
   (B) fraternity
   (C) socialism
   (D) privation
   (E) levity

5. Everything the candidate said publicly was ---- ; he manipulated the media in order to present the image he wanted.

   (A) incendiary
   (B) calculated
   (C) facetious
   (D) scrupulous
   (E) impromptu

GO ON TO THE NEXT PAGE

KAPLAN

6. Most young artists struggle, producing works that have but ---- of future greatness, but Walt Whitman's transformation into a genius was ---- .

   (A) glimmers . . effortless
   (B) shadows . . noteworthy
   (C) features . . protracted
   (D) critiques . . immediate
   (E) aspirations . . unforeseeable

7. Although Sub-Saharan Africa encompasses a large number of ---- cultures, its music is often considered an essentially ---- mass.

   (A) disparate . . homogeneous
   (B) impoverished . . inimitable
   (C) warring . . concrete
   (D) interwoven . . distinctive
   (E) proud . . languid

8. His face was ---- , his features pulled downward by the weight of heavy thoughts.

   (A) morose
   (B) onerous
   (C) contorted
   (D) ossified
   (E) inscrutable

9. The unfortunate demise of the protagonist in the final scene of the movie ---- all possibility of a sequel.

   (A) entertained
   (B) dissembled
   (C) raised
   (D) exacerbated
   (E) precluded

GO ON TO THE NEXT PAGE

Choose the lettered pair of words that is related in the same way as the pair in capital letters.

Example:
FLAKE : SNOW ::
(A)   storm : hail
(B)   drop : rain
(C)   field : wheat
(D)   stack : hay
(E)   cloud : fog

10.   SCAR : INJURY ::

(A)   monument : marble
(B)   fever : illness
(C)   dent : collision
(D)   exhibition : painting
(E)   blood : fistfight

11.   YAWN : BOREDOM ::

(A)   react : surprise
(B)   pout : displeasure
(C)   gasp : breath
(D)   repose : sleep
(E)   cheer : depression

12.   ACTOR : AUDITION ::

(A)   singer : debut
(B)   judge : verdict
(C)   architect : plan
(D)   instrumentalist : solo
(E)   gymnast : tryout

13.   ALIENATE : ESTRANGEMENT ::

(A)   discommode : inconvenience
(B)   sequester : monasticism
(C)   palliate : boredom
(D)   orchestrate : symphony
(E)   aspire : enthusiasm

14.   PUNGENT : SNIFFED ::

(A)   itinerant : traveled
(B)   prickly : touched
(C)   venomous : bitten
(D)   acrid : burned
(E)   belligerent : feuded

15.   DISCONCERT : CONFUSION ::

(A)   fear : superstition
(B)   daunt : discouragement
(C)   spend : extravagance
(D)   remonstrate : reward
(E)   stabilize : imbalance

GO ON TO THE NEXT PAGE

Answer the questions below based on the information in the accompanying passages.

Questions 16–22 are based on the following passage.

The following passage is an excerpt from a book about wolves, written by a self-taught naturalist who studied them in the wild.

Revisionist historians maintain that it was within the power of the United States, in the years during and immediately after the
Line Second World War, to prevent the Cold War
(05) with the Soviet Union. Revisionists suggest that the prospect of impending conflict with the Soviets could have been avoided in several ways. The U.S. could have officially recognized the new Soviet sphere of influence
(10) in Eastern Europe instead of continuing to call for self-determination in those countries. A much-needed reconstruction loan could have helped the Soviets recover from the war. The Americans could have sought to assuage
(15) Soviet fears by giving up the U.S. monopoly of the atomic bomb and turning the weapons over to an international agency (with the stipulation that future nuclear powers do the same).
(20) This criticism of the post-war American course of action fails to take into account the political realities in America at the time, and unfairly condemns the American policy-makers who did consider each of these
(25) alternatives and found them to be unworkable. Recognition of a Soviet Eastern Europe was out of the question. Roosevelt had promised self-determination to the Eastern European countries, and the
(30) American people, having come to expect this, were furious when Stalin began to shape his spheres of influence in the region. The President was in particular acutely conscious of the millions of Polish-Americans who
(35) would be voting in the upcoming election.
Negotiations had indeed been conducted by the administration with the Soviets about

a reconstruction loan, but the Congress refused to approve it unless the Soviets made
(40) enormous concessions tantamount to restructuring their system and withdrawing from Eastern Europe. This, of course, made Soviet rejection of the loan a foregone conclusion. As for giving up the bomb—the
(45) elected officials in Washington would have been in deep trouble with their constituents had that plan been carried out. Polls showed that 82 percent of the American people understood that other nations would
(50) develop bombs eventually, but that 85 percent thought that the U.S. should retain exclusive possession of the weapon. Policy-makers have to abide by certain constraints in deciding what is acceptable and what is
(55) not. They, and not historians, are in the best position to perceive those constraints and make the decisions.
Revisionist historians tend to eschew this type of political explanation of America's
(60) supposed failure to reach a peaceful settlement with the Soviets in favor of an economic reading of events. They point to the fact that in the early post-war years American businessmen and government
(65) officials cooperated to expand American foreign trade vigorously and to exploit investment opportunities in many foreign countries. In order to sustain the lucrative expansion, revisionists assert, American
(70) policy-makers were obliged to maintain an "Open Door" foreign policy, the object of which was to keep all potential trade opportunities open. Since the Soviets could jeopardize such opportunities in Eastern
(75) Europe and elsewhere, they had to be opposed. Hence, the Cold War. But if American policy-makers were simply pawns in an economic game of expansionist capitalism, as the revisionists seem to think,

GO ON TO THE NEXT PAGE

(80) why do the revisionists hold them responsible for not attempting to reach an accord with the Soviets? The policy-makers, swept up by a tidal wave of capitalism, clearly had little control and little choice in (85) the matter.

Even if American officials had been free and willing to make conciliatory gestures toward the Soviets, the Cold War would not have been prevented. Overtures of (90) friendship would not have been reciprocated (as far as we can judge; information on the inner workings of the Kremlin during that time is scanty). Soviet expert George F. Kennan concluded that Russian hostility (95) could not be dampened by any effort on the part of the United States. The political and ideological differences were too great, and the Soviets had too long a history of distrust of foreigners—exacerbated at the time by (100) Stalin's rampant paranoia, which infected his government—to embark on a process of establishing trust and peace with the United States, though it was in their interest to do so.

16. The primary purpose of the passage is to

(A) explode a popular myth
(B) criticize historical figures
(C) refute an argument
(D) analyze an era
(E) reconcile opposing views

17. In line 9, the word *recognized* most nearly means

(A) identified
(B) noticed
(C) acknowledged
(D) distinguished
(E) remembered

18. The author refers to the Polish-Americans (lines 33–35) chiefly to illustrate that

(A) the president had an excellent rapport with ethnic minorities
(B) immigrants had fled from Eastern European countries to escape communism
(C) giving up the idea of East European self-determination would have been costly in political terms
(D) the Poles could enjoy self-determination only in America
(E) the political landscape of the United States had changed considerably since the President was elected

19. A fundamental assumption underlying the author's argument in the second and third paragraphs is that

(A) the Soviets were largely to blame for the failure of conciliatory U.S. initiatives
(B) the American public was very well-informed about the incipient Cold War situation
(C) none of the proposed alternatives would have had its intended effect
(D) the American public was overwhelmingly opposed to seeking peace with the Soviets
(E) the government could not have been expected to ignore public opinion

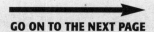

GO ON TO THE NEXT PAGE

20. The phrase *certain constraints* in line 53 most likely refers to

    (A) the etiquette of international diplomacy
    (B) the danger of leaked information about atomic bombs
    (C) the views of the electorate
    (D) the potential reaction of the enemy
    (E) the difficulty of carrying out a policy initiative

21. Which statement best summarizes the revisionist argument concerning the origin of the Cold War (lines 58–76)?

    (A) The United States started the Cold War in order to have a military cover for illegal trading activities.
    (B) The Soviets were oblivious to the negative impact they had on the American economy.
    (C) The economic advantage of recognizing Soviet Europe outweighed the disadvantage of an angry public.
    (D) America could trade and invest with foreign countries only if it agreed to oppose the Soviet Union.
    (E) American economic interests abroad would have been threatened by any Soviet expansion.

22. The question at the end of the fourth paragraph (lines 76–82) serves to

    (A) point out an inconsistency in a position
    (B) outline an area that requires further research
    (C) contrast two different historical interpretations
    (D) sum up a cynical view of post-war economic activity
    (E) restate the central issue of the passage

GO ON TO THE NEXT PAGE

Questions 23–31 are based on the following passage.

James Weldon Johnson was a poet, diplomat, composer and historian of black culture who wrote around the turn of the century. In this narrative passage Johnson recalls his first experience of hearing rag-time jazz.

When I had somewhat collected my senses, I realized that in a large back room into which the main room opened, there was
Line a young fellow singing a song, accompanied
(05) on the piano by a short, thickset black man. After each verse he did some dance steps, which brought forth great applause and a shower of small coins at his feet. After the singer had responded to a rousing encore,
(10) the stout man at the piano began to run his fingers up and down the keyboard. This he did in a manner which indicated that he was a master of a good deal of technique. Then he began to play; and such playing! I stopped
(15) talking to listen. It was music of a kind I had never heard before. It was music that demanded physical response, patting of the feet, drumming of the fingers, or nodding of the head in time with the beat. The dissonant
(20) harmonies, the audacious resolutions, often consisting of an abrupt jump from one key to another, the intricate rhythms in which the accents fell in the most unexpected places, but in which the beat was never lost,
(25) produced a most curious effect . . .

This was rag-time music, then a novelty in New York, and just growing to be a rage, which has not yet subsided. It was originated in the questionable resorts about Memphis
(30) and St. Louis by Negro piano-players who knew no more of the theory of music than they did of the theory of the universe, but were guided by natural musical instinct and talent. It made its way to Chicago, where it
(35) was popular some time before it reached New York. These players often improvised simple and, at times, vulgar words to fit the melodies. This was the beginning of the rag-time song . . .

(40) American musicians, instead of investigating rag-time, attempt to ignore it, or dismiss it with a contemptuous word. But that has always been the course of scholasticism in every branch of art.
(45) Whatever new thing the *people* like is pooh-poohed; whatever is *popular* is spoken of as not worth the while. The fact is, nothing great or enduring, especially in music, has ever sprung full-fledged and unprecedented
(50) from the brain of any master; the best that he gives to the world he gathers from the hearts of the people, and runs it through the alembic* of his genius. In spite of the bans which musicians and music teachers have
(55) placed upon it, the people still demand and enjoy rag-time. One thing cannot be denied; it is music which possesses at least one strong element of greatness: it appeals universally; not only the American, but the
(60) English, the French, and even the German people find delight in it. In fact, there is not a corner of the civilized world in which it is not known, and this proves its originality; for if it were an imitation, the people of
(65) Europe, anyhow, would not have found it a novelty . . .

I became so interested in both the music and the player that I left the table where I was sitting, and made my way through the hall
(70) into the back room, where I could see as well as hear. I talked to the piano player between the musical numbers and found out that he was just a natural musician, never having taken a lesson in his life. Not only could he
(75) play almost anything he heard, but he could accompany singers in songs he had never heard. He had, by ear alone, composed some pieces, several of which he played over for me; each of them was properly proportioned
(80) and balanced. I began to wonder what this man with such a lavish natural endowment would have done had he been trained. Perhaps he wouldn't have done anything at

GO ON TO THE NEXT PAGE

(85) all; he might have become, at best, a mediocre imitator of the great masters in what they have already done to a finish, or one of the modern innovators who strive after originality by seeing how cleverly they *(90)* can dodge about through the rules of harmony and at the same time avoid melody. It is certain that he would not have been so delightful as he was in rag-time.

alembic: scientific apparatus used in the process of distillation

23. In relating his initial impression of rag-time music to the reader, the narrator makes use of

   (A) comparison with the improvisations of classical music
   (B) reference to the audience's appreciative applause
   (C) description of the music's compelling rhythmic effect
   (D) evocation of poignant visual images
   (E) allusion to several popular contemporary tunes

24. In the first paragraph, the narrator portrays rag-time as a type of music that

   (A) would be a challenge to play for even the most proficient musician
   (B) satisfied the narrator's expectations regarding the genre
   (C) violated all of the accepted rules governing musical composition
   (D) made up for a lack of melody with a seductive rhythm
   (E) contained several surprises for the discerning listener

25. In line 29, *questionable* most nearly means

   (A) disreputable
   (B) ambiguous
   (C) doubtful
   (D) approachable
   (E) unconfirmed

26. The narrator's perspective during the second and third paragraphs is that of

   (A) an impartial historian of events in the recent past
   (B) a mesmerized spectator of a musical spectacle
   (C) a knowledgeable critic of the contemporary musical scene
   (D) a commentator reflecting on a unique experience
   (E) an adult reminiscing fondly about his youth

27. In line 32, the reference to "the theory of the universe" serves to

   (A) emphasize that rag-time at its inception was an unconventional musical form
   (B) show that the originators of rag-time were wholly engrossed in their own music
   (C) imply that the attainment of musical proficiency should take priority over academic pursuits
   (D) suggest that those who founded rag-time could not have imagined the extent of its future influence
   (E) demonstrate that level of education is not commensurate with artistic success

GO ON TO THE NEXT PAGE

28. The discussion in the third paragraph of the refusal of American musicians to investigate rag-time suggests that they

    (A) have little or no interest in pleasing people with their music
    (B) need to be made aware of the popularity of rag-time in Europe
    (C) are misguided in their conservative and condescending attitude
    (D) attack rag-time for being merely an imitation of an existing style
    (E) know that it would be difficult to refine rag-time as a musical form

29. Which statement best summarizes the author's argument in the third paragraph?

    (A) Any type of music that is extremely popular should be considered great.
    (B) The two criteria for musical greatness are popularity and originality.
    (C) Music that has become popular overseas cannot be ignored by American musicians.
    (D) Rag-time must be taken up by a musical master and purified to earn critical acclaim.
    (E) Mass appeal in music can be a sign of greatness rather than a stigma.

30. The statement in lines 83–84 ("Perhaps he wouldn't have done anything at all") is best interpreted as conveying

    (A) doubt about the depth of the piano player's skill
    (B) understanding that no amount of talent can compensate for a lack of discipline
    (C) cynicism about the likelihood that a man can live up to his potential
    (D) a recognition that the piano player might have wasted his talent
    (E) frustration at the impossibility of knowing what might have been

31. The author's view (lines 83–92) about the rag-time piano player's lack of formal training can best be summarized as which of the following?

    (A) The piano player's natural talent had allowed him to develop technically to the point where formal training would have been superfluous.
    (B) Formal lessons would have impaired the piano player's native ability to play and compose by ear alone.
    (C) More would have been lost than gained if the piano player had been given formal lessons.
    (D) The piano player's potential to be a truly innovative rag-time artist had been squandered because he had not been formally trained.
    (E) Although dazzling when improvising rag-time, the piano player could never have been more than mediocre as a classical pianist.

If you finish before time is called, you may check your work on this section only. Do not turn to any other section in the test. **STOP**

Time—15 Minutes
10 Questions

Solve each of the following problems, decide which is the best answer choice, and darken the corresponding oval on the answer sheet. Use available space in the test booklet for scratchwork.

Notes:

(1) Calculator use is permitted.

(2) All numbers used are real numbers.

(3) Figures are provided for some problems. All figures are drawn to scale and lie in a plane UNLESS otherwise indicated.

Reference Information

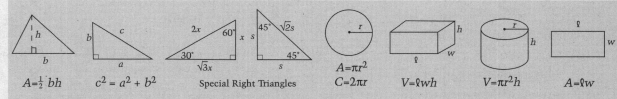

$A=\frac{1}{2}bh$ $c^2 = a^2 + b^2$ Special Right Triangles $A=\pi r^2$ $V=\ell wh$ $V=\pi r^2 h$ $A=\ell w$

$C=2\pi r$

The sum of the degree measures of the angles of a triangle is 180.
The number of degrees of arc in a circle is 360.
A straight angle has a degree measure of 180.

---

1. For all x, $(3x + 4)(4x - 3) =$

    (A) $7x + 1$
    (B) $7x - 12$
    (C) $12x^2 - 12$
    (D) $12x^2 - 25x - 12$
    (E) $12x^2 + 7x - 12$

2. In a certain set of numbers, the ratio of integers to nonintegers is 2:3. What percent of the numbers in the set are integers?

    (A) 20%
    (B) $33\frac{1}{3}\%$
    (C) 40%
    (D) 60%
    (E) $66\frac{2}{3}\%$

3. If $xyz \neq 0$, which of the following is equivalent to $\dfrac{x^2 y^3 z^4}{(xyz^2)^2}$?

    (A) $\dfrac{1}{y}$
    (B) $\dfrac{1}{z}$
    (C) y
    (D) $\dfrac{x}{yz}$
    (E) xyz

4. When the positive integer p is divided by 7, the remainder is 5. What is the remainder when $5p$ is divided by 7?

    (A) 0
    (B) 1
    (C) 2
    (D) 3
    (E) 4

5. What is the *y*-intercept of the line with the equation $2x - 3y = 18$?

    (A) –9
    (B) –6
    (C) –3
    (D) 6
    (E) 9

6. Jan types at an average rate of 12 pages per hour. At that rate, how long will it take Jan to type 100 pages?

    (A) 8 hours and 3 minutes
    (B) 8 hours and 15 minutes
    (C) 8 hours and 20 minutes
    (D) 8 hours and 30 minutes
    (E) 8 hours and 33 $\frac{1}{3}$ minutes

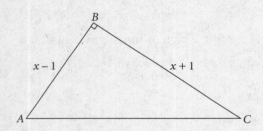

7. In the figure above, *AB* is perpendicular to *BC*. The lengths of *AB* and *BC* are given in terms of *x*. Which of the following represents the area of $\triangle ABC$ for all $x > 1$?

    (A) x
    (B) $2x$
    (C) x^2
    (D) $x^2 - 1$
    (E) $\dfrac{x^2 - 1}{2}$

8. If Jim and Bill have less than $15 between them, and Bill has $4, which of the following could be the number of dollars that Jim has?

    I.   10
    II. 11
    III. 15

    (A) I only
    (B) II only
    (C) I and II only
    (D) II and III only
    (E) I, II, and III

9. Angelo makes *x* dollars for *y* hours of work. Sarah makes the same amount of money for 1 less hour of work. Which of the following expressions represents the positive difference between the two people's hourly wage?

    (A) $\dfrac{x}{y - 1} - \dfrac{x}{y}$
    (B) $\dfrac{x}{y} - \dfrac{x}{y - 1}$
    (C) $\dfrac{x}{y - 1} + \dfrac{x}{y}$
    (D) $\dfrac{y - 1}{x} - \dfrac{y}{x}$
    (E) $\dfrac{y}{x} - \dfrac{y - 1}{x}$

10. Erica has 8 squares of felt, each with area 16. For a certain craft project she cuts the largest circle possible from each square of felt. What is the combined area of the excess felt left over after cutting out all the circles?

    (A) $4(4 - \pi)$
    (B) $8(4 - \pi)$
    (C) $8(\pi - 2)$
    (D) $32(4 - \pi)$
    (E) $16(16 - \pi)$

If you finish before time is called, you may check your work on this section only. Do not turn to any other section in the test. STOP

Time—15 minutes
12 Questions Answer the questions below based on the information in the accompanying passages.

Questions 1–12 are based on the following passages.

These passages present two critics' perspectives on the topic of design museums.

Passage 1

City museums are places where people can learn about various cultures by studying objects of particular historical or artistic
Line value. The increasingly popular "design
(05) museums" that are opening today perform quite a different function. Unlike most city museums, the design museum displays and assesses objects that are readily available to the general public. These museums place
(10) ignored household appliances under spotlights, breaking down the barriers between commerce and creative invention.

Critics have argued that design museums are often manipulated to serve as
(15) advertisements for new industrial technology. But their role is not simply a matter of merchandising—it is the honoring of impressive, innovative products. The difference between the window of a
(20) department store and the showcase in a design museum is that the first tries to sell you something, while the second informs you of the success of the attempt.

One advantage that the design museum
(25) has over other civic museums is that design museums are places where people feel familiar with the exhibits. Unlike the average art gallery patron, design museum visitors rarely feel intimidated or disoriented. Partly
(30) this is because design museums clearly illustrate how and why mass-produced consumer objects work and look as they do, and show how design contributes to the quality of our lives. For example, an exhibit
(35) involving a particular design of chair would not simply explain how it functions as a chair. It would also demonstrate how its various features combine to produce an artistic effect or redefine our manner of
(40) performing the basic act of being seated. The purpose of such an exhibit would be to present these concepts in ways that challenge, stimulate and inform the viewer. An art gallery exhibit, on the other hand,
(45) would provide very little information about the chair and charge the visitor with understanding the exhibit on some abstract level.

Within the past decade, several new
(50) design museums have opened their doors. Each of these museums has responded in totally original ways to the public's growing interest in the field. London's Design Museum, for instance, displays a collection
(55) of mass-produced objects ranging from Zippo lighters to electric typewriters to a show of Norwegian sardine-tin labels. The options open to curators of design museums seem far less rigorous, conventionalized and
(60) pre-programmed than those applying to curators in charge of public galleries of paintings and sculpture. The humorous aspects of our society are better represented in the display of postmodern playthings or
(65) quirky Japanese vacuum cleaners in pastel colors than in an exhibition of Impressionist landscapes.

Passage 2

The short histories of some of the leading technical and design museums make clear an
(70) underlying difficulty in this area. The tendency everywhere today is to begin with present machines and technological processes and to show how they operate and the scientific principles on which they are
(75) based without paying much attention to their historical development, to say nothing of the society that produced them. Only a

GO ON TO THE NEXT PAGE

few of the oldest, largest and best-supported museums collect historical industrial
(80) objects. Most science centers put more emphasis on mock-ups, graphs and multimedia devices. This approach of "presentism" often leads the museum to drop all attempts at study and research; if
(85) industry is called upon to design and build the exhibits, curators may be entirely dispensed with, so that impartial and scientific study disappears, and emphasis is placed on the idea that progress
(90) automatically follows technology.

Industrialization and the machine have, of course, brought much progress; a large portion of humankind no longer works from sunup to sundown to obtain the bare
(95) necessities of life. But industrialization also creates problems—harm to the environment and ecology, neglect of social, cultural and humanistic values, depletion of resources, and even threats of human extinction. Thus
(100) progress needs to be considered critically— from a wider social and humanitarian point of view. Unfortunately, most museums of science and technology glorify machines. Displayed in pristine condition, elegantly
(105) painted or polished, they can make the observer forget the noise, dirt, danger and frustration of machine-tending. Mines, whether coal, iron or salt, are a favorite museum display but only infrequently is
(110) there even a hint of the dirt, the damp, the smell, the low headroom, or the crippling and destructive accidents that sometimes occur in industry.

Machinery also ought to be operated to be
(115) meaningful. Consequently, it should not be shown in sculptured repose but in full, often clattering, action. This kind of operation is difficult to obtain, and few museums can command the imagination, ingenuity, and
(120) manual dexterity it requires. Problems also arise in providing adequate safety devices for

both the public and the machine operators. These, then, are some of the underlying problems of the technical museum—
(125) problems not solved by the usual push buttons, cranks or multimedia gimmicks. Yet attendance figures show that technical museums outdraw all the others; the public possesses lively curiosity and a real desire to
(130) understand science and technology.

1. In line 8, the word *readily* most nearly means

   (A) easily
   (B) willingly
   (C) instantly
   (D) cheaply
   (E) constantly

2. In lines 16–23, the author of Passage 1 suggests that design museums are different from store windows in that

   (A) design museums display more technologically advanced products
   (B) store window displays are not created with as much concern to the visual quality of the display
   (C) design museums are not concerned with the commercial aspects of a successful product
   (D) design museums focus on highlighting the artistic qualities that help sell products
   (E) the objects in store displays are more commercially successful than those in design museums

GO ON TO THE NEXT PAGE

3. From lines 24–34, it can be inferred that the author believes that most museum visitors

(A) are hostile towards the concept of abstract art

(B) prefer to have a context in which to understand museum exhibits

(C) are confused when faced with complex technological exhibits

(D) are unfamiliar with the exhibits in design museums

(E) undervalue the artistic worth of household items

4. The third paragraph of Passage 1 suggests that one important difference between design museums and the art galleries is

(A) the low price of admission at design museums

(B) the amount of information presented with design museum exhibits

(C) the intelligence of the average museum visitor

(D) that art galleries feature exhibits that have artistic merit

(E) the contribution that design museums make to our quality of life

5. In line 58, the word *options* most likely refers to the ability of curators of design museums to

(A) afford large collections of exhibits

(B) attract a wide range of visitors

(C) put together unconventional collections

(D) feature rare objects that interest the public

(E) satisfy their own personal whims in planning exhibitions

6. In lines 66–67, the author most likely mentions "Impressionist landscapes" in order to

(A) provide an example of a typical design museum exhibit

(B) compare postmodern exhibits to nineteenth-century art

(C) point out a decline in the sophistication of the museum-going public

(D) refute the notion that postmodern art is whimsical

(E) emphasize the contrast between two different types of exhibits

7. Which of the following best describes the "underlying difficulty" mentioned in line 70 of Passage 2?

(A) Design museums rarely mention the historical origin of objects they display.

(B) Industrial involvement often forces curators out of their jobs.

(C) Design museums appropriate technology that is essential for study and research.

(D) Technology almost never leads to progress.

(E) Industry places too much emphasis on impartial research.

8. The author of Passage 2 most likely mentions "harm to the environment and ecology" (lines 96–97) in order to

(A) encourage a critical response to the technological age

(B) discourage the reader from visiting technology museums

(C) describe the hazardous conditions in coal, iron and salt mines

(D) dissuade museum visitors from operating the machinery on display

(E) praise museums that present an accurate depiction of technology

GO ON TO THE NEXT PAGE

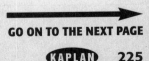

9. The author uses the phrase "sculptured repose" (line 116) in order to

    (A) condemn the curators of design museums for poor planning

    (B) illustrate the greatest problem inherent in design museums

    (C) present an idealized vision of a type of exhibit

    (D) describe the unrealistic way in which machinery is generally displayed

    (E) compare the shape of a machine to a work of art

10. The word *command* (line 119) most nearly means

    (A) oversee

    (B) direct

    (C) control

    (D) summon

    (E) order

11. The author of Passage 2 would probably object to the statement that design "contributes to the quality of our lives" (lines 33–34) on the grounds that

    (A) technical innovation has historically posed threats to our physical and social well-being

    (B) the general public would benefit more from visiting art galleries

    (C) machinery that is not shown in action is meaningless to the viewer

    (D) industry has made a negligible contribution to human progress

    (E) few people have a genuine interest in the impact of science and technology

12. The authors of both passages would probably agree that

    (A) machinery is only enjoyable to watch when it is moving

    (B) most people are curious about the factors behind the design of everyday objects

    (C) the public places a higher value on packaging than it does on quality

    (D) the very technology that is displayed in the museums is likely to cost curators their jobs

    (E) design museums are flawed because they fail to accurately portray the environmental problems that technology sometimes causes

If you finish before time is called, you may check your work on this section only. Do not turn to any other section in the test. **STOP**

ANSWER KEY ON FOLLOWING PAGE

ANSWER KEY

Section 1	Section 2	Section 3	Section 4	Section 5	Section 6
1. E	1. C	1. A	1. D	1. E	1. A
2. E	2. E	2. D	2. B	2. C	2. D
3. C	3. A	3. A	3. B	3. C	3. B
4. A	4. A	4. B	4. B	4. E	4. B
5. A	5. C	5. D	5. B	5. B	5. C
6. D	6. D	6. D	6. A	6. C	6. E
7. C	7. C	7. D	7. A	7. E	7. A
8. A	8. D	8. B	8. A	8. A	8. A
9. C	9. C	9. B	9. E	9. A	9. D
10. A	10. E	10. D	10. C	10. D	10. D
11. E	11. B	11. C	11. B		11. A
12. C	12. E	12. A	12. E		12. B
13. A	13. C	13. A	13. A		
14. D	14. D	14. D	14. B		
15. C	15. A	15. B	15. B		
16. A	16. C	16. 115	16. C		
17. E	17. E	17. .04	17. C		
18. B	18. C	18. 11, 13, 17,	18. C		
19. B	19. B	19, 23, 29,	19. E		
20. B	20. A	31, 37, 41,	20. C		
21. C	21. A	43, or 47	21. E		
22. B	22. B	19. 2/5 or .4	22. A		
23. D	23. E	20. 8	23. C		
24. D	24. C	21. 4	24. E		
25. E	25. A	22. 250	25. A		
	26. D	23. 9	26. C		
	27. C	24. 64	27. A		
	28. C	25. 203	28. C		
	29. A		29. E		
	30. B		30. D		
	31. C		31. C		
	32. D				
	33. B				
	34. B				
	35. B				

COMPUTE YOUR RAW SCORE

First, check your answers against the answer key on the previous page, and count up the number right and the number wrong for each section (there are boxes on your answer sheet to record these numbers). Remember not to count omissions as wrong.

Then figure out your raw scores using the table below. The Verbal raw score is equal to the total right in the three Verbal sections minus one-fourth of the number wrong in those sections. The Math raw score is equal to the total right in the three Math sections minus one-fourth of the number wrong in the two Regular Math sections and minus one-third the number wrong in the QCs. (Remember: There is no deduction for wrong answers in the Grid-ins.) Round each raw score to the nearest whole number.

Finally, use the tables on the next page to convert each raw score to a range of scaled scores.

	Number Right		**Number Wrong**			**Raw Score**
Section 2:	☐	−[.25 ×	☐	]	=	☐
Section 4:	☐	−[.25 ×	☐	]	=	☐
Section 6:	☐	−[.25 ×	☐	]	=	☐
					Verbal Raw Score:	☐
						(Rounded)
Section 3A: Questions 1–15	☐	−[.33 ×	☐	]	=	☐
Section 3B: Questions 16–35	☐	(No wrong-answer penalty)			=	☐
Section 1:	☐	−[.25 ×	☐	]	=	☐
Section 5:	☐	−[.25 ×	☐	]	=	☐
					Math Raw Score:	☐
						(Rounded)

CONVERT YOUR SCORE

Verbal						Math					
Raw	Scaled	Raw	Scaled	Raw	Scaled	Raw	Scaled	Raw	Scaled	Raw	Scaled
−3 or		22	450	48	620	−1 or		19	440	40	600
less	200	23	460	49	630	less	200	20	450	41	610
−2	230	24	470	50	640	0	220	21	460	42	620
−1	270	25	470	51	640	1	240	22	470	43	630
0	290	26	480	52	650	2	260	23	480	44	640
1	300	27	490	53	660	3	280	24	480	45	650
2	310	28	490	54	670	4	300	25	490	46	650
3	320	29	500	55	670	5	310	26	500	47	660
4	330	30	510	56	670	6	330	27	510	48	670
5	330	31	510	57	680	7	340	28	520	49	680
6	340	32	520	58	690	8	350	29	520	50	690
7	350	33	530	59	690	9	360	30	530	51	700
8	360	34	530	60	700	10	370	31	530	52	720
9	370	35	540	61	710	11	380	32	540	53	730
10	370	36	550	62	720	12	390	33	550	54	740
11	380	37	550	63	730	13	400	34	560	55	760
12	390	38	560	64	730	14	410	35	560	56	770
13	390	39	570	65	740	15	420	36	570	57	780
14	400	40	570	66	750	16	430	37	580	58	790
15	410	41	580	67	760	17	430	38	590	59	800
16	410	42	590	68	770	18	440	39	600	60	800
17	420	43	590	69	780						
18	430	44	600	70	790						
19	430	45	600	71 or							
20	440	46	610	more	800						
21	450	47	610								

Don't take these scores too literally. Practice test conditions cannot precisely mirror real test conditions. Your actual SAT scores will almost certainly vary from your practice test scores.

Your score on the practice test gives you a rough idea of your range on the actual exam. If you don't like your score, it's not too late to do something about it. Work your way way through this book again, and turn to Kaplan's *SAT* guide as well as the *SAT Verbal Workbook* and *SAT Math Workbook* for even more help.

Answers and Explanations

SECTION ONE

1. E

Do what's in parentheses first:

$$\left(\frac{1}{5} + \frac{1}{3}\right) \div \frac{1}{2} = \frac{3}{15} + \frac{5}{15} \div \frac{1}{2}$$

$$= \frac{8}{15} \div \frac{1}{2}$$

Then, to divide fractions, invert the one after the division sign and multiply:

$$\frac{8}{15} \div \frac{1}{2} = \frac{8}{15} \times \frac{2}{1} = \frac{16}{15}$$

2. E

Plug in $x = -2$ and see what you get:

$$x^2 - 2x = (-2)^2 - 2(-2)$$
$$= 4 - (-4)$$
$$= 4 + 4$$
$$= 8$$

3. C

To get Vito's rate in pages per hour, take the 96 pages and divide by the time *in hours*. The time is given as "2 hours and 40 minutes." Forty minutes is $\frac{2}{3}$ of an hour, so you can express Vito's time as $2\frac{2}{3}$ hours, or $\frac{8}{3}$ hours:

$$\text{Pages per hour} = \frac{96 \text{ pages}}{\frac{8}{3} \text{ hours}}$$

$$= 96 \times \frac{3}{8} = 36$$

4. A

For $\frac{7}{x}$ to be greater than $\frac{1}{4}$, the denominator x has to be less than 4 times the numerator, or 28. And for $\frac{7}{x}$ to be less than $\frac{1}{3}$, the denominator x has to be greater than 3 times the numerator, or 21. Thus x could be any of the integers 22 through 27, of which there are 6.

5. A

To find the average of three numbers—even if they're algebraic expressions—add them up and divide by 3:

$$\text{Average} = \frac{(2x + 5) + (5x - 6) + (-4x + 2)}{3}$$

$$= \frac{3x + 1}{3}$$

$$= x + \frac{1}{3}$$

6. D

Percent times Whole equals Part:

$$(\text{Percent}) \times 25 = 16$$

$$\text{Percent} = \frac{16}{25} \times 100\% = 64\%$$

7. C

The measures of the interior angles of a triangle add up to 180, so add the two given measures and subtract the sum from 180. The difference will be the measure of the third angle:

$$45 + 70 = 115$$
$$180 - 115 = 65$$

8. A

$$\frac{x^2 + x^2 + x^2}{x^2} = \frac{3x^2}{x^2} = 3$$

9. C

To solve a quadratic equation, put it in the "$ax^2 + bx + c = 0$" form, factor the left side (if you can), and set each factor equal to 0 separately to get the two solutions. To solve $x^2 = 5x - 4$, first rewrite it as $x^2 - 5x + 4 = 0$. Then factor the left side:

$$x^2 - 5x + 4 = 0$$
$$(x - 1)(x - 4) = 0$$
$$x = 1 \text{ or } 4$$

10. A

Picking numbers is the easiest, fastest way to do this problem. Choose a pair of numbers from each set and add them together. If you are unable to prove immediately that a set does not have the property described in the question stem, you may want to choose another pair. In set I, if we add 2 and 4, we get 6. Adding 12 and 8 gives us 20. Adding −2 and 8 gives us 6. Since each sum is a member of the set of even integers, set I seems to be true. For set II, adding 3 and 5 yields 8, which is not an odd integer. Therefore, II is not true. Finally, if we add two primes, say 2 and 3, we get 5. That example is true. If we add 3 and 5, however, we get 8, and 8 is not a prime number. Therefore, only set I has the property and the answer is (A).

11. E

The best way to deal with changing averages is to use the sum. Use the old average to figure out the total of the first 4 scores:

Sum of first 4 scores = (4)(89) = 356

Use the new average to figure out the total he needs after the 5th score:

Sum of 5 scores = (5)(90) = 450

To get his sum from 356 to 450, Martin needs to score 450 − 356 = 94.

12. C

Don't fall for the trap choice (B): You can't add or subtract percents of different wholes. Let the original price $s = 100$. Reducing s by 25% gives you a sale price of 75. This price is then increased by 20%, so the final price is 90. Since $s = 100$, it's easy to see that this is equal to choice (C), $.90s$.

13. A

The prime factorization of 36 is $2 \times 2 \times 3 \times 3$. That factorization includes 2 distinct prime factors, 2 and 3.

14. D

The area of a triangle is equal to one-half the base times the height:

$$\text{Area} = \frac{1}{2}(\text{base})(\text{height})$$
$$36 = \frac{1}{2}(9)(\text{height})$$
$$36 = \frac{9}{2}h$$
$$h = \frac{2}{9} \times 36 = 8$$

15. C

According to the definition, $x \clubsuit = \frac{x}{4} - \frac{x}{6}$. Set that equal to 3 and solve for x:

$$\frac{x}{4} - \frac{x}{6} = 3$$
$$12\left(\frac{x}{4} - \frac{x}{6}\right) = 12(3)$$
$$3x - 2x = 36$$
$$x = 36$$

16. A

Read carefully. This question's a lot easier than you might think at first. It's asking for the total number of coins, not the total value. q quarters, d dimes, and n nickels add up to a total of $q + d + n$ coins.

17. E

Use the points where the line crosses the axes—$(-1, 0)$ and $(0, 2)$—to find the slope:

$$\text{Slope} = \frac{y_2 - y_1}{x_2 - x_1} = \frac{2 - 0}{0 - (-1)} = 2$$

The *y*-intercept is 2. Now plug $m = 2$ and $b = 2$ into the slope-intercept equation form:

$$y = mx + b$$
$$y = 2x + 2$$

18. B

An integer that's divisible by 6 has at least one 2 and one 3 in its prime factorization. An integer that's divisible by 9 has at least two 3's in its prime factorization. Therefore, an integer that's divisible by both 6 and 9 has at least one 2 and two 3's in its prime factorization. That means it's divisible by 2, 3, $2 \times 3 = 6$, $3 \times 3 = 9$, and $2 \times 3 \times 3 = 18$. It's *not* necessarily divisible by 12 or 36, each of which includes *two* 2's in its prime factorization.

You could also do this one by picking numbers. Think of a common multiple of 6 and 9 and use it to eliminate some options. $6 \times 9 = 54$ is an obvious common multiple—and it's not divisible by 12 or 36, but it is divisible by 18. The *least* common multiple of 6 and 9 is 18, which is also divisible by 18. It looks like every common multiple of 6 and 9 is also a multiple of 18.

19. B

Angles *POR* and *ROQ* are adjacent and supplementary, so the measure of $\angle ROP$ is $180° - 50° = 130°$. Now look at ΔPOR:

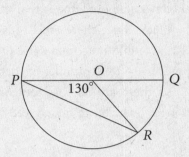

OP and *OR* are radii of the same circle, so they are equal and ΔPOR is isosceles. That means $\angle P$ and $\angle R$ are equal. The two of them need to add up to 50° so that the triangle's 3 interior angles will add up to 180°. If $\angle P$ and $\angle R$ are equal and add up to 50°, then they each measure 25°.

20. B

The volume of a cube is equal to an edge cubed, so $e^3 = 64$ and each edge of the cube has length 4. If the cube is sliced horizontally in two, each of the resulting solids will have two sides of length 4, and one of length 2. So when they are glued together, the resulting figure will have one edge of length 2, one of length 4, and one of length $4 + 4$ or 8.

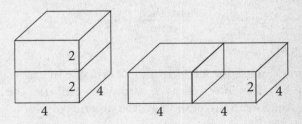

The surface area is the sum of the areas of the solid's six faces. The top and bottom each have area $8 \times 4 = 32$, the front and back each have area $8 \times 2 = 16$, and each side has area $4 \times 2 = 8$. So the surface area of the new solid is $2(32) + 2(16) + 2(8) = 64 + 32 + 16 = 112$.

21. C

Probability equals the number of favorable outcomes over the number of total outcomes. In this case, the favorable outcome is that the chosen sock will be black. Since there are 12 black socks, there are 12 favorable outcomes. The number of total outcomes is the total number of socks. $6 + 12 + 14 = 32$, so there are 32 total outcomes. The probability is $\frac{12}{32}$, which can be reduced to $\frac{3}{8}$.

22. B

This is an average rate problem, so don't just average the two rates. Instead, you have to use total distance and total time to find the average rate. First, pick a distance that is easy to use. For instance, since the speeds for the two halves of the trip are 40 and 60 miles per hour, 120 is an easy number to work with. Using 120 miles as the distance to the store, it would take $\frac{120}{40}$, or 3 hours to go to the store and $\frac{120}{60}$, or 2 hours to return. Thus, it takes 5 hours to complete a round trip of 240 miles. Now find the rate:

$$\text{Average rate} = \frac{\text{distance}}{\text{time}} = \frac{240}{50} = 48$$

23. D

You can use the 2 legs of a right triangle to get the area. Here one leg is a and you can use the Pythagorean theorem to get the other leg:

$$(\text{leg}_1)^2 + (\text{leg}_2)^2 = (\text{hypotenuse})^2$$
$$a^2 + b^2 = c^2$$
$$b^2 = c^2 - a^2$$
$$b = \sqrt{c^2 - a^2}$$

Now plug the legs a and $\sqrt{c^2 - a^2}$ into the triangle area formula:

$$\text{Area} = \frac{1}{2}(\text{base})(\text{height})$$
$$= \frac{1}{2}(\text{leg}_1)(\text{leg}_2)$$
$$= \frac{1}{2}a\sqrt{c^2 - a^2}$$
$$= \frac{a\sqrt{c^2 - a^2}}{2}$$

24. D

The area of a triangle is equal to one-half the base times the height. You can use any of the 3 sides of a triangle for the base—each side has a height to go along with it. It doesn't make any difference which base-height pair you use—a triangle has the same area no matter how you figure it. Thus one-half times PR times QS will be the same as one-half times PS times RT:

$$\frac{1}{2}(PR)(QS) = \frac{1}{2}(PS)(RT)$$
$$\frac{1}{2}(8)(9) = \frac{1}{2}(PS)(7)$$
$$(8)(9) = (PS)(7)$$
$$PS = \frac{72}{7} = 10\frac{2}{7}$$

25. E

In order to find the number of possibilities, multiply the number of possibilities in each step. In other words, there are 3 routes from Bay City to Riverville and 4 routes from Riverville to Straitstown. There are 3 more routes from Straitstown to Frogs Pond, so there are $12 \times 3 = 36$ total routes from Bay City to Frog Pond.

SECTION 2

1. C

The phrase "proves difficult" is a clue: the two missing words have to be nearly opposite in meaning. Choice (C) is correct, because few posters would be **intact** if they were meant to be **destroyed**. None of the other choices makes sense: being (A) **returned** would not stop something from being **recognizable**, being (B) **discarded** would not necessarily stop something from being **relevant**, and so on.

2. E

The phrases "long considered" and "finally" suggest contrast. The missing word is probably the opposite of "making some headway in its battle against extinction." (E) **imperiled**, "in danger," is the best answer. (A) **elusive** means "hard to find"; (B) **prevalent** means "common"; (C) **combative** means "eager to fight"; (D) **voracious** means "having a huge appetite."

3. A

The sentence sets up a contrast between the situation before the invention of the tape recorder, and the situation after. We need a word that's the opposite of "paraphrased," which means "expressed in different words." The answer is **verbatim**, "word-for-word."

4. A

The phrase "encouraged hopes" suggests that the two missing words will be somewhat related in meaning. Choice (A) is the best answer, because we expect **a serious** novelist to use **subtle** characterizations. The other choices make less sense; in fact, it's not clear what (C) **accurate** or (D) **fictional** or (E) **authentic** characterizations would be. (C) **prolific** means "highly productive"; (D) **accomplished** means "skillful, experienced"; (E) **reclusive** means "unsociable."

5. C

The missing word has to be related in meaning to "extended tenure." (C) **longevity** is the best choice. (A) **acumen** and (B) **savvy** both mean "skill" or "knowledge." (D) **decorum** means "proper behavior"; (E) **celebrity** means "fame."

6. D

The word *although* indicates contrast: the two missing words have to be opposite in meaning. This is the case with **buoyant**, "light-hearted, cheerful," and **subdued**, "quiet." In (A), **introverted** means "reserved, not outgoing." In (B), **imperious** means "commanding," and **incensed** means "angry."

7. C

The phrase "failure to" establishes the negative tone of the sentence. An agency ought to "fix" or "get rid of" flawed policies. Possible answers for the first blank are (C) **rescind** or "remove, cancel," and (D) **amend** or "fix." Failure to do this is a bad thing, so we need a negative word for the second blank. The best choice is **lackadaisical**, "careless, sloppy."

8. D

"Rapid turnover" would tend to increase "inconsistency," so we need a word that means "increased" or "worsened." **Exacerbated** means "made worse."

9. C

What claim would be "belied" or contradicted by a record of contributing to only one party? A claim of **impartiality**, of not favoring one side over the other.

10. E

"Repeated breakdown of negotiations" would tend to "support" or **reinforce** the view that the sides "were not truly committed to" "preventing" or **averting** a military confrontation. In (A) and (D), **established** and **strengthened** fit the first blank, but **escalating** and **initiating** are wrong for the second. In (B), **avoiding** fits the second blank, but **undermined** is wrong for the first.

11. B

The phrase "now that" suggests a similarity of tone between the two missing words, and the word "painful" tells us that the words will be negative. Only (B) provides a negative word for both blanks. A painful **decline** would indeed tend to cause budgetary **stringency** or tightness.

12. E

The word in the second blank has to relate in some logical way to "fear of causing leaves to fall," and the only word that does so is **durable**, "tough, not fragile." If the plant has become more **durable**, that should be a **relief** to those who were afraid of damaging it. In (A), **consternation** is "concern or worry," and **amorphous** means "shapeless."

13. C

Words like "unchanging" and "eternal" provide a definition of the missing word, (C) **static**. (D) **Holistic** means "functioning as a whole," and (E) **homogeneous** means "all of one kind"; neither word implies species being unchanging and no new species coming into existence.

14. D

A **LABORATORY** is by definition a place where you **EXPERIMENT**. A **graveyard** is by definition a place where you **inter**, or bury, people. Choices (A) and (B) are wrong because you can do things in a **garage** besides **repair** things, and you can do things on a **beach** besides **sunbathe**.

15. A

To **EXONERATE** someone is to remove **BLAME** from him or her. To **disinfect** something is to remove **contamination** from it. To (B) **divert** a **stream** is to change its course; to (C) **indict** someone is to assert that person's **guilt**. Choice (E) is a bridgeless pair.

16. C

By definition, to **SCRUTINIZE** something is to **LOOK** at it very carefully. To **peruse** something is to **read** it very carefully. In (D), **importune** means the same thing as **plead**.

17. E

A **GULLIBLE** person is easy to **DUPE** or fool. A **submissive** person is easy to **control**. In (A), a **fallible** person has a tendency to **err**; this is a different bridge. Choice (B) is a bridgeless pair. In (C), a **dejected** person is already **disheartened**. In choice (D) a **headstrong** person is difficult to **coax**.

18. C

A **CONVERSATION** is carried on by two or more **INTERLOCUTOR**s, the people who participate in a conversation. A **game** is carried on by two or more **players**. The other choices have different bridges. An (A) **orator** makes a **speech** and an (E) **doctor** makes a **diagnosis**. Choices (B) and (D) have weak bridges: a **prosecutor** can take part in a **hearing**, and a **publisher** can publish a **novel**.

19. B

ENTOMOLOGY is, by definition, the study of **INSECTS**. **Pedagogy** is the study of **education**. In each of the other choices, there is a connection between the two words, but not the same connection as in the stem pair.

20. A

A **SKIRMISH** is, by definition, a minor **BATTLE**. A **misdemeanor** is a minor **crime**.

21. A

FORENSIC means "having to do with **LITIGATION**," or legal procedure (you've probably heard of "forensic medicine," medical procedure used in the investigation of a crime). (A) **Maritime** means "having to do with the **sea**." Choice (D) may be tempting, but **exemplary** means "ideal," not "having to do with an **example**." Choice (C) simply combines two words that are often paired, but have no necessary relation. In (B), **euphoria** is an example of a **feeling**. In (E), something **illusory** does not necessarily have to do with **magic**.

22. B

By definition, to **FEIGN** is to give a false **IMPRESSION**. To **perjure** is to give false **testimony**. In (C), (D), and (E), the first word has connotations of falsehood, but it does not specifically mean falsifying the second word.

23. E

A **POLEMIC** is a speech or piece of writing that advocates a particular point of view; by definition, it is not **IMPARTIAL**. Similarly, an **extrovert**, a sociable, outgoing person, is not **retiring** or shy and withdrawn. In (A), an **antidote** is **curative**. In the other choices, **discipline** may or may not be **harsh**, a **heretic** may or may not be **persecuted**, and a **defendant** may or may not be **guilty**.

The Wolves Passage

This Science passage is written by a naturalist who recounts how he went into the wilderness and, through trial and error experimentation and observation, learned some new and surprising things about the way wolves live. For example, wolves are a lot less suspicious and aggressive than people think they are, and contrary to popular belief, wolf families are not nomadic—they live and stay in territories with very definite boundaries.

24. C

In the first paragraph, the author explains how the wolves were aware of his presence but ignored him. That's why the author's precautions were superfluous. (C) basically paraphrases that idea: the author's precautions were unnecessary because the wolves weren't interested in him. (A) doesn't work because the author never really says how long it was before he encountered the wolves. (B) is out because the author never mentions any wild animals other than wolves. Contrary to (D), even after the author interfered with the wolves' boundaries, they never bothered him. (E) is out because it's never suggested that the wolves have poor eyesight.

25. A

The author's basic point in paragraph 1 is that he was surprised at the way the wolves behaved towards him: they sized him up quickly right at the beginning and, from then on, ignored him. He found this behavior disconcerting, or **strange**, as (A) puts it. (B) sounds exaggerated—the author never really suggests that he was fearful of attack. With (C), the author says that he took longer to assess the wolves than they took to assess him, but his basic point is not to emphasize his own ignorance. (D) doesn't work because the wolves left the author alone—precautions weren't necessary. (E), like (B), isn't suggested—that the author thinks he has a lot of courage.

26. D

In paragraph 3 the author describes how the wolf was so preoccupied that he came within 15 yards of his tent without seeing it. It wasn't until the author made noise that the wolf suddenly became aware of its surroundings. (D) paraphrases this idea: that the wolf was not **on its guard**—it was self-absorbed. The author expresses no surprise about the wolf traveling alone (A) or hunting at night (C). As for (B), the point is not that the wolf lacks energy—it does respond when the author startles it. (E) is out because the author doesn't really mention any fear of attack.

27. C

The first sentence of paragraph 3 describes the wolf as "anxious to go home to bed." The idea is that he was **eager** to get home (C). **Distressed** (A), **afraid** (B), **uneasy** (D), and **worried** (E) are other definitions of *anxious*, but they don't fit the idea in the sentence.

28. C

In paragraph 4, the author explains that one of the things he learned is that, contrary to popular belief, the wolves were "settled beasts" rather than "nomadic hunters." The idea, in other words, is that the wolves were **stable**—they had established homes. **Decided** (A) and **resolute** (B) are other meanings of *settled*, but they don't work in the sentence. Neither **inflexible** (D) nor **confident** (E) fits when plugged in.

29. A

The idea at the beginning of paragraph 4 is that the wolves, contrary to what people generally think, are not nomadic. (A) catches the idea: the author is countering a popular myth or belief about the behavior of wolves. (B) is tricky, but there's really no paradox or ambiguity: the idea is that the wolves are NOT nomadic. (C) is tricky too, but the passage never says that the idea that wolves are nomadic is an established fact. As for (D), there's no indication that what the author observed—that the wolves live in established territories—is an exception to a general rule. (E) doesn't work because there's really no summary of any conclusions in the quoted lines. (A) is the best choice.

30. B

In the middle of paragraph 5 the author describes how the wolf family regularly made the rounds of their lands and "freshened up the boundary markers." He guessed that this was done because there were other wolves living in adjacent areas, although he never saw any sign of trouble between the neighboring wolf families. Then you get the quoted idea: since he never witnessed any disputes, he figured that it was all basically a ritual activity. (B) catches the idea. The idea that the activity was a ritual isn't related to the fact that it was repeated (A), that the boundaries were marked by geographic features (C), that they were marked at the same time each week (D)—that's never suggested, or that the whole family participated (E). The wrong choices miss the point.

31. C

One of the author's discoveries is that the wolves live in territories with clearly marked boundaries. So, contrary to what most people think, they aren't nomadic—they don't travel endlessly from place to place looking for food and sleeping in new areas. The idea in (C), if it were true, would contradict or weaken that idea. The idea in (A) would strengthen the thesis—if there were disputes over boundaries, that would suggest that the wolves are protective of their territory. The idea in (B)—the particular size of the wolves' territory—is irrelevant—it doesn't really relate to the question. (D) is tricky, but it doesn't work: the author finds that the wolves are territorial even though they actually don't have conflicts with their neighbors. The idea in (E) is irrelevant: the passage never discusses whether or not wolves are alert when encountering other animals.

32. D

The phrase "invisible wall" occurs in paragraph 7, and the point is that the wolf, who was plodding home as preoccupied as usual, was suddenly stopped in its tracks when it encountered the spot where the author had left his own markings. So the idea about the invisible wall is that the wolf was stopped suddenly (D), as if it had suddenly banged up against it. The idea of an invisible wall has nothing to do with delight in getting the wolf's attention (A), annoyance on the part of the wolf (B), high speed (C)—the wolf was "padding," not running—or exhaustion after a night of hunting (E).

33. B

In the very same sentence in paragraph 7, the author says that the wolf, upon finding the author's marks, immediately became bewildered. (B) restates that. The passage says nothing about **combativeness** (A), **anxiety** (C), **wariness** (D), or **dread** (E).

34. B

Temerity is a tough vocabulary word—it means impetuousness or **rashness** (B). But you really didn't have to know that definition to pick the right answer. All you have to do with Definition-in-Context questions is plug in each of the answer choices, and eliminate the ones that don't fit the sentence's meaning. If you do that here, none of the other choices works. With (A), it's not that the author's being discourteous. That sounds strange. Rather, he's being too bold—only (B) makes sense. Remember, if you're stumped with any hard question, work backwards by eliminating any wrong choices you can—and then guess.

35. B

At the end of paragraph 8, the author states that he turned his back on the wolf "in an effort to break the impasse." In other words, he did it to bring about a change in the situation (B). Nothing suggests that he did it to show his power over the wolf (A); make the wolf recognize his existence (C)—the wolf already did; look for a weapon (D); or avoid the wolf's "hypnotic" gaze (E).

SECTION 3

1. A

Don't calculate. Compare piece by piece. The first fraction in Column A is greater than the first fraction in Column B, and the second fraction in Column A is greater than the second fraction in Column B. Therefore the sum in Column A is also greater.

2. D

Try a few numbers. Plugging in $\frac{1}{2}$ for x, you get $\frac{1}{2}$ in Column A, but in Column B you get 1 over $\frac{1}{2}$, which is 1 divided by $\frac{1}{2}$, which is 2. Here Column B is greater. But when you plug in a negative number, things change. Plugging in $-\frac{1}{2}$ gives you $-\frac{1}{2}$ in Column A, and 1 over $-\frac{1}{2}$, which is the same as -2, in Column B. More than one relationship exists, so the answer is (D).

3. A

Don't calculate. Compare Column A to a percent of 34 that's easy to find. Think of 52% as just a bit more than 50%, or $\frac{1}{2}$. 52% of 34, then, is just a bit more than half of 34, so it's more than 17.

4. B

Expand Column A to make it look more like Column B. Distribute the 3 and you get $3x - 6$. No matter what x is, subtracting 6 from $3x$ will leave you with less than subtracting 4 from $3x$.

5. D

There are several pairs of integers that have a product of 10. You don't need to find every pair. Just try to find a pair that has a sum greater than 6 and another pair that has a sum less than 6. An example of the former is 5 and 2. An example of the latter is -5 and -2. The answer is (D).

6. D

We know that x and y are integers that do not equal zero, but that's all we know. First instinct may tell you that Column B is larger because the squares of x and y are both positive, and the product of two positive integers is usually greater than the quotient. However, what if $y = 1$? In this case, $\dfrac{x^2}{y^2} = x^2y^2$. Since there is more than one possible relationship between Column A and Column B, the answer is (D).

7. D

It looks at first glance like B and C divide the segment into three equal pieces. But check the mathematics of the situation to be sure. You're given that $AC = BD$:

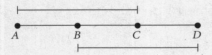

What can you deduce from that? You can subtract BC from both equal lengths and you'll end up with another equality: $AB = CD$. But what about BC? Does it have to be the same as AB and CD? No. The diagram could be resketched like this:

Now you can see that it's possible for AC and BD to be equal but for BC to be longer than AB. It's also possible for BC to be shorter:

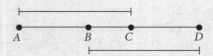

More than one relationship is possible, so the answer is (D).

8. B

If you try picking numbers, you'll find that Column B is always greater. It has to be, because $y > 1$, and multiplying a positive number x by something greater than 1 will result in something greater than x.

9. B

First figure out what the simplified form of Column B is. Since x^3 is squared, you must multiply the exponents, leaving you with x^6. Since x is greater than 1, the number gets larger as it is raised to higher powers. Since x^6 has a larger exponent than x^5, and since x is greater than 1, Column B must be greater.

10. D

First simplify Column B by dividing both the numerator and denominator by y. Thus you're left comparing $\dfrac{1}{y}$ in Column A to y in Column B. Don't jump to the conclusion that Column A is a fraction and Column B is an integer. It could be the other way around. If $y = 2$, then Column A is $\dfrac{1}{2}$ and Column B is 2. On the other hand, if $y = \dfrac{1}{2}$, then Column A is 2 and Column B is $\dfrac{1}{2}$. More than one possible relationship means that the answer is (D).

11. C

The first step in this problem is finding the values you must compare. Column A equals the area of a square with side 6, so plug 6 into the formula for the area of a square:

$$A = s^2$$
$$A = 6^2$$
$$A = 36$$

Now find the value of Column B by plugging 9 into the formula for the perimeter of a square:

$$P = 4s$$

$$P = 4(9)$$

$$P = 36$$

Since the columns are equal, the answer is (C).

12. A

The key to this problem is knowing how to find the median and mode of the scores. The mode is the value occurring most often, which is 93 for this set of scores. The median is the middle value, so the first thing you have to do is to rearrange the scores into numerical order:

82, 85, 88, 90, 93, 93, 94, 98

Now take the middle value. Since there is an even number of scores, you'll have to take the average of the two middle scores for the median. In this case, the two middle scores are 90 and 93. $90 + 93 = 183$, which when divided by 2 is 91.5. Therefore, the mode, 93, is greater than the median, 91.5, and Column A is greater than Column B.

13. A

The area of the circle is $\pi r^2 = \pi(3)^2 = 9\pi$. The area of the rectangle is 9×3. Don't think of it as 27; it's easier to compare in the form 9×3. π is more than 3, so 9π is more than 9×3.

14. D

Re-express both columns. In each case you can turn 1 into $\frac{1+y}{1+y}$. Column A, then, becomes

$\frac{1+y}{1+y} - \frac{y}{1+y}$, which is equal to $\frac{1+y-1}{1+y}$,

or $\frac{1}{1+y}$. Column B becomes $\frac{1+y}{1+y} - \frac{1}{1+y}$,

which is equal to $\frac{1+y-1}{1+y}$ or $\frac{y}{1+y}$. Now both

columns have the same positive denominator, so

the larger quantity will be the one with the larger numerator. (You could think of it as multiplying both columns by the positive quantity $1 + y$.) All you have to do now is compare 1 to y. Which is bigger? You don't know. All you know is that y is positive, but because it could be less than, more than, or even equal to 1, the answer is (D).

15. B

First consider Column B. If a square has a perimeter of 32, the length of each side must be 8. Therefore the area is $8^2 = 64$. Now consider Column A. Since $AB > BC$, one dimension of the rectangle must be larger than the other. To get an idea of how the area of a rectangle changes as its dimensions change, pick numbers for the dimensions. Since the perimeter of $ABCD$ is 32, the sum of one length and one width is half of that, or 16. Pick numbers that add up to 16, but also give you a clear idea of how the area changes. To do this, pick one pair of numbers which represents something near a square and one pair which represents a very elongated rectangle. You could choose 9 and 7 for the first pair and 15 and 1 for the second, for instance. Now find the areas of the rectangles with your chosen dimensions. Multiplying the first pair gives you $9 \times 7 = 63$, while multiplying the second yields $15 \times 1 = 15$. As the dimensions get closer to the square, the area gets larger. However, a square with a certain perimeter has a greater area than any other rectangle with the same perimeter, so Column B is larger than Column A.

16. 115

Since lines p and q are parallel, we can use the rule about alternate interior angles to fill in the following:

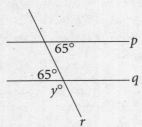

Since the angle marked $y°$ is adjacent and supplementary to a 65° angle, $y = 180 - 65 = 115$.

17. .04

Be careful. The question is not asking: "What is $\frac{1}{4}$ of 16?" It's asking: "What is $\frac{1}{4}$ percent of 16?" One-fourth of 1 percent is 0.25%, or 0.0025: $\frac{1}{4}$% of 16 $= 0.0025 \times 16 = 0.04$

18. 11, 13, 17, 19, 23, 29, 31, 37, 41, 43, or 47

In order for each of these fractions to be in its simplest form, a would have to be a number that has no prime factors in common with 3, 5, or 14. So just find a value between 2 and 50 that fits that description. Your best bet is to use a prime number, such as 11. That's one of 11 acceptable answers.

19. 2/5 or .4

If there are 36 men and 24 women in the group, then the total number of group members is 60. The women make up $\frac{26}{40}$ of the group. Since this fraction cannot be gridded, reduce it or turn it into a decimal. To reduce it, divide both the numerator and denominator by 12, and you end up with $\frac{2}{5}$. To turn it into a decimal, divide 60 into 24, and you end up with .4.

20. 8

To evaluate this expression when $s = 9$, simply plug 9 in for s. Substituting 9 into the expression yields:

$$\frac{3(9) + 5}{4} = \frac{27 + 5}{4} = \frac{32}{4} = 8$$

21. 4

The easiest way to get the answer here is to pick numbers. Pick a number for x that has a remainder of 2 when divided by 6, such as 8. Increase the number you picked by 8. In this case, $8 + 8 = 16$. Now divide 16 by 6, which gives you 2 remainder 4. Therefore, the answer is 4.

22. 250

Percent times Whole equals Part:

$(15\%) \times (\text{take-home pay}) = \$37.50$

$(0.15) \times (\text{take-home pay}) = \$37.50$

$\text{take-home pay} = \dfrac{\$37.50}{0.15} = \$250.00$

23. 9

The area of a triangle is equal to one-half the base times the height. Here the base (along the x-axis) is 6 and the height (perpendicular to the base—i.e., parallel to the y-axis) is 3, so the area is $\frac{1}{2}bh = \frac{1}{2}(6)(3) = 9$.

24. 64

You cannot find the area of the square without finding the length of a side, so use the information you are given about the rectangles to find the length of the square's sides. Since the rectangles have the same dimensions, we know that the side of the square must be twice the length of the shorter side of either rectangle. The side of the square must also be the longer side of either rectangle.

Call the length of a side of the square, which is also the length of a longer side of either rectangle, x. Then the shorter side of either rectangle is $\frac{x}{2}$. Now use the formula for the perimeter:

$$P = 2l + 2w$$

For either rectangle, you have

$$24 = 2x + 2\left(\frac{x}{2}\right)$$
$$24 = 2x + x$$
$$24 = 3x$$
$$8 = x$$

To find the area of the square, simply multiply 8 by 8. The answer is 64.

25. 203

This looks like a physics question, but in fact it's just a "plug-in-the-number-and-see-what-you-get" question. Be sure you plug 95 in for C (not F):

$$C = \frac{5}{9}(F - 32)$$
$$95 = \frac{5}{9}(F - 32)$$
$$\frac{9}{5} \times 95 = F - 32$$
$$F - 32 = 171$$
$$F = 171 + 32 = 203$$

SECTION 4

1. D

The word in the first blank has to be similar in meaning to "controversy": (C) **belligerent**, (D) **scandalous**, and (E) **provocative** would fit. The band wouldn't do this if they didn't find that the strategy worked, so (B) **rewarding** and (D) **effective** fit for the second blank. Only (D) fits for both blanks.

2. B

The correct answer is implied by "numerous scribbled edits that cover even his supposed final drafts." In other words, Joyce attached great importance to (B) **revision**.

3. B

The key is that the players "now charge for their signatures." Either the fans who believe that the players are not "greedy" would be "surprised" or "disappointed," or the fans who believe that the players are not "ungreedy" would be "confirmed." Choice (B) fits the former prediction.

4. B

The words *though* and *absence* indicate contrast, so the missing word has to be nearly opposite in meaning to "isolation and the longing for connection." **Fraternity**—brotherhood or fellowship—is the best choice. Choice (D) may be tempting, but the term **socialism** refers to a specific set of political and economic doctrines, not just to any sort of society.

5. B

The part of the sentence after the semicolon pretty basically defines the missing word. The word is **calculated**, consciously planned. (A) **Incendiary** means "inflaming"; (C) **facetious** means "joking"; (D) **scrupulous** means "honest"; (E) **impromptu** means "unplanned."

6. A

The word *but* after the comma indicates that the word in the second blank contrasts with "struggle." (A) **Effortless** and (D) **immediate** are possibilities. The word "but" before the first blank means something like "merely," so the word in the first blank has to suggest something small, like a faint prediction. **Glimmers** fits the meaning.

7. A

The word *although* indicates contrast, and the words "large number" and "mass" provide a clue to what's missing. We need something that means "different" for the first blank, and something that means "the same" for the second blank. This is basically what **disparate** and **homogeneous** mean.

8. A

We need something here that goes with "heavy thoughts." **Morose**, "gloomy," is the best choice.

9. E

The "demise" or death of the protagonist presumably "eliminated" all possibility of a sequel. That's what **precluded** means.

10. C

A **SCAR** is the mark left by an **INJURY**. A **dent** is the mark left by a **collision**. In (E), blood is not a permanent mark, and it is not always the result of a **fistfight**.

11. B

To **YAWN** to display **BOREDOM**. To **pout** is to display **displeasure**. One can **react** to any number of things; to **react** is not necessarily to show **surprise**.

12. E

An **ACTOR**'s tryout is called an **AUDITION**. A **gymnast**'s audition is called a **tryout**. In each of the other choices, there is a valid bridge, but not the stem bridge. In (A), a **debut** is a **singer's** first performance.

13. A

To **ALIENATE** is to impose **ESTRANGEMENT**, making people aliens or strangers. To **discommode** is to impose **inconvenience**. In (B), **monasticism** is the life of monks and nuns; these people are usually **sequestered** or separated from other people, not everyone who is **sequestered** enters a life of **monasticism** (for example, juries are often sequestered). In (C), **palliate** is to relieve **boredom**.

14. B

Something **PUNGENT** or foul-smelling is, by definition, unpleasant to be **SNIFFED**. Something **prickly** is unpleasant to be touched. Something (C) **venomous** does not necessarily work by being **bitten**.

15. B

To **DISCONCERT** is to cause **CONFUSION**. To **daunt** is to cause **discouragement**. Note that (D) is a bridgeless pair.

The Cold War Passage

The author of this passage has one overarching strategy: Set up the arguments of the revisionist historians and then knock 'em down. Paragraph 1 explains the things that, according to the revisionists, could have been done to avoid the Cold War, which are 1) the U.S. could have just accepted Soviet domination in Eastern Europe, 2) the U.S. could have given them money for reconstruction, and 3) the U.S. could have given up its monopoly of the bomb. Paragraphs 2 and 3 outline the author's refutation of these arguments; he concentrates on the American political atmosphere as the main reason that the revisionists' ideas were not really workable at the time. Revisionists, he then asserts in paragraph 4, would reject this politics-based argument and claim instead that it was the economic situation that forced American policy makers to oppose the Soviets. The author of course then knocks down this new argument; it is contradictory, he says, to say that American officials were caught in an economic tide and then to blame them for not doing things differently. The author concludes in the final paragraph by stating that there was essentially no way, given the climate in the Soviet Union, that the Cold War could have been avoided.

16. C

As we noted above, the author of this passage is primarily engaged in setting up and knocking down the arguments of the revisionist historians of the Cold War. This makes (C) correct and (E) wrong (the author is definitely not interested in reconciling his view with that of the revisionists). (A) is wrong because the ideas of the revisionists are not, as far as we know, a popular myth. (B) is out because the author is defending historical figures—the policy makers—for what they did, not criticizing them. (D) is too neutral a choice for this passage; the author does engage in analysis of the era of the beginning of the Cold War, but his purpose is to do far more than just analyze events. He wants to poke holes in revisionist theories.

17. C

When revisionists say that the U.S. could have "recognized" the Soviet influence in Eastern Europe, they mean that the U.S. could have formally **acknowledged** this Soviet presence. (C) is correct.

18. C

Look back to the second half of the second paragraph. The author says there that Roosevelt could never have recognized a Soviet Eastern Europe because the American people did not like the idea of the Soviets holding sway in that region. In particular, the president would have lost the votes of the Polish Americans who, you can infer, did not want the Soviets controlling their "old country." (C) spells out this point. Each of the other choices is a misreading of the context of the sentence about the Polish American voters.

19. E

In the second and third paragraphs, the author refutes the suggestions of the revisionists primarily by saying that the policy-makers couldn't do what was necessary to avoid the Cold War because the American people were against it. The assumption the author makes is that the policy makers **could not have been expected to ignore public opinion** (E). The author never says in the second and third paragraphs that the Soviets were to blame for failed U.S. peace initiatives (A), or that none of the alternatives would work (C)—what he does say, in a later paragraph, is that if peace initiatives had not run aground due to American politics, then they would have run aground due to the Soviet climate. The author also does not say in the second and third paragraphs that the American public was **well-informed** (B) or **overwhelmingly opposed to seeking peace** (D); all we know is that they opposed Soviet influence in Eastern Europe as well as the idea of giving up the atom bomb monopoly.

20. C

This question is closely linked to the previous one. The author refers to the "certain constraints" at the end of the third paragraph, in the midst of the discussion on the impact of public opinion on the policy-makers. From context, then, you know that the constraints the author is talking about are the opinions of the people—in other words, **the views of the electorate** (C). If you didn't put the sentence about "constraints" in context, any of the other choices might have looked appealing.

21. E

This question centers on the fourth paragraph, which is where the author explains the revisionists' view that American policy makers decided to oppose the Soviet Union because Soviet expansion could jeopardize U.S. trade and investment opportunities in Eastern Europe and elsewhere. (E) captures this idea. The author says nothing about illegal trading activities (A), nor does he indicate whether or not the Soviets knew about the negative impact they could have on the American economy (B). (C) is out because the Soviet Union was not recognized by the United States, so this could not possibly have had anything to do with the origin of the Cold War. (D) is wrong because there is no evidence in the paragraph to support it.

22. A

The author poses the question in order to show that there is a problem with the revisionists' economic interpretation of the Cold War: you can't blame the policy-makers if they didn't have any control. Thus the question serves to **point out an inconsistency** (A) in the revisionists' position. (D) might be tempting since the revisionists' view is pretty cynical, but the author is questioning that view here, not summing it up.

The James Weldon Johnson Passage

Johnson, the author of this autobiographical piece, does not just describe the experience he had watching the piano-player playing rag-time; he also uses the scene as a jumping-off point from which to comment on the origin of rag-time (second paragraph), to disparage American musicians for refusing to accept rag-time (third paragraph), and to speculate on what the piano player could have amounted to under different circumstances (fourth paragraph).

23. C

The author's initial impression of rag-time can be found in the first paragraph. He emphasizes how the beat demanded a physical response and meshed with the "dissonant harmonies," etc., to produce a "curious effect." (C) is the correct answer. The only other choice that has anything to do with the first paragraph is (B). (B) is wrong because the audience is said to have applauded the singer's dance steps, not the rag-time music.

24. E

Let's go through the choices one-by-one, keeping in mind that we're focusing exclusively on the first paragraph. Although the piano player is "master of a good deal of technique," choice (A) is too extreme to be correct. We know nothing in the first paragraph of the author's expectations of rag-time, so (B) is out too. (C), (D), and (E) are different interpretations of the author's description of the piano player's playing. While it is certainly true that rag-time has dissonant harmonies and jumps from one key to another, you cannot infer from this that rag-time violates every rule of musical composition (C) or that it has no melody at all (D). (E) is correct since the narrator notes that "the accents fell in the most unexpected places."

25. A

In the context of the phrase "questionable resorts about Memphis and St. Louis," the word *questionable* means **disreputable** (A).

26. C

Choice (B) might have jumped right out at you since the narrator's perspective in paragraph 1 is that of a mesmerized spectator, but his perspective in paragraphs 2 and 3 changes. He steps back from the description of his first encounter with rag-time and begins to discuss rag-time's history, appeal, and impact on the contemporary musical scene. Therefore, (C) is the correct answer. (A) is wrong because the author is not impartial; he thinks highly of rag-time. Watching rag-time playing is not a "unique experience," which eliminates (D). As for (E), the narrator says nothing about his youth in the second and third paragraphs.

27. A

Put the reference to the "theory of the universe" in the context of the second paragraph. The author says that the players who first developed rag-time knew "no more of the theory of music than they did of the theory of the universe"—in other words, they had no formal music education—but their natural talent guided them. Since they had no conventional schooling in music, you can infer that their invention, rag-time, was **an unconventional musical form** (A).

(B) and (E) are the close wrong answers. (B) is out because the originators of rag-time could have been interested in other people's music even though they had no formal music education. (E) is wrong since it misunderstands the overall point of the paragraph; the author is not interested in making general statements about the relationship between education and artistic success. (C) is the sort of choice you can rule out by common sense; no SAT question is going to have a correct answer that downplays the importance of academics. Finally, there is no evidence that indicates (D) could be true.

28. C

The narrator argues in the third paragraph that rag-time should not be ignored or dismissed by American musicians just because it is popular. All great music, he states, comes from the hearts of the people. In other words, he is saying that the **conservative and condescending attitude** of American musicians is misguided (C). There is no evidence in the third paragraph to support any of the other choices. (B) is perhaps the most tempting, since the author talks in the third paragraph about rag-time's popularity in Europe, but it seems as though American musicians do know about rag-time's popularity and find it distasteful.

29. E

This question is a follow-up on the previous one. As we've said, the author's argument in the third paragraph is that music should not be dismissed by serious musicians just because it happens to be popular. (E) paraphrases this idea. (A) stretches the author's argument way too far. (B) is wrong because the author does not try to establish criteria for musical greatness. (C) focuses too narrowly on the author's mention of the fact that rag-time was popular abroad. (D) is clearly wrong since rag-time gained popularity even though it had not been "taken up by a musical master."

30. D

The narrator poses to himself the question about what might have become of the piano player had he been properly trained and then answers himself by saying "perhaps he wouldn't have done anything at all." The narrator goes on to say that even if the piano player achieved some success as an imitator of the greats or as an innovator, he still would not have been as "delightful" as he was playing rag-time. Thus the statement that "perhaps he wouldn't have done anything at all" can best be interpreted as a **recognition that the piano player might have wasted his talent** (D) had he been formally trained. (A) and (B) are wrong because the narrator thinks highly of the piano player's skill even if that skill is not genius-level or particularly disciplined. (C) and (E) are both far too broad and too negative to be the correct answer.

31. C

The correct answer here is going to be a paraphrase of the idea that no matter how far the piano player would have gone if trained, he would not have been as delightful as he was as a rag-time player. (C) is the choice you're looking for. (E) is the most tempting wrong answer since the author's statements at the end of the passage can easily be misconstrued to mean that the piano player could never have been more than mediocre as a classical artist. However, "never" is too strong a word here—

the narrator is not, and cannot be, as sure as that—so this choice is wrong.

Section 5

1. E

Use FOIL:

$$(3x + 4)(4x - 3)$$
$$= (3x \times 4x) + [3x \times (-3)] + (4 \times 4x) + [4 \times (-3)]$$
$$= 12x^2 - 9x + 16x - 12$$
$$= 12x^2 + 7x - 12$$

2. C

When you know that the given parts add up to the whole, then you can turn a part-to-part ratio into 2 part-to-whole ratios—put each term of the ratio over the sum of the terms. In this case, since all the numbers in the set must be either integers or nonintegers, the parts do add up to the whole. The sum of the terms in the ratio 2:3 is 5, so the two part-to-whole ratios are 2:5 and 3:5.

$$\frac{\text{integers}}{\text{numbers}} = \frac{2}{5} = \frac{2}{5}(100\%) = \frac{200\%}{5} = 40\%$$

3. C

Get rid of the parentheses in the denominator, and then cancel factors the numerator and denominator have in common:

$$\frac{x^2 y^3 z^4}{(xyz^2)^2} = \frac{x^2 y^3 z^4}{x^2 y^2 z^4}$$
$$= \frac{x^2}{x^2} \times \frac{y^3}{y^2} \times \frac{z^4}{z^4}$$
$$= y$$

4. E

If p divided by 7 leaves a remainder of 5, you can say that $p = 7n + 5$, where n represents some integer. Multiply both sides by 5 to get $5p = 35n + 25$. The remainder when you divide 7 into $35n$ is 0. The reminder when you divide 7 into 25 is 4, so the remainder when you divide $5p$ by 7 is $0 + 4 = 4$.

For most people this one's a lot easier to do by picking numbers. Think of an example for p and try it out. p could be 12, for example, because when you divide 12 by 7, the remainder is 5. (p could also be 19, 26, 33, or any of infinitely many more possibilities.) Now multiply your chosen p by 5: $12 \times 5 = 60$. Divide 60 by 7 and see what the remainder is: $60 \div 7 = 8$, remainder 4.

5. B

To find the y-intercept of a line from its equation, put the equation in slope-intercept form:

$$2x - 3y = 18$$
$$-3y = -2x + 18$$
$$y = \frac{2}{3}x - 6$$

In this form, the y-intercept is what comes after the x—in this case it's -6.

6. C

Set up a proportion:

$$\frac{12 \text{ pages}}{1 \text{ hour}} = \frac{100 \text{ pages}}{x \text{ hours}}$$
$$12x = 100$$
$$x = \frac{100}{12} = 8\frac{1}{3}$$

One-third of an hour is $\frac{1}{3}$ of 60 minutes, or 20 minutes. So $8\frac{1}{3}$ hours is 8 hours and 20 minutes.

7. E

With a right triangle you can use the 2 legs as the base and the height to figure out the area. Here the leg lengths are expressed algebraically. Just plug the 2 expressions in for b and h in the triangle area formula:

$$\text{Area} = \frac{1}{2}(x-1)(x+1)$$

$$= \frac{1}{2}(x^2 - 1) = \frac{x^2 - 1}{2}$$

8. A

The easiest way to do this problem is to subtract Bill's money from the total of the money that Jim and Bill have. Doing this gives you $15 - 4 = 11$. However, the problem states that they have LESS THAN 15 dollars. Therefore, Jim must have less than 11 dollars. Of I, II, and III, the only value that is less than 11 is I, so the answer must be (A).

To solve this problem algebraically, set up an inequality where J is Jim's money and B is Bill's money:

$J + B < 15$ where $B = 4$

$J + 4 < 15$

$J < 11$

Again, be wary of the fact that this is an inequality, NOT an equation.

9. A

Pick numbers for x and y. For instance, say that Angelo makes 20 dollars for working 5 hours and Sarah makes 20 dollars for working 4 hours. In this case, Angelo makes \$4 per hour and Sarah makes \$5. The difference between their wages is \$1 per hour. Now plug 20 in for x and 5 in for y in each of the answer choices. Which ones give you a result of 1? Only (A), which is the answer.

10. D

A square with area 16 has sides of length 4. Therefore the largest circle that could possibly be cut from such a square would have a diameter of 4.

Such a circle would have a radius of 2, making its area 4π. So the amount of felt left after cutting such a circle from one of the squares of felt would be $16 - 4\pi$, or $4(4 - \pi)$. There are 8 such squares, so the total area of the left over felt is $8 \times 4(4 - \pi) = 32(4 - \pi)$.

SECTION 6

The Design Museums Passages

Passage 1   The position of the author of this passage starts to become clear in the second paragraph: she likes design museums and is willing to defend them against critics. She thinks design museums are not just advertisements for new technology but places where new products can be honored. Design museums, she asserts, are comfortable for visitors because the exhibits provide a lot of information about the objects displayed—information you wouldn't get in an art gallery. Another advantage of design museums, she says, is that their curators have more freedom than do the curators of public art galleries.

Passage 2   Author 2 does not hold technical and design museums in the same high regard as author 1 does, you soon find out in this passage. Author 2 complains about several things: 1) technical museums concentrate on present technology and ignore historical study and research; 2) they glorify machines and industrialization when these things do harm as well as good; and 3) they do not (and cannot safely and imaginatively) show machinery in action. Author 2 does admit at the very end, however, that the public has shown a healthy curiosity about science and technology.

1. A

To say that something is "readily available to the general public" is to say that it is **easily** available. (A) is the correct answer.

2. D

Author 1 says that department store windows try to sell you something whereas design exhibits try to give you an appreciation of the aesthetic value of something. (D) paraphrases this idea. (A), (B), and (E) can be readily eliminated. Be careful with (C), though. Even though design museums focus on the artistic qualities of products, it does not automatically follow from this that design museums are not concerned at all with the commercial aspects of a successful product. (C) is wrong.

3. B

In the third paragraph of Passage 1, the author argues that design museums make visitors feel comfortable because the exhibits illustrate the purpose behind the look and function of the displayed object; art gallery exhibits, by contrast, provide no such information. From this argument you can infer that author 1 thinks that visitors want to be informed about the object they are viewing. This makes (B) correct. There is no evidence to support any of the other choices, all of which are misreadings of paragraph 3. (A) can be eliminated as soon as you see "hostile towards . . . abstract art." (C) and (D) contradict the author, who says that visitors are not confused by technological exhibits since they are familiar and informative. (E) is an unwarranted inference based on the author's statement that design exhibits point out the artistic qualities of the displayed items; you cannot conclude from this that most museum visitors undervalue the artistic worth of household items.

4. B

Since you just reviewed paragraph 3 for the last question, the answer to this one should jump right out at you. The difference between a design museum exhibit and an art gallery exhibit is that a design museum exhibit provides you with information about the object being displayed, whereas the art gallery exhibit does not. (B) is correct. None of the other choices has any basis in the passage.

5. C

After mentioning the collection of Zippo lighters, etc., in London's Design Museum, author 1 says that curators of design museums have options that are far less rigorous, conventionalized and pre-programmed than those open to curators of art galleries. This is a fancy way of saying that the curators of design museums have more freedom to put together unconventional collections (C). (E) is the tempting wrong answer to this question. It's wrong because it goes too far: the design curators have freedom, but not, as far as we know, the freedom to satisfy "their own personal whims."

6. E

In the very last sentence of passage 1, the author says that design museums ("the display of postmodern playthings or quirky Japanese vacuum cleaners") are better able to represent humor than art galleries ("an exhibition of Impressionist landscapes"). The author is emphasizing the contrast between design museum and art gallery exhibits (E). (B) is the trickiest wrong answer. It misses the point of the last sentence because the author is not comparing "postmodern playthings" with Impressionist art; she is comparing the different ways these two things are exhibited.

7. A

The answer to this question will be the choice that summarizes paragraph 1. Since the author spends paragraph 1 complaining that design museums ignore the historical aspect of technology, choice

(A) is the best answer. (B) focuses too narrowly on the last part of the paragraph, where the author says that since industry builds the exhibits, curators may be dispensed with. This is not the underlying difficulty referred to at the beginning of the paragraph. The other choices have nothing to do with the first paragraph.

8. A

Author 2's point in the second paragraph is that industrialization and "progress" have not been all good and should be considered critically, but technology museums just glorify them. He mentions industrialization's harm to the environment and ecology to support this point and to encourage **a critical response** to technology, so (A) is correct. (B) is wrong because it's too negative even for this author. (C) is a distortion of a detail at the end of the second paragraph, while (D) is a distorted idea from the third paragraph. (E) is out because author 2 doesn't do any praising in the second paragraph.

9. D

Put the phrase in context. Author 2 says that displayed machinery should be in action, not in "sculptured repose," as is the case with the machinery in technology museums. To author 2, you can infer, the "sculptured repose" is meaningless and **unrealistic** (D). (A) is out because the author is not condemning the curators for poor planning; in fact, the author admits that displaying operating machinery would be extremely difficult. (B) can be eliminated because it's too extreme. The author never says which—if any—of the problems he discusses is the "greatest problem." (C) and (E) miss the author's point and the context in which the phrase "sculptured repose" is found.

10. D

Choices (A), (B), (C), and (E) are common synonyms for "command," but none of them works in the context of the phrase "command the imagination, ingenuity and manual dexterity it requires." Only choice (D) can do the job.

11. A

Predict the answer to the question before you go looking through the choices. You know that author 2 thinks that technology has had a lot of negative consequences, so you can assume that he would point this out in response to author 1's optimistic statement. This makes (A) the best answer. We don't know what author 2's position on art galleries is, so (B) is out. (C) comes from passage 2 but is irrelevant to the question asked in the stem. (D) and (E) contradict specific things author 2 says in the course of his passage.

12. B

In questions like this one, wrong answer choices are often statements that one author, but not both, would agree with. For example, author 2 would probably agree with choice (A) and would definitely agree with (D) and (E), but author 1 would most likely not agree with any of these three. That narrows the field to (B) and (C). (C) is a very general statement that really has no basis in either passage. (B), on the other hand, is an idea that can be found in both passages, so it is the correct answer.

APPENDIX A

SAT Math in a Nutshell

The math on the SAT covers a lot of ground—from arithmetic to algebra to geometry.

Don't let yourself be intimidated. We've highlighted the 100 most important concepts that you'll need for SAT Math and listed them in this appendix.

You've probably been taught most of these in school already, so this list is a great way to refresh your memory.

A MATH STUDY PLAN

Use this list to remind yourself of the key areas you'll need to know. Do four concepts a day, and you'll be ready within a month. If a concept continually causes you trouble, circle it and refer back to it as you try to do the questions.

Need more help? The math reference list comes from Kaplan's *SAT Math Workbook*. For more help with the Math section of the SAT, the workbook is a great place to start.

NUMBER PROPERTIES

1. Integer/Noninteger

Integers are **whole numbers**; they include negative whole numbers and zero.

2. Rational/Irrational Numbers

A rational number is a number that can be expressed as **a ratio of two integers**. Irrational numbers are real numbers—they have locations on the number line; they just **can't be expressed precisely as fractions or decimals**. For the purposes of the SAT, the most important irrational numbers are $\sqrt{2}$, $\sqrt{3}$, and π.

3. Adding/Subtracting Signed Numbers

To **add a positive and a negative**, first ignore the signs and find the positive difference between the number parts. Then attach the sign of the original number with the larger number part. For example, to add 23 and –34, first we ignore the minus sign and find the positive difference between 23 and 34—that's 11. Then we attach the sign of the number with the larger number part—in this case it's the minus sign from the –34. So, $23 + (-34) = -11$.

Make **subtraction** situations simpler by turning them into addition. For example, think of $-17 - (-21)$ as $-17 + (+21)$.

To **add or subtract a string of positives and negatives**, first turn everything into addition. Then combine the positives and negatives so that the string is reduced to the sum of a single positive number and a single negative number.

4. Multiplying/Dividing Signed Numbers

To multiply and/or divide positives and negatives, treat the number parts as usual and **attach a minus sign if there were originally an odd number of negatives**. For example, to multiply –2, –3, and –5, first multiply the number parts: $2 \times 3 \times 5 = 30$. Then go back and note that there were three—an odd number—negatives, so the product is negative: $(-2) \times (-3) \times (-5) = -30$.

5. PEMDAS

When performing multiple operations, remember **PEMDAS**, which means **Parentheses** first, then **Exponents**, then **Multiplication and Division** (left to right), and lastly, **Addition and Subtraction** (left to right). In the expression $9 - 2 \times (5 - 3)^2 + 6 \div 3$, begin with the parentheses: $(5 - 3) = 2$. Then do the exponent: $2^2 = 4$. Now the expression is: $9 - 2 \times 4 + 6 \div 3$. Next do the multiplication and division to get: $9 - 8 + 2$, which equals 3. If you have difficulty remembering PEMDAS, use this sentence to recall it: **Please Excuse My Dear Aunt Sally**.

6. **Counting Consecutive Integers**

To count consecutive integers, **subtract the smallest from the largest and add 1**. To count the integers from 13 through 31, subtract: $31 - 13 = 18$. Then add 1: $18 + 1 = 19$.

DIVISIBILITY

7. Factor/Multiple

The factors of integer n are the positive integers that divide into n with no remainder. The multiples of n are the integers that n divides into with no remainder. For example, 6 is a factor of 12, and 24 is a multiple of 12. 12 is both a factor and a multiple of itself, since $12 \times 1 = 12$ and $12 \div 1 = 12$.

8. Prime Factorization

To find the prime factorization of an integer, just keep breaking it up into factors until **all the factors are prime**. To find the prime factorization of 36, for example, you could begin by breaking it into 4×9, then break that into $2 \times 2 \times 3 \times 3$.

9. Relative Primes

Relative primes are integers that have no common factor other than 1. To determine whether two integers are relative primes, break them both down to their prime factorizations. For example: $35 = 5 \times 7$, and $54 = 2 \times 3 \times 3 \times 3$. They have **no prime factors in common**, so 35 and 54 are relative primes.

10. Common Multiple

A common multiple is a number that is a multiple of two or more integers. You can always get a common multiple of two integers by **multiplying** them, but, unless the two numbers are relative primes, the product will not be the *least* common multiple. For example, to find a common multiple for 12 and 15, you could just multiply: $12 \times 15 = 180$.

11. Least Common Multiple (LCM)

To find the least common multiple, check out the **multiples of the larger integer** until you find one that's **also a multiple of the smaller**. To find the LCM of 12 and 15, begin by taking the multiples of 15. 15 is not divisible by 12; 30 is not; nor is 45. But the next multiple of 15, 60, *is* divisible by 12, so it's the LCM.

12. Greatest Common Factor (GCF)

To find the greatest common factor, break down both integers into their prime factorizations and multiply **all the prime factors they have in common**. $36 = 2 \times 2 \times 3 \times 3$, and $48 = 2 \times 2 \times 2 \times 2 \times 3$. What they have in common is two 2s and one 3, so the GCF is $2 \times 2 \times 3 = 12$.

13. Even/Odd

To predict whether a sum, difference, or product will be even or odd, just **take simple numbers such as 1 and 2 and see what happens**. There are rules—"odd times even is even," for example—but there's no need to memorize them. What happens with one set of numbers generally happens with all similar sets.

14. Multiples of 2 and 4

An integer is divisible by 2 (which is even) if the **last digit is even**. An integer is divisible by 4 if the **last two digits form a multiple of 4**. The last digit of 562 is 2, which is even, so 562 is a multiple of 2. The last two digits form 62, which is *not* divisible by 4, so 562 is not a multiple of 4. The integer 512, however, is divisible by four because the last two digits form 12, which is a multiple of 4.

15. Multiples of 3 and 9

An integer is divisible by 3 if the **sum of its digits is divisible by 3**. An integer is divisible by 9 if the **sum of its digits is divisible by 9**. The sum of the digits in 957 is 21, which is divisible by 3 but not by 9, so 957 is divisible by 3 but not by 9.

16. Multiples of 5 and 10

An integer is divisible by 5 if the **last digit is 5 or 0**. An integer is divisible by 10 if the **last digit is 0**. The last digit of 665 is 5, so 665 is a multiple of 5 but *not* a multiple of 10.

17. Remainders

The remainder is the **whole number left over after division**. 487 is 2 more than 485, which is a multiple of 5, so when 487 is divided by 5, the remainder will be 2.

FRACTIONS AND DECIMALS

18. Reducing Fractions

To reduce a fraction to lowest terms, **factor out and cancel** all factors the numerator and denominator have in common.

$$\frac{28}{36} = \frac{4 \times 7}{4 \times 9} = \frac{7}{9}$$

19. Adding/Subtracting Fractions

To add or subtract fractions, first find a **common denominator**, then add or subtract the numerators.

$$\frac{2}{15} + \frac{3}{10} = \frac{4}{30} + \frac{9}{30} = \frac{4+9}{30} = \frac{13}{30}$$

20. Multiplying Fractions

To multiply fractions, **multiply** the numerators and **multiply** the denominators.

$$\frac{5}{7} \times \frac{3}{4} = \frac{5 \times 3}{7 \times 4} = \frac{15}{28}$$

21. Dividing Fractions

To divide fractions, **invert** the second one and **multiply**.

$$\frac{1}{2} \div \frac{3}{5} = \frac{1}{2} \times \frac{5}{3} = \frac{1 \times 5}{2 \times 3} = \frac{5}{6}$$

22. Converting a Mixed Number to an Improper Fraction

To convert a mixed number to an improper fraction, **multiply** the whole number part by the denominator, then **add** the numerator. The result is the new numerator (over the same denominator). To convert $7\frac{1}{3}$, first multiply 7 by 3, then add 1, to get the new numerator of 22. Put that over the same denominator, 3, to get $\frac{22}{3}$.

23. Converting an Improper Fraction to a Mixed Number

To convert an improper fraction to a mixed number, divide the denominator into the numerator to get a **whole number quotient with a remainder**. The quotient becomes the whole number part of the mixed number, and the remainder becomes the new numerator— with the same denominator. For example, to convert $\frac{108}{5}$, first divide 5 into 108, which yields 21 with a remainder of 3. Therefore, $\frac{108}{5} = 21\frac{3}{5}$.

24. Reciprocal

To find the reciprocal of a fraction, **switch the numerator and the denominator**. The reciprocal of $\frac{3}{7}$ is $\frac{7}{3}$. The reciprocal of 5 is $\frac{1}{5}$. The product of reciprocals is 1.

25. Comparing Fractions

One way to compare fractions is to **re-express them with a common denominator.** $\frac{3}{4} = \frac{21}{28}$ and $\frac{5}{7} = \frac{20}{28}$. $\frac{21}{28}$ is greater than $\frac{20}{28}$, so $\frac{3}{4}$ is greater than $\frac{5}{7}$. Another way to compare fractions is to **convert them both to decimals.** $\frac{3}{4}$ converts to .75, and $\frac{5}{7}$ converts to approximately .714.

26. Converting Fractions to Decimals

To convert a fraction to a decimal, **divide the bottom into the top**. To convert $\frac{5}{8}$, divide 8 into 5, yielding .625.

27. Converting Decimals to Fractions

To convert a decimal to a fraction, set the decimal over 1 and **multiply the numerator and denominator by 10 raised to the number of digits to the right of the decimal point.** For instance, to convert .625 to a fraction, you would multiply $\frac{.625}{1}$ by $\frac{10^3}{10^3}$, or $\frac{1000}{1000}$. Then simplify: $\frac{625}{1000} = \frac{5 \times 125}{8 \times 125} = \frac{5}{8}$.

28. Repeating Decimal

To find a particular digit in a repeating decimal, note the **number of digits in the cluster that repeats.** If there are 2 digits in that cluster, then every second digit is the same. If there are three digits in that cluster, then every third digit is the same. And so on. For example, the decimal equivalent of $\frac{1}{27}$ is .037037037..., which is best written $.\overline{037}$. There are three digits in the repeating cluster, so every third digit is the same: 7. To find the 50th digit, look for the multiple of three just less than 50—that's 48. The 48th digit is 7, and with the 49th digit the pattern repeats with 0. The 50th digit is 3.

29. Identifying the Parts and the Whole

The key to solving most fractions and percents story problems is to identify the part and the whole. Usually you'll find the **part** associated with the verb *is/are* and the **whole** associated with the word *of*. In the sentence, "Half of the boys are blonds," the whole is the boys ("of the boys"), and the part is the blonds ("are blonds").

PERCENTS

30. Percent Formula

Whether you need to find the part, the whole, or the percent, use the same formula:

Part = Percent × Whole

Example:	What is 12% of 25?
Setup:	Part = .12 × 25

Example:	15 is 3% of what number?
Setup:	15 = .03 × Whole

Example:	45 is what percent of 9?
Setup:	45 = Percent × 9

31. Percent Increase and Decrease

To increase a number by a percent, **add the percent to 100 percent**, convert to a decimal, and multiply. To increase 40 by 25 percent, add 25 percent to 100 percent, convert 125 percent to 1.25, and multiply by 40. 1.25 × 40 = 50.

32. Finding the Original Whole

To find the **original whole before a percent increase or decrease, set up an equation**. Think of the result of a 15 percent increase over x as $1.15x$.

Example:	After a 5 percent increase, the population was 59,346. What was the population before the increase?
Setup:	$1.05x = 59,346$

33. Combined Percent Increase and Decrease

To determine the combined effect of multiple percent increases and/or decreases, **start with 100 and see what happens.**

Example:	A price went up 10 percent one year, and the new price went up 20 percent the next year. What was the combined percent increase?
Setup:	First year: 100 + (10 percent of 100) = 110. Second year: 110 + (20 percent of 110) = 132. That's a combined 32 percent increase.

RATIOS, PROPORTIONS, AND RATES

34. Setting up a Ratio

To find a ratio, put the number associated with the word *of* **on top** and the quantity associated with the word *to* **on the bottom** and reduce. The ratio of 20 oranges to 12 apples is $\frac{20}{12}$, which reduces to $\frac{5}{3}$.

35. Part-to-Part Ratios and Part-to-Whole Ratios

If the parts add up to the whole, a part-to-part ratio can be turned into two part-to-whole ratios by putting **each number in the original ratio over the sum of the numbers**. If the ratio of males to females is 1 to 2, then the males-to-people ratio is $\frac{1}{1+2} = \frac{1}{3}$ and the females-to-people ratio is $\frac{2}{1+2} = \frac{2}{3}$. In other words, $\frac{2}{3}$ of all the people are female.

36. Solving a Proportion

To solve a proportion, **cross-multiply**:

$$\frac{x}{5} = \frac{3}{4}$$

$$4x = 3 \times 5$$

$$x = \frac{15}{4} = 3.75$$

37. Rate

To solve a rates problem, **use the units** to keep things straight.

Example: If snow is falling at the rate of one foot every four hours, how many inches of snow will fall in seven hours?

Setup: $$\frac{1 \text{ foot}}{4 \text{ hours}} = \frac{x \text{ inches}}{7 \text{ hours}}$$

$$\frac{12 \text{ inches}}{4 \text{ hours}} = \frac{x \text{ inches}}{7 \text{ hours}}$$

$$4x = 12 \times 7$$

$$x = 21$$

38. Average Rate

Average rate is *not* simply the average of the rates.

$$\text{Average A per B} = \frac{\text{Total } A}{\text{Total } B}$$

$$\text{Average Speed} = \frac{\text{Total distance}}{\text{Total time}}$$

To find the average speed for 120 miles at 40 mph and 120 miles at 60 mph, **don't just average the two speeds**. First figure out the total distance and the total time. The total distance is 120 + 120 = 240 miles. The times are two hours for the first leg and three hours for the second leg, or five hours total. The average speed, then, is $\frac{240}{5}$ = 48 miles per hour.

AVERAGES

39. Average Formula

To find the average of a set of numbers, **add them up and divide by the number of numbers**.

$$\textbf{Average} = \frac{\textbf{Sum of the terms}}{\textbf{Number of terms}}$$

To find the average of the five numbers 12, 15, 23, 40, and 40, first add them: 12 + 15 + 23 + 40 + 40 = 130. Then divide the sum by 5: 130 ÷ 5 = 26.

40. Average of Evenly Spaced Numbers

To find the average of evenly spaced numbers, just **average the smallest and the largest**. The average of all the integers from 13 through 77 is the same as the average of 13 and 77:

$$\frac{13 + 77}{2} = \frac{90}{2} = 45$$

41. Using the Average to Find the Sum

$$\textbf{Sum = (Average)} \times \textbf{(Number of terms)}$$

If the average of 10 numbers is 50, then they add up to 10 × 50, or 500.

42. Finding the Missing Number

To find a missing number when you're given the average, **use the sum**. If the average of four numbers is 7, then the sum of those four numbers is 4 × 7, or 28. Suppose that three of the numbers are 3, 5, and 8. These three numbers add up to 16 of that 28, which leaves 12 for the fourth number.

43. Median

The median of a set of numbers is the **value that falls in the middle of the set**. If you have five test scores, and they are 88, 86, 57, 94, and 73, you must first list the scores in increasing or decreasing order: 57, 73, 86, 88, 94.

The median is the middle number, or 86. If there is an even number of values in a set (six test scores, for instance), simply take the average of the two middle numbers.

44. Mode

The mode of a set of numbers is the **value that appears most often**. If your test scores were 88, 57, 68, 85, 99, 93, 93, 84, and 81, the mode of the scores would be 93 because it appears more often than any other score. If there is a tie for the most common value in a set, the set has more than one mode.

POSSIBILITIES AND PROBABILITY

45. Counting the Possibilities

The fundamental counting principle: If there are **m ways** one event can happen and **n ways** a second event can happen, then there are **$m \times n$ ways** for the two events to happen. For example, with five shirts and seven pairs of pants to choose from, you can put together $5 \times 7 = 35$ different outfits.

46. Probability

$$\text{Probability} = \frac{\text{Favorable outcomes}}{\text{Total possible outcomes}}$$

For example, if you have 12 shirts in a drawer and nine of them are white, the probability of picking a white shirt at random is $\frac{9}{12} = \frac{3}{4}$. This probability can also be expressed as .75 or 75 percent.

POWERS AND ROOTS

47. Multiplying and Dividing Powers

To multiply powers with the same base, **add the exponents and keep the same base:**
$$x^3 \times x^4 = x^{3+4} = x^7$$

To divide powers with the same base, **subtract the exponents and keep the same base:**
$$y^{13} \div y^8 = y^{13-8} = y^5$$

48. Raising Powers to Powers

To raise a power to a power, **multiply the exponents:**

$$(x^3)^4 = x^{3 \times 4} = x^{12}$$

49. Simplifying Square Roots

To simplify a square root, **factor out the perfect squares** under the radical, unsquare them, and put the result in front.

$$\sqrt{12} = \sqrt{4 \times 3} = \sqrt{4} \times \sqrt{3} = 2\sqrt{3}$$

50. Adding and Subtracting Roots

You can add or subtract radical expressions **when the part under the radicals is the same:**

$$2\sqrt{3} + 3\sqrt{3} = 5\sqrt{3}$$

Don't try to add or subtract when the radical parts are different. There's not much you can do with an expression like:

$$3\sqrt{5} + 3\sqrt{7}$$

51. Multiplying and Dividing Roots

The product of square roots is equal to the **square root of the product:**

$$\sqrt{3} \times \sqrt{5} + \sqrt{3 \times 5} = \sqrt{15}$$

The quotient of square roots is equal to the **square root of the quotient:**

$$\frac{\sqrt{6}}{\sqrt{3}} = \sqrt{\frac{6}{3}} = \sqrt{2}$$

ALGEBRAIC EXPRESSIONS

52. Evaluating an Expression

To evaluate an algebraic expression, **plug in** the given values for the unknowns and calculate according to **PEMDAS**. To find the value of $x^2 + 5x - 6$ when $x = -2$, plug in -2 for x: $(-2)^2 + 5(-2) - 6 = 4 - 10 - 6 = -12$.

53. Adding and Subtracting Monomials

To combine like terms, **keep the variable part unchanged while adding or subtracting the coefficients:**

$$2a + 3a = (2 + 3)a = 5a$$

54. Adding and Subtracting Polynomials

To add or subtract polynomials, **combine like terms**.

$$(3x^2 + 5x - 7) - (x^2 + 12) =$$
$$(3x^2 - x^2) + 5x + (-7 - 12) =$$
$$2x^2 + 5x - 19$$

55. Multiplying Monomials

To multiply monomials, **multiply the coefficients and the variables separately:**

$$2a \times 3a = (2 \times 3)(a \times a) = 6a^2$$

56. Multiplying Binomials—FOIL

To multiply binomials, use **FOIL**. To multiply $(x + 3)$ by $(x + 4)$, first multiply the **First** terms: $x \times x = x^2$. Next the **Outer** terms: $x \times 4 = 4x$. Then the **Inner** terms: $3 \times x = 3x$. And finally the **Last** terms: $3 \times 4 = 12$. Then add and combine like terms:

$$x^2 + 4x + 3x + 12 = x^2 + 7x + 12$$

57. Multiplying Other Polynomials

FOIL works only when you want to multiply two binomials. If you want to multiply polynomials with more than two terms, make sure you **multiply each term in the first polynomial by each term in the second.**

$$(x^2 + 3x + 4)(x + 5) =$$
$$x^2(x + 5) + 3x(x + 5) + 4(x + 5) =$$
$$x^3 + 5x^2 + 3x^2 + 15x + 4x + 20 =$$
$$x^3 + 8x^2 + 19x + 20$$

After multiplying two polynomials together, the number of terms in your expression before simplifying should equal the number of terms in one polynomial multiplied by the number of terms in the second. In the example above, you should have $3 \times 2 = 6$ terms in the product before you simplify like terms.

FACTORING ALGEBRAIC EXPRESSIONS

58. Factoring out a Common Divisor

A factor common to all terms of a polynomial can be **factored out**. Each of the three terms in the polynomial $3x^3 + 12x^2 - 6x$ contains a factor of $3x$. Pulling out the common factor yields $3x(x^2 + 4x - 2)$.

59. Factoring the Difference of Squares

One of the test maker's favorite factorables is the **difference of squares**.

$$a^2 - b^2 = (a - b)(a + b)$$

$x^2 - 9$, for example, factors to $(x - 3)(x + 3)$.

60. Factoring the Square of a Binomial

Learn to recognize polynomials that are squares of binomials:

$$a^2 + 2ab + b^2 = (a + b)^2$$
$$a^2 - 2ab + b^2 = (a - b)^2$$

For example, $4x^2 + 12x + 9$ factors to $(2x + 3)^2$, and $n^2 - 10n + 25$ factors to $(n - 5)^2$.

61. Factoring Other Polynomials—FOIL in Reverse

To factor a quadratic expression, **think about what binomials you could use FOIL on to get that quadratic expression**. To factor $x^2 - 5x + 6$, think about what First terms will produce x^2, what Last terms will produce $+6$, and what Outer and Inner terms will produce $-5x$. Some common sense—and a little trial and error—lead you to $(x - 2)(x - 3)$.

62. Simplifying an Algebraic Fraction

Simplifying an algebraic fraction is a lot like simplifying a numerical fraction. The general idea is to **find factors common to the numerator and denominator and cancel them**. Thus, simplifying an algebraic fraction begins with factoring.

For example, to simplify $\dfrac{x^2 - x - 12}{x^2 - 9}$, first factor the numerator and denominator:

$$\frac{x^2 - x - 12}{x^2 - 9} = \frac{(x - 4)(x + 3)}{(x - 3)(x + 3)}$$

Canceling $x + 3$ from the numerator and denominator leaves you with $\dfrac{x - 4}{x - 3}$.

SOLVING EQUATIONS

63. Solving a Linear Equation

To solve an equation, do whatever is necessary to both sides to **isolate the variable**. To solve the equation $5x - 12 = -2x + 9$, first get all the xs on one side by adding $2x$ to both sides: $7x - 12 = 9$. Then add 12 to both sides: $7x = 21$. Then divide both sides by 7: $x = 3$.

64. Solving "in Terms of"

To solve an equation for one variable **in terms of** another means to **isolate the one variable on one side of the equation**, leaving an expression containing the other variable on the other side of the equation. To solve the equation $3x - 10y = -5x + 6y$ for x in terms of y, isolate x:

$$3x - 10y = -5x + 6y$$
$$3x + 5x = 6y + 10y$$
$$8x = 16y$$
$$x = 2y$$

65. Translating from English into Algebra

To translate from English into algebra, **look for the key words and systematically turn phrases into algebraic expressions and sentences into equations**. Be careful about order, especially when subtraction is called for.

Example: The charge for a phone call is r cents for the first three minutes and s cents for each minute thereafter. What is the cost, in cents, of a phone call lasting exactly t minutes? $(t > 3)$

Setup: The charge begins with r, and then something more is added, depending on the length of the call. The amount added is s times the number of minutes past three minutes. If the total number of minutes is t, then the number of minutes past three is $t - 3$. So the charge is $r + s(t - 3)$.

66. Solving a Quadratic Equation

To solve a quadratic equation, put it in the "$ax^2 + bx + c = 0$" form, **factor** the left side (if you can), and set each factor equal to 0 separately to get the two solutions. To solve $x^2 + 12 = 7x$, first rewrite it as $x^2 - 7x + 12 = 0$. Then factor the left side:

$$(x - 3)(x - 4) = 0$$
$$x - 3 = 0 \text{ or } x - 4 = 0$$
$$x = 3 \text{ or } 4$$

67. Solving a System of Equations

You can solve for two variables only if you have two distinct equations. Two forms of the same equation will not be adequate. **Combine the equations** in such a way that **one of the variables cancels out**. To solve the two equations $4x + 3y = 8$ and $x + y = 3$, multiply both sides of the second equation by -3 to get: $-3x - 3y = -9$. Now add the two equations; the $3y$ and the $-3y$ cancel out, leaving: $x = -1$. Plug that back into either one of the original equations and you'll find that $y = 4$.

68. Solving an Inequality

To solve an inequality, do whatever is necessary to both sides to **isolate the variable**. Just remember that when you **multiply or divide both sides by a negative number**, you must **reverse the sign**. To solve $-5x + 7 < -3$, subtract 7 from both sides to get: $-5x < -10$. Now divide both sides by -5, remembering to reverse the sign: $x > 2$.

COORDINATE GEOMETRY

69. Finding the Distance Between Two Points

To find the distance between points, use the **Pythagorean theorem or special right triangles**. The difference between the xs is one leg and the difference between the ys is the other.

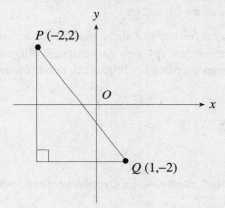

In the figure above, PQ is the hypotenuse of a 3-4-5 triangle, so $PQ = 5$.

You can also use the **distance formula**:

$$d = \sqrt{(x^1 - x^2)^2 + (y^1 - y^2)^2}$$

To find the distance between $R(3, 6)$ and $S(5, -2)$:

$$d = \sqrt{(3 - 5)^2 + [6 - (2)]^2}$$
$$= \sqrt{(-2)^2 + (8)^2}$$
$$= \sqrt{68} = 2\sqrt{17}$$

70. Using Two Points to Find the Slope

$$\text{Slope} = \frac{\text{Change in } y}{\text{Change in } x} = \frac{\text{Rise}}{\text{Run}}$$

The slope of the line that contains the points $A(2, 3)$ and $B(0, -1)$ is:

$$\frac{y_A - y_B}{x_A - x_B} = \frac{3 - (-1)}{2 - 0} = \frac{4}{2} = 2$$

71. Using an Equation to Find the Slope

To find the slope of a line from an equation, put the equation into the **slope-intercept** form:

$$y = mx + b$$

The **slope is m**. To find the slope of the equation $3x + 2y = 4$, rearrange it:

$$3x + 2y = 4$$
$$2y = -3x + 4$$
$$y = \frac{3}{2}x + 2$$

The slope is $-\frac{3}{2}$.

72. Using an Equation to Find an Intercept

To find the y-intercept, you can either put the equation into $y = mx + b$ (slope-intercept) form—in which case b is the y-intercept—or you can just **plug $x = 0$** into the equation and **solve for y**. To find the x-intercept, **plug $y = 0$** into the equation and **solve for x**.

LINES AND ANGLES

73. Intersecting Lines

When two lines intersect, **adjacent angles are supplementary and vertical angles are equal**.

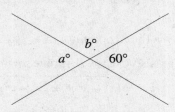

In the figure above, the angles marked $a°$ and $b°$ are adjacent and supplementary, so $a + b = 180$. Furthermore, the angles marked $a°$ and $60°$ are vertical and equal, so $a = 60$.

74. Parallel Lines and Transversals

A transversal across parallel lines forms **four equal acute angles and four equal obtuse angles.**

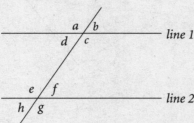

In the figure above, line 1 is parallel to line 2. Angles *a*, *c*, *e*, and *g* are obtuse, so they are all equal. Angles *b*, *d*, *f*, and *h* are acute, so they are all equal.

Furthermore, **any of the acute angles is supplementary to any of the obtuse angles.** Angles *a* and *h* are supplementary, as are *b* and *e*, *c* and *f*, and so on.

TRIANGLES—GENERAL

75. Interior Angles of a Triangle

The three angles of any triangle add up to 180°.

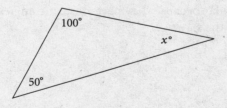

In the figure above, $x + 50 + 100 = 180$, so $x = 30$.

76. Exterior Angles of a Triangle

An exterior angle of a triangle is equal to the **sum of the remote interior angles.**

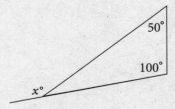

In the figure above, the exterior angle labeled $x°$ is equal to the sum of the remote angles: $x = 50 + 100 = 150$.

The three exterior angles of a triangle add up to 360°.

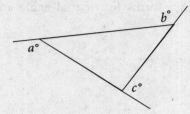

In the figure above, $a + b + c = 360$.

77. Similar Triangles

Similar triangles have the same shape; **corresponding angles are equal and corresponding sides are proportional.**

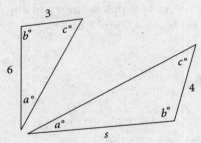

The triangles above are similar because they have the same angles. The 3 corresponds to the 4 and the 6 corresponds to the *s*.

$$\frac{3}{4} = \frac{6}{s}$$

$$3s = 24$$

$$s = 8$$

78. Area of a Triangle

$$\text{Area of Triangle} = \frac{1}{2}(\text{base})(\text{height})$$

The height is the perpendicular distance between the side that's chosen as the base and the opposite vertex.

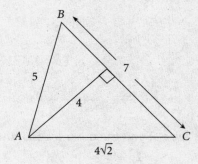

In the triangle above, 4 is the height when the 7 is chosen as the base.

$$\text{Area} = \frac{1}{2}bh = \frac{1}{2}(7)(4) = 14$$

79. Triangle Inequality Theorem

The length of one side of a triangle must be **greater than the difference and less than the sum** of the lengths of the other two sides. For example, if it is given that the length of one side is 3 and the length of another side is 7, then you know that the length of the third side must be greater than $7 - 3 = 4$ and less than $7 + 3 = 10$.

80. Isosceles Triangles

An isosceles triangle is a triangle that has **two equal sides**. Not only are two sides equal, but the angles opposite the equal sides, called base angles, are also equal.

81. Equilateral Triangles

Equilateral triangles are triangles in which **all three sides are equal.** Since all the sides are equal, all the angles are also equal. All three angles in an equilateral triangle measure 60 degrees, regardless of the lengths of sides.

RIGHT TRIANGLES

82. Pythagorean Theorem

For all right triangles:

$$(\text{leg}_1)^2 + (\text{leg}_2)^2 = (\text{hypotenuse})^2$$

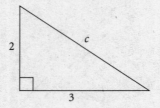

If one leg is 2 and the other leg is 3, then:

$$2^2 + 3^2 = c^2$$
$$c^2 = 4 + 9$$
$$c = \sqrt{13}$$

83. The 3-4-5 Triangle

If a right triangle's leg-to-leg ratio is 3:4, or if the leg-to-hypotenuse ratio is 3:5 or 4:5, it's a 3-4-5 triangle and you don't need to use the Pythagorean theorem to find the third side. Just figure out what multiple of 3-4-5 it is.

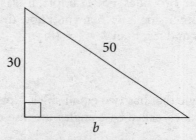

In the right triangle shown, one leg is 30 and the hypotenuse is 50. This is 10 times 3-4-5. The other leg is 40.

84. The 5-12-13 Triangle

If a right triangle's leg-to-leg ratio is 5:12, or if the leg-to-hypotenuse ratio is 5:13 or 12:13, then it's a 5-12-13 triangle. You don't need to use the Pythagorean theorem to find the third side. Just figure out what multiple of 5-12-13 it is.

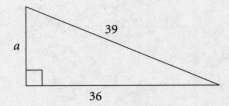

Here one leg is 36 and the hypotenuse is 39. This is 3 times 5-12-13. The other leg is 15.

85. The 30-60-90 Triangle

The sides of a 30-60-90 triangle are in a ratio of $x : x : x\sqrt{3} : 2x$; the Pythagorean theorem is not necessary.

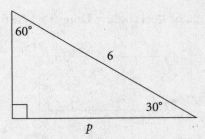

If the hypotenuse is 6, then the shorter leg is half that, or 3; and then the longer leg is equal to the short leg times $\sqrt{3}$, or $3\sqrt{3}$.

86. The 45-45-90 Triangle

The sides of a 45-45-90 triangle are in a ratio of $x : x : x : \sqrt{2}$.

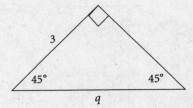

If one leg is 3, then the other leg is also 3, and the hypotenuse is equal to a leg times $\sqrt{2}$, or $3\sqrt{2}$.

OTHER POLYGONS

87. Characteristics of a Rectangle

A rectangle is a **four-sided figure with four right angles**. Opposite sides are equal. Diagonals are equal.

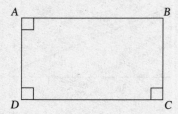

Quadrilateral *ABCD* above is shown to have three right angles. The fourth angle therefore also measures 90°, and *ABCD* is a rectangle. The perimeter of a rectangle is equal to the sum of the lengths of the four sides, which is equivalent to 2(length + width).

88. Area of a Rectangle

Area of Rectangle = Length × Width

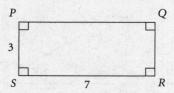

The area of a 7-by-3 rectangle is $7 \times 3 = 21$.

89. Characteristics of a Parallelogram

A parallelogram has **two pairs of parallel sides**. Opposite sides are equal. Opposite angles are equal. Consecutive angles add up to 180°.

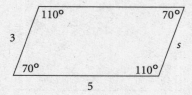

In the figure above, *s* is the length of the side opposite the 3, so $s = 3$.

90. Area of a Parallelogram

Area of Parallelogram = Base × Height

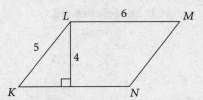

In parallelogram *KLMN* above, 4 is the height when *LM* or *KN* is used as the base. Base × height = 6 × 4 = 24.

91. Characteristics of a Square

A square is a **rectangle with four equal sides**.

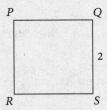

If *PQRS* is a square, all sides are the same length as *QR*. The perimeter of a square is equal to four times the length of one side.

92. Area of a Square

Area of Square = (Side)^2

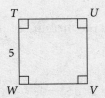

The square above, with sides of length 5, has an area of $5^2 = 25$.

93. Interior Angles of a Polygon

The **sum of the measures of the interior angles of a polygon = $(n - 2) \times 180$**, where *n* is the number of sides.

Sum of the Angles = $(n - 2) \times 180$

The eight angles of an octagon, for example, add up to $(8 - 2) \times 180 = 1{,}080$.

CIRCLES

94. Circumference of a Circle

Circumference = $2\pi r$

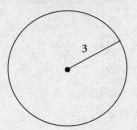

In the circle above, the radius is 3, and so the circumference is $2\pi(3) = 6\pi$.

95. Length of an Arc

An **arc** is a piece of the circumference. If n is the degree measure of the arc's central angle, then the formula is:

$$\textbf{Length of an Arc} = \left(\frac{n}{360}\right)\!\left(2\pi r\right)$$

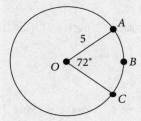

In the figure above, the radius is 5 and the measure of the central angle is 72°. The arc length is $\frac{72}{360}$ or $\frac{1}{5}$ of the circumference:

$$\left(\frac{72}{360}\right)(2\pi)(5) = \frac{1}{5}(10\pi) = 2\pi$$

96. Area of a Circle

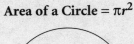

Area of a Circle = πr^2

The area of the circle is $\pi(4)^2 = 16\pi$.

97. Area of a Sector

A **sector** is a piece of the area of a circle. If n is the degree measure of the sector's central angle, then the formula is:

$$\textbf{Area of a Sector} = \left(\frac{n}{360}\right)\left(\pi r^2\right)$$

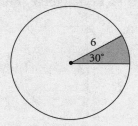

In the figure above, the radius is 6 and the measure of the sector's central angle is 30°. The sector has $\frac{30}{360}$ or $\frac{1}{12}$ of the area of the circle:

$$\left(\frac{30}{360}\right)(\pi)(6^2) = \left(\frac{1}{12}\right)(36\pi) = 3\pi$$

SOLIDS

98. Surface Area of a Rectangular Solid

The surface of a rectangular solid consists of three pairs of identical faces. To find the surface area, find the area of each face and add them up. If the length is l, the width is w, and the height is h, the formula is:

Surface Area = $2lw + 2wh + 2lh$

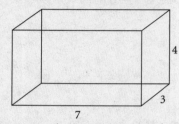

The surface area of the box above is: $2 \times 7 \times 3 + 2 \times 3 \times 4 + 2 \times 7 \times 4 = 42 + 24 + 56 = 122$

99. Volume of a Rectangular Solid

Volume of a Rectangular Solid = lwh

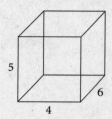

The volume of a 4-by-5-by-6 box is $4 \times 5 \times 6 = 120$.

A cube is a rectangular solid with length, width, and height all equal. If e is the length of an edge of a cube, the volume formula is:

Volume of a Cube = e^3

The volume of this cube is $2^3 = 8$.

100. Volume of a Cylinder

Volume of a Cylinder $= \pi r^2 h$

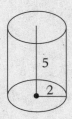

In the cylinder above, $r = 2$, $h = 5$, so:

$$\text{Volume} = \pi(2^2)(5) = 20\pi$$

A Special Note for International Students

If you are an international student considering attending an American university, you are not alone. Over 582,000 international students pursued academic degrees at the undergraduate, graduate, or professional school level at U.S. universities during the 2001–2002 academic year, according to the Institute of International Education's *Open Doors* report. Almost half of these students were studying for a bachelor's or first university degree. This number of international students pursuing higher education in the United States is expected to continue to grow. Business, management, engineering, and the physical and life sciences are particularly popular majors for students coming to the United States from other countries.

If you are not a U.S. citizen and you are interested in attending college or university in the United States, here is what you'll need to get started.

- If English is not your first language, you'll probably need to take the TOEFL (Test of English as a Foreign Language) or provide some other evidence that you are proficient in English in order to complete an academic degree program. Colleges and universities in the United States will differ on what they consider to be an acceptable TOEFL score. A minimum TOEFL score of 213 (550 on the paper-based TOEFL) or better is often required by more prestigious and competitive institutions. Because American undergraduate programs require all students to take a certain number of general education courses, all students— even math and computer science students—need to be able to communicate well in spoken and written English.

- You may also need to take the SAT or the ACT. Many undergraduate institutions in the United States require both the SAT and TOEFL of international students.

- There are over 3,400 accredited colleges and universities in the United States, so selecting the correct undergraduate school can be a confusing task for anyone. You will need to get help from a good advisor or at least a good college guide that gives you detailed information on the different schools available. Since admission to many undergraduate programs is quite competitive, you may want to select three or four colleges and complete applications for each school.

- You should begin the application process at least one year in advance. An increasing number of schools accept applications throughout the year. In any case, learn the application deadlines and plan accordingly. Although September (the fall semester) is the traditional time to begin university study in the United States, you can begin your studies at many schools in January (the spring semester).

In addition, you will need to obtain an I-20 Certificate of Eligibility from the school you plan to attend if you intend to apply for an F-1 Student Visa to study in the United States.

KAPLAN INTERNATIONAL PROGRAMS

If you need more help with the complex process of university admissions, assistance preparing for the SAT, ACT, or TOEFL, or help building your English language skills in general, you may be interested in Kaplan's programs for international students.

Kaplan International Programs were designed to help students and professionals from outside the United States meet their educational and career goals. At locations throughout the United States, international students take advantage of Kaplan's programs to help them improve their academic and conversational English skills, raise their scores on the TOEFL, SAT, ACT, and other standardized exams, and gain admission to the schools of their choice. Our staff and instructors give international students the individualized attention they need to succeed. Here is a brief description of some of Kaplan's programs for international students:

General Intensive English

Kaplan's General Intensive English classes are designed to help you improve your skills in all areas of English and to increase your fluency in spoken and written English. Classes are available for beginning to advanced students, and the average class size is 12 students.

General English Self-Study

For students needing a flexible schedule, this course helps improve general fluency skills. Kaplan's General English Self-Study course employs the communicative approach and focuses on vocabulary building, reading and writing. You will receive books, audio and video materials as well as three hours of instructor contact per week.

TOEFL and Academic English

This course provides you with the skills you need to improve your TOEFL score and succeed in a U.S. university or graduate program. It includes advanced reading, writing, listening, grammar, and conversational English. You will also receive training for the TOEFL using Kaplan's exclusive computer-based practice materials.

TOEFL TEST PREPARATION COURSE

Kaplan's TOEFL course can help you learn test taking skills and strategies to raise your TOEFL score. This course is for intermediate to advanced English learners with a TOEFL score of at least 517 (187 computer).

SAT Test Preparation Course

The SAT is an important admission criterion for U.S. colleges and universities. A high score can help you stand out from other applicants. This course includes the skills you need to succeed on each section of the SAT, as well as access to Kaplan's exclusive practice materials.

Other Kaplan Programs

Since 1938, more than 3 million students have come to Kaplan to advance their studies, prepare for entry to American universities, and further their careers. In addition to the above programs, Kaplan offers courses to prepare for the ACT, GMAT, GRE, MCAT, DAT, USMLE, NCLEX, and other standardized exams at locations throughout the United States.

Applying to Kaplan International Programs

To get more information, or to apply for admission to any of Kaplan's programs for international students and professionals, contact us at:

> **Kaplan International Programs**
> 700 South Flower, Suite 2900
> Los Angeles, CA 90017, USA
> Phone (if calling from within the United States): 800-818-9128
> Phone (if calling from outside the United States): 213-452-5800
> Fax: 213-892-1364
> Email: world@kaplan.com
> Web: www.kaplaninternational.com

Kaplan is authorized under federal law to enroll nonimmigrant alien students. Kaplan is accredited by ACCET (Accrediting Council for Continuing Education and Training).

Test names are registered trademarks of their respective owners.

How Did We Do? Grade Us.

Thank you for choosing a Kaplan book. Your comments and suggestions are very useful to us. Please answer the following questions to assist us in our continued development of high-quality resources to meet your needs.

The title of the Kaplan book I read was: _____

My name is: _____

My address is: _____

_____

My e-mail address is: _____

What overall grade would you give this book?   Ⓐ Ⓑ Ⓒ Ⓓ Ⓕ

How relevant was the information to your goals?   Ⓐ Ⓑ Ⓒ Ⓓ Ⓕ

How comprehensive was the information in this book?   Ⓐ Ⓑ Ⓒ Ⓓ Ⓕ

How accurate was the information in this book?   Ⓐ Ⓑ Ⓒ Ⓓ Ⓕ

How easy was the book to use?   Ⓐ Ⓑ Ⓒ Ⓓ Ⓕ

How appealing was the book's design?   Ⓐ Ⓑ Ⓒ Ⓓ Ⓕ

What were the book's strong points? _____

How could this book be improved? _____

Is there anything that we left out that you wanted to know more about?

Would you recommend this book to others?   ☐ YES   ☐ NO

Other comments: _____

_____

_____

Do we have permission to quote you?   ☐ YES   ☐ NO

Thank you for your help.
Please tear out this page and mail it to:

Managing Editor
Kaplan, Inc.
1440 Broadway, 8th floor
New York, NY 10018

Thanks!

KAPLAN®

<ins>NOTES</ins>

<ins>NOTES</ins>

NOTES

NOTES

NOTES

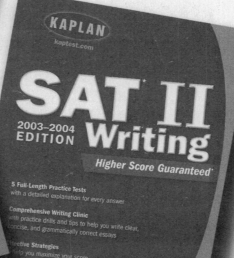

Want a High Score on the SAT?

We've got a guide for every student need.